D0063366

INKLINGS OF REALITY:

Essays Toward a Christian Philosophy of
Letters

by

Donald T. Williams, PhD

Pastor and Church-Planter, Trinity Fellowship
(E.F.C.A.)
Assoc. Prof. of English, Toccoa Falls College,
Toccoa Falls, Ga.

INKLINGS OF REALITY

by

Donald T. Williams, PhD

Toccoa Falls College Press, Toccoa Falls, Ga. 30598

1996

ISBN: 1-885729-07-3

Cover Photo:

Portrait of Erasmus of Rotterdam by
Hans Holbein the Younger, ca. 1523

DEDICATION

for *David Stott Gordon:*

Best and most faithful of Friends;

Comrade-in-arms in the Cause;

Fellow Reader;

In honor of the Camp Cameron Accords.

1

TABLE OF CONTENTS:

ACKNOWLEDGMENTS

Earlier versions of some of the following material have been previously published as follows: a greatly abbreviated version of the introduction appeared in Alliance Life, March 17, 1993, pp. 6-7; an earlier version of chapter two appeared in Leland Ryken and David C. Barratt, eds., The Discerning Reader (London: Brit. IVP & Grand Rapids: Baker, 1996); of chapter three in Trinity Journal, 5 (1976), pp. 67-78; of chapter four in Michael Bauman and Marty Klauber, eds., Historians of the Christian Tradition: Their Methodologies and Impact on Western Culture (Nashville: Broadman & Holman, 1995); of chapter six in Christian Scholar's Review, 19:3 (March, 1990), pp. 271-85; and of the conclusion in Eternity, Oct. 1986, pp. 34-36. The book reviews in the appendix originally appeared in Eternity or The Journal of the Evangelical Theological Society. All of that material has been revised and expanded to a greater or lesser extent; I am grateful to the various publishers for permission to reuse it.

A number of people have read all or part of the manuscript and offered valuable suggestions, though any errors of fact or interpretation that remain are assuredly my own. They include Leland Ryken, David C. Barratt, Michael Bauman, David S. Gordon, Wil Shorb, Frank J. Warnke, John D. Woodbridge, Jim Kilgo, Marion Montgomery, Kay Ludwigson, Donna Fletcher Crow, and most importantly, *Inklings II* (Inklings Too, Inklings to . . .), the writers' and artists' support group of Trinity Fellowship Evangelical Free Church of Toccoa, Ga.: Mike and Anna Sharp, Mark and Debby Gerl, Sarah Binger, Jaime Fredericks, Phil Brande, Matt Preston, and others on occasion. They give me hope that biblical consciousness and wholeness of vision may not indeed perish from the earth.

Technical support was provided by Clarence Wulf, Kelly Vickers, and Sharon Farley, who either gave me access to computers or provided useful advice in their operation. A special word of thanks must go to Mike Sharp, formerly professor of Christian Education at Toccoa Falls College, whose legendary skill at wheedling recalcitrant computers saved at least much valuable time, and possibly the whole book from oblivion on more than one occasion.

"To think well is to serve God in the interior court."

--Thomas Traherne, <u>Five Centuries of Meditations</u>

"We present you with this Book, the most valuable thing that this world affords. Here is wisdom; this is the royal Law; these are the lively Oracles of God."

--Presentation of the Holy Bible, English Coronation Service

"Consider, too, that none of those things you see with your eyes and touch with your hands are as real as the truths you read there [in Scripture]. . . . Remember that men lie, that they are deceived, but that the truth of God neither misleads nor is itself misled."

--Erasmus, <u>Enchiridion</u>

"Literature shapes and invigorates the youthful character and prepares one marvelously well for understanding Holy Scripture. . . . Jerome chides the effrontery of those who, coming straight out of secular studies, dare to expound the Scriptures; but how much more impudent is the behavior of those people who presume to do that very same thing without even a taste of those disciplines."

--Erasmus, <u>Enchiridion</u>

"No man, who knows nothing else, knows even his Bible."

--Matthew Arnold, <u>Culture and Anarchy</u>

"Why have we [no grace] for books, those spiritual repasts-- a
grace before Milton--a grace before Shakespeare--a devotional
exercise proper to be said before reading the <u>Faerie Queene</u>?"

--Charles Lamb, "Grace before Meat"

For him was lever have at his beddes heed
Twenty bokes, clad in blak or reed,
Of Aristotle and his philosophye
Than robes rich, or fithele, or gay sautrye.

--Geoffrey Chaucer, "General Prolog" to <u>The Canterbury Tales</u>

For out of olde feldes, as men seith,
Cometh all this newe corn from yeer to yeer;
And out of olde bokes, in good feith,
Cometh all this newe science that men lere.

--Chaucer, <u>Parlement of Foules</u>

"Be sure that you go to the author to get at his meaning, not to find yours."

--John Ruskin, Sesame and Lilies, Lecture 1

"There has never been a great revelation of the word of God unless He has first prepared the way by the rise and prosperity of languages and letters, as though they were John the Baptists."

--Martin Luther, Letter to Eoban Hess, March 29, 1523.

"A good book is the purest essence of the human soul."

--Thomas Carlyle, Speech in Support of the London Library

"Hear them, read, mark, learn, and inwardly digest them."

--Book of Common Prayer, Collects, Second Sunday in Advent

PRELUDE

THE CONVERSION OF AUGUSTINE

Villanelle no. 13

The Voice cried out in answer to his need
    To take the plunge, to be converted *now*,
    Singing, "*Tolle, Lege*, take and read."
For years he'd stumbled over the hard creed
    Of Jesus in the flesh--who could see how?
    But nothing else would answer to his need.
His mother's prayers were destined to succeed
   Through Ambrose' preaching, his own quest, and Thou
    Singing, "*Tolle, lege*, take and read."
"But can you live without us?" they would plead--
    His mistresses--as if to disallow
    The Voice that cried in answer to his need.
"Yes! Rather, put on Christ, who came to bleed,
    And make no plans the field of flesh to plow."
    Such was the Answer he took up to read.
At last, the Hound of Heaven had him treed,
    Weeping, broken, and prepared to bow.
    The Voice cried out in answer to his need,
Singing, "*Tolle, lege*, take and read."

--D.T.W.

INTRODUCTION

The Conversation

"In the evening, I return to my house and go into my study. At the door I take off the clothes I have worn all day, mud-spotted and dirty, and put on regal and courtly garments. Thus appropriately clothed, I enter into the ancient courts of ancient men, where, being lovingly received, I feed on that food which alone is mine, and which I was born for; for I am not ashamed to speak with them and to ask the reasons for their actions, and they courteously answer me."

--Niccolo Machiavelli

The classical concept of education that inspired men of the Renaissance like Machiavelli involved growing out of the provincialism of one's own time and place to become a citizen of the ages. Such people heard around them the echoes of a great Conversation as old as the race, in which the great Minds wrestled with the great Questions: Who are we? Where did we come from? Why are we here? What is ultimately real? What is the greatest good? And, not least importantly, how do we know? They strove to acquire the intellectual equipment-- languages, logic, rhetoric, hermeneutics, etc.--which would enable them to enter into the Conversation themselves, to benefit from the wisdom of the Ancients, and perhaps even to make a small contribution of their own for the use of future generations. It was in books that the Conversation took place, and in their own books it would continue when they themselves had faded into dust.

The Christian vision of education is both broader and deeper than that of the Ancients. It is more, but not less; it includes the classical ideal while going beyond it. We too seek to join a great Conversation already going on around us. It contains many of the same voices and deals with all of the same questions. But our Conversation is guided by the Voice of Scripture more surely toward the Truth, and it has as its goal not just personal enrichment and fulfillment but the glory of God in practical service. As Milton summarized it, "The end, then, of learning is to repair the ruins of our first parents by regaining to know God aright, and out of that knowledge to love him, to imitate him, to be like him." Nothing less than a "complete and generous" dose of such learning could fit us to "perform justly, skillfully, and magnanimously all the offices, both private and public, of peace and war."[1]

Perhaps then the greatest service Christian teachers can perform is to introduce their students to the participants in the Conversation and enable them to take their place in it so their service can be informed by it. It is, in other words, to make them lovers of books: the Bible supremely, and the classics of course, and a host of heroes of the faith who have blazed the trail before us as well.

As a *People of the Book*, Christians have always been a community to whom reading was important. They have staked their souls, their eternities, and the priorities which govern their daily lives on a set of radical and interrelated premises: that God exists as a personal and articulate Being whose innermost nature is eternally expressed as the *Logos*, the Word; that we were created in the image of this articulate Word; that the Word became flesh and dwelt among us to live our life and die our death and redeem us; and that this Word was enscripturated in a *Book* whose propositions meaningfully communicate to us still the essence of who He is.

Christians are, in other words, a people who have experienced the fact that the living Word is mediated by the written Word. All their thinking about life--and about thought--

begins from the fact that this *Book* has *communicated* to them the thoughts of the prophets, the experience of Christ's original followers, and the truths about Him out of which those experiences flowed. They may argue *to,* but first they argue *from,* the fact that, as Erasmus put it, the text of Scripture can "render [Christ] so fully present that you would see less if you gazed upon him with your very eyes."[2]

Hence, Christians know in their bones that in the acts of writing and reading an Author--or an author--can communicate across millennia his experience, his personality, his ideas. Of *course* God can do it. "Who made man's mouth? Is it not I, the Lord?" He asked Moses. And because we were made in His image, we can receive it. And if He can do it, then human beings made in his image can do it too, though not infallibly without His inspiration, and we can receive that as well.

For a Christian who understands his own roots, then, life is a decidedly logocentric (word-centered) enterprise. If God and human authors have communicated with us through the written word, reading is central to all of our existence. As a People of the Book, therefore, Christians have always had to wrestle with what reading means and how it relates to education, character formation, and every area of life. They have often done so constructively, even profoundly. This book looks at several key moments in the history of that wrestling in order to uncover the elements of a Christian philosophy of letters, a biblical view of reading and its place in the Christian life. It does not claim to be that philosophy, only to take the first steps toward it. But they are steps that desperately need to be taken once again.

For we live in a generation which has come to doubt profoundly the ability of language to convey meaning, much less truth. Deconstructionists, and others only less radical, tell us that language refers solely to itself, not to anything in the outside world; that readers *create* the meaning of the texts they read rather than *receiving* it; and that the most minute analysis of the details of a text, rather than uncovering the author's intended meaning, only serves to show that all language of necessity leads to inherent contradiction.

The author has thus been banished from his own text, and readers are praised not for their faithfulness to his meaning but for the originality with which they create their own. Those "readings" are valued in which the reader performs the most impressive intellectual gymnastics for which the text is merely the playing field. Interpretations are valued, in other words, for their sophistication rather than their fidelity, their subtlety rather than their truth. (It is not, of course, that sophistication and subtlety are not valuable. But in the present climate, they are valued for their own sake, not because they can help us toward an understanding of the text that is truer at the same time as it is fuller and richer. And when these good things are cut loose from their allegiance to truth, sophistication becomes mere sophistry and subtlety mere obfuscation.)

Such values now dominate the academic study of literature, which I can hardly characterise better than with the following sonnet:

Horace, Sir Philip Sidney, and Matthew Arnold,
Looking Down on Earth from Elysium,
Scratch their Heads

Sonnet LXXI

The purpose, by delighting thus to teach
And then by teaching also to delight?
Nothing but a lame excuse to preach
Oppressive values--how naive, how trite!
The good of history and philosophy,
The concrete and the abstract unified?
A quaint, archaic curiosity

From European white males who have died.
To see the thing for what it really is,
To know the best that has been thought and done?
Merely factual answers for a quiz,
No more a map for any race we run.
It's how the academic game is played--
And Goodness, Truth, and Beauty are betrayed.

--D.T.W.

Such values now dominate the academic study of literature and are beginning to spill over into biblical studies and theology. No longer valued for the traditional humane reasons because its meaning is held to be inaccessible anyway, literature becomes a mere excuse for academic prostitutes who were hired to do other things to push leftist agendas and attack the very foundations of the Western civilization which makes their sheltered academic lives possible. It is no wonder then that, in such a context, illiteracy is on the rise again in the general population, and biblical illiteracy is on the rise even among believers. Why bother to read carefully or at all if all texts are only self-referential anyway?[3] It is high time for the voices of sanity to be heard once again.

The purpose of this book is not to refute the contentions of the Deconstructionists or their other "post-modern" cohorts. That job does not require a book.[4] It can be done in one paragraph--and here it is.

People who claim that literary texts are purely self-referential make this claim in books. In these books, they refer to other books, analyzing them in an attempt to prove that what we once took for attempts at communication are really "self-consuming artifacts."[5] But if their claim is true, then the other texts were not actually ever referred to at all. Hence their analysis proves nothing, since their claims, if true, could not refer to anything outside their own books. In other words, the only thing

Deconstruction *can* deconstruct is Deconstruction--on its own premises! The position is radically self-defeating. And its proponents will not be happy if you try to use their hermeneutic on their own writings as I have suggested. They would insist that they are *communicating* that communication is impossible. They *mean* to say that the author's meaning cannot be recovered and is irrelevant. People who are unwilling even to make the attempt to live by their own philosophy do not deserve the dignity of a refutation. They do not deserve to be taken seriously, and I do not propose to grant them any further dignity than I have already done in this paragraph. They are Naked Emperors plain and simple, and that is all that finally needs to be said about them.

The purpose of this book therefore is not to refute those who deny the existence of objective meaning in literary texts but simply to remind us that there is an alternative way of looking at things. (After all, the best refutation of harlotry is not ethical argument--though that has its place--but a good marriage.) That alternative is ancient and wise and has been developed with profundity and sanity and splendor by better minds than mine. I just want to bring those minds back into the Conversation once again. I want, by reminding us of what they can communicate, to make us lovers of books: the Bible supremely, and the classics of course, and a host of heroes of the faith who have blazed the trail before us as well.

A scholar's (or any serious reader's) books are not only the tools of his trade; they are also his environment, his friends, and his security blanket. He never feels quite at home unless they are all displayed on their shelves, surrounding his desk with their familiar, well-worn covers. Though they are legion, he knows the position of each one and can reach out his hand to it almost with his eyes closed.

Each has a different role to play, and some play more than one. Some are allies, troops he can muster in support of the Cause. Some are sparring partners against which he sharpens his wits. Some are teachers whose well of wisdom never runs dry. Some are librarians, efficient repositories of information. Some are merely playmates for idle moments. Some take all these roles in turn.

None is there except by invitation, for each has had to clear a fearful set of hurdles to win its place. A host of others wait patiently for admission, and the scholar would like to let them in. But shelf space is always limited--there is no such thing as enough. Money is in even shorter supply. And as middle age approaches, moving becomes more and more of an ordeal, and spouses may be less and less understanding about the necessity of allotting any of the family budget at all to the augmentation of what already looms as an awesome pile of obviously non-functional dead weight. Cramped up in boxes piled to the ceiling awaiting the van, temporarily shorn of all their beauty and power, they lie silent and offer no defense. But the scholar is loyal; he cannot rest until they are uncaged and arranged on their shelves once more.

He sees to the task himself, setting all other matters aside. He is deliberate and meticulous and downright fussy. It is a different study, a different set of shelves, and the old arrangement cannot be reproduced exactly. He gropes toward the new one slowly, guided somewhat by utility but even more by a mysterious principle of aesthetic order and harmony. He could not tell you what it is, but somehow he knows when he has hit it. He may then sit for days in satisfied contemplation of the ordered universe of thought which now orbits around his head. Only then can real work begin.

For the Christian scholar--at least for this one--his books thus arranged take on a further significance. Some of mine remind me of nothing so much as the great Cloud of Witnesses of Hebrews 12:1. Like those saints in the honor roll of faith in chapter eleven, they inspire me to more faithful service.

I look up from my typewriter and catch the eye, as it were, of Athanasius with his dogged devotion to the truth. There sits Martin Luther, alive still with his passionate and desperate search for justification before God. John Calvin fills a whole shelf with his careful exegesis and penetrating thought (even the very ratio of his works on my shelves: twenty-two volumes of commentary to two of systematic theology--no wonder the Institutes are still the place to begin in dogmatics!). Opposite from him sits Wesley with his thirst for holiness and concern for the common people. And the list goes on.

Augustine, Anselm, and Aquinas; Baxter, Owen, and Edwards; Hodge, Warfield, and Machen; Westcott, Hort, and Lightfoot; Dante, Spenser, and Milton; Herbert, Donne, and Hopkins; Newton, Cowper, and Watts; Lewis, Tolkien, and Francis Schaeffer: their example and legacy impels me to lay aside every encumbrance and the sin which so easily besets us and run with endurance the race which is set before us, fixing my eyes (as they did) on Jesus, the Author and Finisher of our faith.

I enter into the courts of these men and they lovingly receive me. I ask them the reasons for their actions and they courteously answer me. They remind me that the shoddy standards of both piety and thought in our own day are irrelevant to my work. They keep me from forgetting either Whom I serve or with whom I serve. They are fellow lovers of Scripture and the Lord who enrich my knowledge and experience of both. And they are joined by a host of others who did not know the Lord but whose experience of the human condition forms an essential part of the larger context within which the writings of those who did can best be understood.

All these writers help me tremendously when I read them, but in some ways I think the reminder provided by their mere presence stacked around my head is the greatest help of all (though it wouldn't be, of course, if I had not read and absorbed them). And if I can just introduce my students to them--if I can just get the Conversation started--I shall consider my life (and their tuition) well spent indeed.

The following pages will attempt to provide an overview of the history of Christian thinking about the meaning and purpose of reading and writing and then peer at selected moments of that history in more detail, seeking to discern their relevance for Christian life and ministry today. But first, I would like to begin, in traditional Evangelical fashion, with my testimony: the story of how I first became a *reader* (as opposed to a mere consumer of print) and the difference it has made in my life as a servant of Jesus Christ. For I would never have stumbled upon anything else that is of value here had it not been for the awakening that is chronicled in chapter one.

The paths to awakening are varied; the Lord works in mysterious ways. But the darkness out of which we all must emerge is the same, and the Light that dawns is One. Hence, though the experiences in the first chapter are mine, the pilgrimage they embody in many ways mirrors that of the Evangelical movement itself. But to find those connections, we must first take the journey the Renaissance wanted to take: *ad fontes*, back to the sources.

Once upon a time. . .

Notes to Introduction

1.John Milton, "Of Education," in Witherspoon and Warnke, eds., <u>Seventeenth-Century Prose and Poetry</u>, 2nd ed. (San Diego: Harcourt Brace Jovanovich, 1982), pp. 389-90.

2.Desiderius Erasmus, <u>Paraclesis</u>, qtd. in Marjorie O'Rourke Boyle, <u>Erasmus on Language and Method in Theology</u> (Toronto: Univ. of Toronto Pr., 1977), p. 137.

3.For excellent analyses of the decline of reading in the modern/post-modern world and the failure of Evangelicalism adequately to resist it, see David F. Wells, <u>No Place for Truth; Or, Whatever Happened to Evangelical Theology</u> (Grand Rapids: Eerdmans, 1993) and Gene Edward Veith, <u>Loving God with All Your Mind: How to Survive and Prosper as a Christian in the Secular University and Post-Christian Culture</u> (Westchester, Il.: Crossway, 1987). For concise and insightful analyses of Deconstruction and other anti-literary trends in the study of letters, see Clarence Walhout and Leland Ryken, eds., <u>Contemporary Literary Theory: A Christian Appraisal</u> (Grand Rapids: Eerdmans, 1991), especially the essays by Michael Vander Weele and Alan Jacobs; David S. Dockery, ed., <u>The Challenge of Postmodernism: An Evangelical Engagement</u> (Wheaton: Bridgepoint, 1995); and Gene Edward Veith, <u>Postmodern Times: A Christian Guide to Contemporary Thought and Culture</u> (Wheaton: Crossway, 1994). Also good is Veith's <u>Reading Between the Lines: A Christian Guide to Literature</u> (Wheaton: Crossway, 1990).

4.But if you want to see such a refutation done a bit more thoroughly than in a paragraph, see Michael Bauman, <u>Pilgrim Theology: Taking the Path of Theological Discovery</u> (Grand Rapids: Zondervan, 1992), pp. 125-135. For a brilliant book-length defense of the possibility of objective and recoverable meaning, see E. D. Hirsch, <u>Validity in Interpretation</u> (New Haven, Ct.: Yale Univ. Pr., 1967).

5. To steal a phrase from Stanley Fish, <u>Self-Consuming Artifacts: The Experience of Seventeenth-Century Literature</u> (Berkeley: Univ. of California Pr., 1972). Fish is perhaps the best known proponent of the thesis that meaning resides in the reader rather than the text. He tries to avoid solipsism by appealing to the restraints provided by a "competent" interpretive community; but the author still ends up being unable to communicate directly with the reader.

<blockquote>
"I never," protested Stan Fish,
"Said that readers can make what they wish
Of a text. The community
Has that impunity."
Slippery animals, fish.
--D.T.W.
</blockquote>

INTERLUDE

THE GOAL OF THE TRIVIUM

Commentary, Prvb. 9:1-6
Sonnet LXXV

Old mysteries await fresh revelation.
    Such ideas ought of right to be presented
    In royal garments, rich and ornamented,
Befitting their high lineage and station.
Heraldic manuscript illumination
    In Celtic knotwork swirled and brightly tinted
    For metaphors and the meanings they have hinted:
The setting beckons us, an invitation.

What now seems quaint and esoteric lore
    Was once the simple bedrock of our thought:
    First principles and their elucidation.
That's partly what the wondrous words were for--
    Despite our darkness, they can still be caught:
    Faint echoes of the ancient Conversation.

--D.T.W.

Chapter 1

MORNING:
Reading and the Awakening of Biblical Consciousness

"Confusion heard His voice, and wild uproar
Stood ruled, stood vast infinitude confined;
Till at His second bidding darkness fled,
Light shone, and order from disorder sprung."
--Milton, Paradise Lost, iii.710-713.

"The millions," said Henry David Thoreau, "are awake enough for physical labor; but only one in a million is awake enough for effective intellectual exertion, only one in a hundred millions to a poetic or divine life."[1]

Grant that his statistics are exaggerated and elitist. I have certainly met more people who had at least a glimmer of light beneath their eyelids than they would have given me a right to expect--though not as many, certainly, as one might desire. But his point is worth some thought.

"To be awake," he continued, "is to be alive. I have never yet met a man who was quite awake. How could I have looked him in the face?"

How indeed?

I think I know what such a man would look like. His hair would be white as snow, his eyes like coals of fire, and there would be a sharp sword coming from his mouth. The effect of the whole would shine more brightly than the sun.

To look on such a face would either send a person screaming into the abyss with eyes blasted forever blind by a painful searing which could never be forgotten, or it would shock him so fully awake that he could look unflinching like the eagle on the sun and not need sleep again for all eternity. And all of us, whether we recognize it or not, spend our lives either looking for glimpses of that face wherever we can find them, or pulling the covers up around our heads and wishing the dreaded morning would go away.

Seen thus from the distance of eternity, the spiritual topography of the world lays out in lines hard and clear. But viewed from the immediate perspective of time, some of the clarity is lost in swirling mists and tangled thickets. Not all those who seem to be looking for the light, or even who are able to point out glimpses of it to others, find it, or accept it when they do. And some who are destined to spend eternity bathed in its splendor can be heard snoring most contentedly here and now.

Some of this discrepancy must no doubt be attributed to the fallibility of human judgment, surely a large part to the mystery of sovereign grace; but much is to the shame and disgrace of a Church that ought to be responding better to the Light which has theoretically begun to dawn in its hearts.

I know this problem well, for I can trace it in all its paradoxical complexity in the annals of my own life. I cannot yet claim to be very much awake, but I am far more than I once was. I had "known the Lord," as we say, for years before I took the least notice of the wonder, the glory, and the pathos of the world he had made and of life lived within it or connected these marvels with his hand in them. At the age of five, in simple, childlike faith, I had walked the aisle of a little Baptist church, confessed my sins, and asked Jesus to be my personal Savior. I intend no disparagement of that very real, very biblical, and very necessary experience; but I have since learned both by experience and observation that it guarantees no vision of anything much beyond itself.

You might say that I was too young, too immature to expect my conversion to be much of a window on the world, that this would inevitably come with time. But I saw too many of my peers "mature" by falling into such a stupor that even their conversion was all but forgotten. They simply became like most of their elders, reminiscent of the old lady in Edith Sitwell's poem "Solo for Ear-Trumpet."[2] The narrator is visiting a "rich relation" when suddenly the heavy silence is shattered by Gabriel's horn: Eternity has actually dawned.

> . . . Down the horn
> Of her ear-trumpet I convey
> The news that: "It is Judgment Day!"
> "Speak louder; I don't catch, my dear."
> I roared: *"It is the Trump we hear!"*
> "The *What*?" "The TRUMP!"
> "I shall complain--
> Those boy-scouts practicing again!"

Time alone brings only deafness and blindness, not only to "spiritual things" but even to Creation; and it happens to the saved as well as to the lost.

Something else is needed: not some particular and definitive "second blessing" or "taste of new wine" necessarily, but *something* to keep us constantly waking up to the reality of what we believe, of what it was we received when we accepted Christ. From the perspective of eternity, it is the work of the Holy Spirit: sanctification, illumination--essentially and simply, making Jesus real to us day by day.[3] From the perspective of time, he uses some strange instruments.

READING:

In my case, the process of awakening began with the writings of three men--only one of which was clearly a Believer in touch with the Source of the dawn. The pathos and the tragedy--and surely the Lord, who loved the Rich young Ruler but sent him away sorrowing, must feel it too--is this: that the other two, seekers after and in some sense even seers of the light, must now be feared to be in eternal blackness, their need for the Blood being the one thing they fatally could or would not see. Yet apart from them, my own eyes would still be largely shut.

HENRY DAVID THOREAU

The first was Thoreau. In so far as he had a theology, he was vaguely pantheistic. Christ was to him a great man, more "awake" no doubt than most, perhaps uniquely in tune with the Oversoul--but not Lord, not a savior from *sin*. You would think that a man who could miss that most crucial of truths would miss everything; yet few men have more clearly sensed or more truly expressed the certainty of that luminescent mystery behind the surface appearances of life that makes the whole throb with a purpose just beyond our grasp and the confidence that the business of life is to cut through the trivia and find out what it is.

Men's lives, he saw, are "frittered away by detail."[4] Most of them have "somewhat hastily concluded"[5] that the purpose of life is to serve God and enjoy him forever. It was the haste that troubled him--how did they *know*? And if those who followed that path had really found the truth, why did it lead usually only to frittering? Unfortunately, he never found out; but he went to Walden Pond to try.

I must have been in about the tenth grade. I had always been a dutiful student, not as yet from any particular love of learning so much as from the Protestant work ethic my parents had instilled in me and from the fact that diagraming sentences and memorizing facts for tests were among the few things I excelled at. So when we were assigned to read Walden, I did. And this is what I saw:

> I went to the woods because I wished to live deliberately, to front only the essential facts of life, and see if I could not learn what it had to teach, and not, when I came to die, discover that I had not lived.. . . I wanted to live deep and suck out all the marrow of life . . . and reduce it to its lowest terms, and, if it proved to be mean, why then to get the whole and genuine meanness of it, and publish its meanness to the world; or if it were sublime, to know it by experience and be able to give a true account of it.[6]

I saw a passion for truth for its own sake--not the desire to edify or to establish a position but simply to follow the *truth* wherever it might lead--which I had never encountered in the church. I was among those who had concluded (hastily, one might even say, at the advanced philosophical age of five) that the chief end of man was to glorify God and enjoy him forever. I did not abandon that conclusion, but I began to wonder--without knowing exactly how to proceed--whether it might be possible to conclude it more slowly and deliberately. I realized, with some fear, that once the question had been raised, you had to be prepared to abandon the conclusion should it turn out to be false--else you could not in real honesty make the claim that it was true.

That all had to stay on the back burner for awhile, but in the meantime, life had suddenly become an adventure. To see and admit and face the theoretical possibility of meanness made the sublimity suddenly precious. I became more attentive both to books and nature. I began, like Thoreau, to take walks on which I kept appointments with trees. I began to be attuned to the great mystery in the fact that the world is there, is beautiful, yet is terrible and cruel, and to be hungry for deeper insights into that mystery.

I began, in other words, to understand what Thoreau meant when he wrote,

> Time is but the stream I go a-fishing in. I drink at it; but while I drink I see the sandy bottom and detect how shallow it is. Its thin current slides away, but eternity remains. I would drink deeper; fish in the sky, whose bottom is pebbly with stars.[7]

I began to awake.

ROBERT FROST

Then there was Robert Frost. There is no clear evidence that he knew the Lord (cryptic phrases in his letters give hope,[8] but there was no clear testimony), but he certainly loved the world the Lord had made, and he lived close to it and reveled in its objective reality. He liked to lean his weight on it until it left the marks of grass stems in his hand, and longed "for weight and strength / To feel the earth as rough / To all my length."[9] Maybe it was the length and harshness of the New England winters that gave such special poignancy to his understanding of the meaning of the changing seasons as the poet of both inner and outer weather;[10] at any rate, he had the gift in his deceptively simple poems of focussing the sense of mystery behind nature which Thoreau had spoken of until it became so powerful it could knock the wind out of you.

It was autumn of the same year. My family had taken advantage of a long weekend to go camping in the mountains of north Georgia. We followed a little dirt road which winds its way into the hills past the Tallulah River and Tate Branch campgrounds and then on into North Carolina, where it dwindles to a footpath that eventually climbs to join the Appalachian Trail. We didn't get that far; we set up our camper at Tallulah River and the rest of the family enjoyed grilling hot dogs on the fire and building dams out of stones in the mountain stream while I, having contracted some stomach bug, lay in the camper and experienced the meanness of life. The sublimity was about to follow. On the last day my illness departed only a few hours before we all were scheduled to, and I used my short reprieve amidst the blazing glory of that Georgia fall in the best Thoreauvian fashion: I went for a walk.

I followed the road or trail (the distinction was becoming increasingly arbitrary) as it wound its way further into the hills. It followed the Tallulah River, among the most playful of mountain streams, as it alternately hugged the curb, leapt under a bridge to reappear on the other side, or dropped a couple hundred feet beneath as the valley deepened. It was one of those glorious days we often get in Georgia autumns, with the sun conspiring with the leaves to remind you what red and gold really mean and the air just cool enough to make exertion pleasant. There was only one problem: the finitude of time, which insisted on floating away like a leaf on the surface of the stream.

I was supposed to be back at camp at a particular time--what particular time I don't remember, nor does it matter. To accomplish that feat was simple enough: just divide the time you did have in half, which would yield the precise moment at which you had to turn around and retrace your steps. The difficulty was that that time was clearly going to arrive before I had gotten anywhere near the place I wanted to get to, which I suppose had something to do with the source of the stream, the heart of the mountains, and the very root of all existence. I cheated, stretching it by five minutes, promising myself I would make it up by walking faster on the return trip. But there finally came the bend in the road I was not going to see around and the hill I was not going to see over. And in that brief moment of equilibrium between going and coming, I learned something inexpressible about the nature of life, the mystery of time, the significance of choice, and the cost of commitment. It was like a seed resting within me on the long ride home, and I did not know what manner of thing it would grow into.

As Providence would have it, there was another literary assignment waiting for me when I returned to school. If you know Frost at all, you must have already guessed what it was:

> Two roads diverged in a yellow wood,
> And sorry I could not travel both
> And be one traveler, long I stood
> And looked down one as far as I could
> To where it bent in the undergrowth;
>
> Then took the other, as just as fair,
> And having perhaps the better claim
> Because it was grassy and wanted wear;
> Though as for that, the passing there
> Had worn them really about the same,
>
> And both that day equally lay
> In leaves no step had trodden black.
> Oh, I kept the first for another day!
> Yet, knowing how way leads on to way,
> I doubted if I should ever come back.
>
> I shall be telling this with a sigh
> Somewhere ages and ages hence:
> Two roads diverged in a wood, and I--
> I took the one less traveled by,
> And that has made all the difference.[11]

How did he *know*?

This was a real eye-opener. Somebody else had stood in the same kind of silence with the yellow leaves sifting through the air as I had, and had seen the same thing. The poem about stopping by a wood on a snowy evening[12] followed and confirmed my hunch.

I did not then know that Frost had already died just a few years earlier. But I did know that if I ever met him, and we got to talking about walking in the woods, we would understand each other. What we had seen was an inexpressible mystery of beauty made tragic by time and mortality which lies at the heart of things and somehow makes choices matter.[13] Only, for Frost, it wasn't-- or, at least it wasn't *quite*--inexpressible. In his writings he had leapt across space and time to share with me his own glimpses of the mystery in a magical act of communication.

It was well that Frost had gotten to me first, before the English Teachers; for many of them would try to get me to see poems as something else--as puzzles to be solved by clever interpreters, for example. By this method, they would efficiently make most of my peers into confirmed haters of poetry. But I had been fortified against their evil machinations by my own experience of poetry as shared experience, shared life, shared vision.[14]

Yes, the miracle was that for Frost, the mystery of life wasn't quite inexpressible. His poems helped to focus it for me, to get me a little closer to it. And that fact introduced another mystery, the mystery of words (or of *the Word*, as I was later to realize).

Here then were two truths I was sure of, two pillars I could build on as foundational from here on out: There was a mysterious and tragic beauty and purpose bound up in creation that made life worth living, and language, when used just right, was the lens which could bring that mystery into focus. If I was going to eschew the unexamined life as not worth living, if I was going to be awake--if I was going to be a philosopher, I would also have to be a poet.

Not that only those with the gift for writing verse could be awakened; but in this realm at least I was not content to be a hearer of the Word only, and not a doer. And so I began to write. All of it was juvenile, of course, and much of it was trash. But it helped to keep me in touch with my masters--Frost, then Hopkins, then Spenser, Milton, Shakespeare--and follow them at least from afar.

Now all this time I believed that Jesus was Lord and that he had died for my sins, and I was trying to live for him. But there was no connection between those commitments and the intellectual and aesthetic life that was waking up and trying out its muscles within me--at least, none that I as yet could see. And that fact began to make me slightly uneasy.

It was clear that if Jesus was really the Son of God, his claims on life must be all-encompassing. Yet, as a general rule, the people I knew who were most committed to him were also the most narrow in their field of interests. They certainly had no time for the kind of things I was coming alive to, and were in fact positively threatened by them. They weren't exactly *Fritterers*; they were alive to that greatest of tasks, taking the Gospel of Christ to a lost world, something I also cared about. But they weren't even coming close to being able to communicate it to the people I wanted to reach, the young seekers of Lakeshore High School. The reason was that they were *Hasty Concluders* and satisfied to be, and anyone who wasn't was obviously unspiritual. As a consequence, I was getting more confused and, against my own will, more alienated from the Faith. Fortunately, it was the next year that the Tolkien craze of the Sixties hit our campus.

J. R. R. TOLKIEN

The Lord's method of supplying the missing piece to my puzzle was a masterstroke of divine pedagogy. I read <u>The Lord of the Rings</u> like everybody else in our school's intellectual subculture, and like everyone else enjoyed the game of interpreting all our experience in terms of its characters and events. We all took on the identity of one of the characters in the book: I was Aragorn, and my best friends included Gandalf, Legolas, and Sam Gamgee.

Perhaps I responded more enthusiastically to the spell than most, for I was finding Tolkien's imaginary world to be one more powerful lense to bring into some kind of focus the whole mystery of life which Thoreau and Frost had been showing me. The building blocks of Middle Earth were the same as those of our own world: tree and mountain, water, wood and stone, starlit distances, beauty made poignant by the passage of time; but here also, with much greater clarity than in the other authors, the conflict of Good and Evil, Light and Darkness, the heroic and sacrificial nature of the Quest. This element gave an added depth, both of joy and sorrow, to the thing. The vision was more tragic, yet simultaneously more hopeful; it was bracing, like a breath of wind from the sea. The thought even began vaguely coalescing in my mind that if a *Christian* ever really saw the mystery of life and became awake to the mystery of words, this would be how he might write. But of course all my experience denied the notion that such a thing could be.

Well, I proceeded to do what you do when you find a writer who moves you deeply: I read everything by him that I could get my hands on. In Tolkien's case at that time, outside The Hobbit and the Ring trilogy that wasn't very much. But there was a thing called The Tolkien Reader, and it did include a piece called "An Essay on Faerie Stories." And if so far I had been yawning and rubbing my eyes as the sunlight streamed in through the window, now I sat bolt upright in bed and looked out upon the day.

"On Faerie Stories" was about the writer's craft and contained tantalizing suggestions about the composition of The Lord of the Rings, and as such was interesting enough. Tolkien was coming to one more argument for taking fantasy literature as a serious art-form--and the alarm clock went off without warning.

Although now long estranged,
Man is not wholly lost nor wholly changed.
Dis-graced he may be, yet is not de-throned,
And keeps the rags of lordship once he owned:
Man, Sub-creator, the refracted Light
Through whom is splintered from a single White
To many hues, and endlessly combined
In living shapes that move from mind to mind.
Though all the crannies of the earth we filled
With elves and goblins, though we dared to build
Gods and their houses out of dark and light,
And sowed the seed of dragons--'twas our right
(Used or misused). That right has not decayed:
We make still by the law in which we're made.[15]

My hands still shake with excitement when I read the note I scribbled into the margin: "I.e., Tolkien's theory is inherently Christian and assumes the *imago Dei*." And as if he had known that such a revelation might seem too good to be true, he confirmed the poetry in plain prose only one page later: "We make ... because we are made: and not only made, but made in the image and likeness of a Maker."[16]

There was only one thing to do: I slammed the book shut and went for a walk to think and to rejoice and to worship.

"We make still by the law in which we're made." It was one of those rare moments of white-hot insight that illuminates the whole dark world like a lightning bolt at midnight, drives away the shadows, and etches the true shape of things in your consciousness forever. The energy of it drove both my feet and my thoughts at a rapid pace as I tried to analyze it into its component parts.

So: The life of the mind outside the narrow range of what was considered "spiritual," awake to nature and art and the mystery of life, was *not* incompatible with Christianity after all.

In fact (what was really staggering), it *depended* for its meaning and validity on the truth of specifically Christian doctrine. Genesis, creation, the image of God had been in both my Bible and my mind for a long time. Why had I never seen the connection? Apparently, the Bible had the answers, but if you read *only* the Bible you might miss some of the questions.

But there was more. What needed explanation was not my interest in philosophy and literature after all, but rather the Church's lack of it. Here they had a monopoly on the key to that whole dimension of human life which separates man from the animals, and they not only didn't know it but wouldn't have seen why it mattered if they had. (As old mysteries were cleared up, new ones stepped forward to take their place.)

But there was more. Christianity *had* to be true! Either the *imago Dei* explained who I was and why I was here, or life was totally absurd, meaningless, and futile. There were no other alternatives. (Francis Schaeffer and Tolkien's friend C. S. Lewis would later help me see fuller ramifications of this insight, but the germ of it was here.)

And there was more, in fact the greatest of all: The original Great Mystery, the mystery of life I had glimpsed and which had started the whole pilgrimage with Thoreau and Frost, was simultaneously clarified, focussed, and deepened. For running right through the heart of it was the scarlet thread of Creation, Fall, Redemption, and Restoration in Christ.

The two worlds I had been living in rushed together and met, not with the crash of collision but with the embrace of marriage, and became one flesh. There was only one world, more full of wonder than ever, and I was at home in it. The glory of its making, the tragedy of its fall, and the joy of its redemption: All were revealed in the part and the whole once you had the eyes to see. And what those eyes saw once the blinders had been removed was the glory of God in the face of Jesus Christ. And once you have seen that *that* is what the Christian faith is all about, nothing matters more than seeing more of it and communicating that vision to others.

AND THE AWAKENING OF
BIBLICAL CONSCIOUSNESS

And the vision came from *reading*. Not just any words, but the right words, were the laser that removed the cataracts and let me see what had been there all along. I would never have become a lover of nature or a lover of God to the extent that I did had I not been also a lover of books. Not all books would do it, but if you weren't prepared to go through quite a lot of them, you would never run into the ones that did.

But why didn't I catch this vision of the glory of God just from reading the Bible? The vision is certainly there, and there with sufficient--no, with powerful--clarity. Perhaps it is because we have learned to view reading the Bible as a "religious" exercise, with the result that what we read there gets compartmentalized along with the rest of our religion (one of the dangers of living in a secular world) and does not interact with our other thoughts. It is not the fault of the Bible, but of our whole approach to faith.

Hence I (like many others, I believe) had to learn to *read* outside the Bible so I could go back later and really read the Bible with open eyes, with the walls of the old compartments now knocked flat. I need the Bible as the central plumb line that keeps the mixture of truth and error, wisdom and folly, etc. in my other reading from leading me astray; but I also need the other reading to keep my vision fresh and expanding--including my vision of the Bible itself. Then I have a chance to develop what we might call *biblical consciousness*: a mind structured as well as informed and nourished by the experience of reading the world through words, with the Word of Scripture in the central, controlling place.[17]

Thus, for biblical consciousness to be born in us--for the Bible to begin to play the role in our lives it was designed to have, and play it fully--we must first and foremost become *readers*. (If we remain merely readers, without the influence of the Bible and Regeneration, we develop what we might call *textual consciousness*, which remains incomplete until the text of Scripture transforms it into the fuller and richer mind set of biblical consciousness).

And this fact should not be surprising. It is one of the most basic motifs of biblical theology--along with Creation, Fall, Incarnation, and Redemption--that the Living Word is Mediated by the Written Word. Our minds, after all, were made in the image of the One who *spoke* the universe into existence. When Genesis mentions our creation in the image of God, only two of the divine attributes have been at that point revealed: He is *creative* and he is *articulate*--and speech is the means by which he creates. Hence the image of God in us must be the fact that we too are articulate and creative. We alone among all the physical creatures can use language to change our thoughts, feelings, perceptions. Ultimately, our ability to change not only our view of the world, but even the world itself, depends on language. Its creative power is what separates us from the rest of the animal creation and makes us able to relate to God.

It is, therefore, not until we come awake to the power of language--until we become *readers*, interpreting the world through language consciously, deliberately, and (as Christians) in obedience to Scripture--that we begin fully to develop our capacity for vision, for good or evil. For all do interpret the world through some grid that is ultimately linguistic, whether they know it or not, and most do it simply haphazardly, if not rebelliously. So why not do it deliberately, based on the Scriptural language we know we can trust as the divinely inspired grid that will let us see the world as it really is? For language is *not* an arbitrary system unrelated to reality (though its individual symbols are in a sense arbitrary); it is the *basis* of reality. For the Word *said*, "Let there be light" . . . and there *was*. And then he said that it was *good*.

Hence for those who look at the world from the standpoint of biblical consciousness, both *ontology* (being) and *ethics* (values) are based on *philology* (language).[18] That is why words--used and understood or abused and distorted--matter so much.[19]

Now, there has been a method in all this autobiographical madness. It has been a highly personal, and perhaps somewhat eccentric, account of the sanctifying work of the Holy Spirit in the subject I happen to know best. We might have developed the doctrine biblically from John 15:26, 16:13-15, etc.: The Spirit will bear witness of Christ by glorifying him, and glorify him by communicating to us all that is his and the Father's.

In other words, the Holy Spirit will wake us up to and keep us awake to the reality of that which we received when we received Christ--which is simply *everything*, for all that the Father has belongs to the Son. When God the Father is said to possess everything, the word must surely be taken in its most literal sense, lest we deny the doctrine of creation. So what the Spirit does is keep the believer awake to the fact that the presence of Christ, the interests of Christ, the claims of Christ, the redeeming grace of Christ, and the lordship of Christ cannot be excluded from any area of life. No one would want to claim out loud that they should be. But nevertheless, we continue to hear from every segment of the American church, whether traditional or charismatic, whether Catholic or Protestant, loudly and clearly, the sounds of snoring.

It is, then, not enough to avoid committing a list of sins or even to be excited about some small list of "spiritual" activities. The person who is filled with the Spirit is a person who cannot escape the fact that his conversion to Christ compels him to something we might call *wholeness of vision*. And wholeness of vision is something that cannot be had apart from *biblical consciousness*, for it is mediated by the Spirit who inspired Scripture, and mediated through words (Jn. 17:17): the Word supremely, but other words as well.

But ought not such realizations to be a normative part of any genuinely Christian religious awakening? Not in terms of details, of course; the question really is, does true spirituality have anything to do with wholeness of vision? If this definition of the Spirit's work is accurate, then the most disturbing fact about American Evangelical Christianity, whether charismatic or traditional, is the almost total absence of that work from the scene.

One need only reflect for a moment about the history of the Spirit's work to see that our own experience of it has been anomalous, to say the least. We have been using the metaphor of "awakening" to describe his operations, and it is an appropriate metaphor for us; we are supposed to have had two great ones in our past. But come to them for a moment from the perspective of some of the other great movements of the Spirit in the history of salvation.

The Awakening of Israel in the Exodus experience produced not only the Law but also the Song of Moses (from which eventually descends the whole poetic achievement of the Hebrew Psalter), the dance of Miriam, and the artistic and architectural skill of Bezalel and Oholiab (which is explicitly attributed to the Spirit in Ex. 35:31). From the reawakening of Christendom to the Gospel in the Protestant Reformation flowed not only the theology of Luther and Calvin but also the music of Bach and Handel and the poetry of Edmund Spenser, George Herbert, and John Milton. Even the revivals of the Eighteenth Century in England gave us not only the preaching of John Wesley but also the unsurpassed hymnody of his brother Charles, John Newton, William Cowper, and Isaac Watts.

And if you ask what is the cultural legacy of the greatest Awakening of all time, the one that began at Pentecost, I would simply point you to the New Testament itself: inspired and inerrant revelation to be sure, but simultaneously a literary achievement of unparalleled proportions. A brand new genre, the Gospel; the Gospel of Luke, often called the most beautiful prose ever written; the impassioned reasoning and the exalted doxologies of Paul; the epic sweep of the Apocalypse: Had familiarity and generations of prooftexting not bred contempt, we would find it as inspired aesthetically as it is doctrinally.

Well, where is the comparable cultural legacy of American revivalism? It is a question that has no answer. Something--the pragmatic and utilitarian bent of our whole society, perhaps--has been allowed to block the full effects of the Spirit's work among us. We have had great zeal, large movements, grand organizations, royal battles; but no Bach, no Spenser, no Milton, not even a Tolkien or a C. S. Lewis--for we have not, for the most part, had wholeness of vision. And it is not just that we have missed it. We have resisted it like the plague.

When Francis Schaeffer came talking about the Lordship of Christ over the whole person and the total culture, we looked at him as if he were saying something new and strange. He was not; he was just calling us to wholeness of vision. We desperately need reformation and revival, perhaps even a third Great Awakening. Perhaps the way to prepare for it is for believers to become really open to the fullness of the Spirit, which is not speaking in tongues or other ecstasies[20] but wholeness of vision. For this to happen, we must become *readers*--of the Bible, of other books, and of the world as interpreted by the right kind of language,[21] not just passive consumers of electronic images.[22] What is the "right kind of language?" Language that is consistent with Scripture and harmonious with its profound soteriological and Christocentric vision. We are not talking about "high culture," necessarily: more pictures nobody can understand on the walls of our churches or more highbrow music in their services. We are talking about men and women who, as whole persons, live all of life Christocentrically seven days a week. We are talking about wholeness of vision.

In short, we need to wake up, and apart from becoming readers in pursuit of biblical consciousness we cannot fully do that. To be awake is to be alive. We claim to know as Savior One in whom is life eternal and inexhaustible, and that life is the light of men. Let us look him full in the face, and recognize him also as Creator and King, and begin to see the whole world in the light of that Light. Let us pull back the shades and throw open the windows and breathe, as the Light streams in, the sweet, unsullied air of morning. Let us make by the law in which we're made, take the road less traveled by, and fish in the sky, whose bottom is pebbly with stars.

Let us do it now, lest the dawn should pass us by.

Notes to Chapter One

1. Henry David Thoreau, Walden, in Sculley Bradley, Richard Croom Beatty, & E. Hudson Long, eds., The American Tradition in Literature, vol. 1 (N. Y.: Norton, 1967), p. 1302.

2. In Louis Untermeyer, ed., Modern American and Modern British Poetry, rev., shorter ed. (N. Y.: Harcourt, Brace, & World, 1955), p. 558.

3. For a more comprehensive treatment of the work of the Holy Spirit from a biblical and theological perspective, see my The Person and Work of the Holy Spirit (Nashville: Broadman, 1994).

4. Thoreau, op. cit., p. 1303.

5. Ibid.

6. Ibid., pp. 1302-3.

7. Thoreau, op. cit., p. 1308.

8. See Lawrance Thompson, ed., Selected Letters of Robert Frost (N. Y.: Holt, Rinehart, & Winston, 1964), pp. 221, 482, 497-8 (but see the next letter), 530-31, 596. The difficulty is not only the crypticness (what does he mean by "orthodoxy"?) but also trying to discern the tone. Perhaps we can only say he combined a stubborn refusal to repudiate Christian orthodoxy with a powerful reticence about personal revelations, and let it go at that.

9. Robert Frost, "To Earthward," in Edward Connery Lathem, ed., The Poetry of Robert Frost (N. Y.: Holt, Rinehart, & Winston, 1969), p. 227.

10. See "Tree at My Window," in Lathem, op. cit., p. 251.

11. Frost, "The Road not Taken," in Lathem, op. cit., p. 105.

12. Lathem, op. cit., p. 224.

13. For other Frost poems with a particularly powerful tincture of this quality, see "In Hardwood Groves," "Reluctance," "Two Tramps in Mudtime," and "Directive," in Lathem, op. cit., pp. 25, 29, 275, 377.

14. I am not, of course, suggesting that all poetry is autobiography. Writers often speak through a *persona*; the speaker is naively identified with the author only at great interpretive peril. But I would insist that even the *persona* is a device the author uses in order to *say* something, and that this something is recoverable, usually through common sense interpretation.

15. J. R. R. Tolkien, "On Fairy Stories," in The Tolkien Reader (N. Y.: Ballantine, 1966), p. 54.

16. Ibid., p. 55.

17. We might define the kind of mind structured and nurtured by the experience of reading as *textual consciousness*; the ability to manipulate the world through language comes from this, but can easily be used for evil purposes (whether the moral corruption of pornography or the equally immoral prostitutions of the mind that come from ideological thinking or nihilism and

Deconstruction). When *textual consciousness* centers humbly, obediently, and teachably on the Bible as the central standard for truth and meaning, *biblical consciousness*, the kind of mind God designed us to have, can be born. But for this to happen, something more than reading is required: spiritual regeneration must also occur. See the conclusion, "Regeneration and Right Thinking," for further development of this idea.

18. For an outstanding exposition of this point, see Marjorie O'Rourke Boyle, Erasmus on Language and Method in Theology (Toronto: Univ. of Toronto Pr., 1977).

19. The merely *textually* conscious have no reason beyond their own individual experience to believe that language can accurately reflect reality--hence their tendency, greater than that of the unlearned, to slide into false sophistication and relativism. The *biblically* conscious, on the other hand, know the *Logos* as the ground of both language and existence, and consequently have a stable epistemological foundation on which to stand. Curiously, one of the great "evils" according to post-modern literary analysis is "privileged" discourse/language/texts (like the traditional literary canon). Christians are people who have *chosen*, for good and sufficient reasons, to "privilege" the text of Scripture and view all other discourse from that standpoint. If Scripture is indeed inspired by the Creator of the universe, then only those whose textual consciousness, by this privileging, has become biblical consciousness, can hope to see the world as it really is.

20. Not that these things are necessarily excluded from the experience of the Spirit's fullness--but they are not its essence. See my The Person and Work of the Holy Spirit, op. cit., for further exposition of all these points related to sanctification from a more specifically theological perspective.

21. I do not mean to say that illiterate peoples are excluded from spirituality; but they are handicapped in their pursuit of it. There is the Word heard and preached as well as the Word read. In each case the Word must work if wholeness of vision is to be engendered and nourished. One can thus be a Reader (in the special sense in which I am using the word) without being a reader (in the general sense); but the ability to read (in the common meaning) obviously enhances one's access to the Word and the words which can breed biblical consciousness.

22. For an excellent analysis of the difference between active reading and the passive consumption of images, see Gene Edward Veith, Reading Between the Lines: A Christian Guide to Literature (Wheaton: Crossway, 1990), esp. pp. 17-25.

INTERLUDE

THE HELLENE AND THE HEBREW

Commentary, Rom. 12:1 (KJV)
Sonnet LXVIII

So where does Athens meet Jerusalem?
    Tertullian couldn't find a single place,
    And thus condemned the blind and groping Race
To groping blindness. Greeks? Well, as for them,
They asked the Questions brilliantly, but slim
    Or none the odds that they would ever trace
    The Answers, which the Jew in every case
Possessed; the Questions never occurred to him.

Separate, they both remain opaque,
    A price we pay for our ancestral treason.
    The unexamined life will never find
A *Cross* between the two is what can make
    The sacrifice of self an act of Reason:
    To love the Lord your God with all your mind.

--D.T.W.

Chapter 2

CHRISTIAN POETICS, PAST AND PRESENT
The Story of Christian Thinking about Literature

"[I] sing of Knights and Ladies gentle deeds;
Whose prayses hauing slept in silence long,
Me, all too meane, the sacred Muse areeds
To blazon broad emongst her learned throng."
--Edmund Spenser, <u>Faerie Queene</u>, Prolog to Book I

Biblical consciousness and the wholeness of vision it produces are endangered species in the modern world. But there was a time when they ruled the earth--or at least the minds of thinking Christians. This chapter will introduce us to a number of such Christians, to the fruits of their thinking, and to the Great Tradition of Reading they left as their legacy to us.

The story of Christian poetics--that is, the story of Christians thinking consciously *as* Christians about the nature and significance of literary art--is the tale of a movement struggling almost in spite of itself to come to grips with its own doctrine that human beings are created in the image of God. The faith was born into a pagan culture and has survived into a secular one which shows signs of returning to paganism. The Church has perforce used the languages, the markets, and the forms of the surrounding culture. It has transformed them and been transformed by them. In the West, as the faith and the culture grew up together, this process has at times made them all but indistinguishable. But the relationship has always been ambivalent. "What has Athens to do with Jerusalem?" asked Tertullian; and the answers, while legion, have never been simple or easy.[1]

Specifically, Christians have struggled to apply to literature the general biblical principle about being in the world but not of it (Jn. 17:11-16). They were rightly wary of a culture based on idolatry--hence of its literature--hence of literature in general. But they could not escape the literary foundations of their own origin, nor the fact that they, and all humankind, were created in the image of One who expressed his inmost nature from the Beginning as the Word. This tension gives rise to the seeming contradictions of their collective response: condemning literature as dangerous at worst and a waste of time at best while producing some of the greatest poems the world has ever seen. And in the process, a few of them have found in the *imago Dei* the only coherent explanation of why the human race is, for better or worse, a tribe of incorrigible makers.

THE BEGINNINGS: AUGUSTINE

St. Augustine, the most profound and articulate of their early spokesmen, is in his own writings a microcosm of their larger, continuing discussion. There has never been a more outstanding example of a person in whom biblical consciousness produced wholeness of vision; on every page of his masterpiece, The Confessions, a profoundly God-centered view of the world shines forth. Yet he struggled mightily with how to relate his extra-Biblical reading to that vision. As the real starting point of the ongoing discussion of these issues, he requires extended treatment.

The negative side is more well known. In Book I of the Confessions, he seems to look back on his study of Virgil with nothing but regret for lost time. The exercise of imitating his poetic lies (*figmentorum poeticorum*) was "mere smoke and wind"; Augustine's time would have been better spent on God's praises in Scripture than such "empty vanities"; his labor on them was in effect nothing more than a "sacrifice offered up to the collapsed angels."[2] He had wept for Dido who killed herself for love while staying dry-eyed over his own spiritual death, but now thinks of his enjoyment of her fictional sorrow as madness (*dementia*).[3] In Book III he confesses that when he attended theaters in his youth he "sympathized together with the lovers when they wickedly enjoyed one another."[4] To enjoy in tragedy that which one would not willingly suffer in reality is "miserable madness" (*miserabilis insania*). Literary experience does not lead to virtue because true mercy is practical. The emotional catharsis of the theater, though, is a sham, for by it one is not "provoked to help the sufferer, but only invited to be sorry for him."[5]

The complaints are the familiar ones which would be repeated again and again throughout history. The fictions of the poets are lies; they are a waste of time, distracting us from more profitable pursuits; and they are an enticement to evil. Yet even as we read these passages, we cannot believe that for Augustine they tell the whole story. Where, we ask, would the felicitous style of the Confessions have come from if he had never studied the classics from the standpoint of rhetorical analysis? And where would he have found such a perfect concrete example for his point about the ironies of misplaced human emotion had he remained ignorant of the dolors of Dido? Indeed, if we just keep reading, we find that there is more to Augustine's view of literature than at first meets the eye.

Even in the Confessions we find hints of factors in Augustine's upbringing which help explain the vehemence of his negative statements and nuance our understanding of their significance. His education was rhetorical and sophistic; he was trained, in other words, to be a lawyer, a professional maker of the worse to appear the better reason and a teacher of others to do the same. He was taught to scour the classics for examples of eloquence which could be used cynically to sway juries in court cases with no concern for the truth. And in this eloquence his "ambition was to be eminent, all out of a damnable and vain-glorious end, puffed up with a delight of human glory."[6] It is little wonder then that in his post-conversion reaction he felt compelled to resign that profession and ended up at times appearing to toss the baby of literature out along with the bath water of sophistry. Yet even the very terms of his rejection testify to the power of words well used.

It is evident on every page of his writings that Augustine was impacted for the good by his classical reading in spite of his cynical teachers and his own scruples, and sometimes he is not unaware of it. The pagan Cicero's Hortensius was a major influence leading to his conversion to Christ. It "quite altered my affection, turned my prayers to thyself, O Lord, and made me have clean other purposes and desires." It had this effect, he interestingly notes, because he made use of it not to "sharpen his tongue" but "for the matter of it."[7]

He had, then, moments in which he recognized something of value even in pagan literature, something which the abuses that also exist ought not to deter us from seeking. Elsewhere he expounds the principle implicit here and defines explicitly what the something is:

> We [Christians] should not abandon music because of the superstitions of pagans if there is anything we can take from it that might help us understand the Holy Scriptures. . . . Nor is there any reason we should refuse to study literature because it is said that Mercury discovered it. That the pagans have dedicated temples to Justice and Virtue and prefer to worship in the form of stones things which ought to be carried in the heart is no reason we should abandon justice and virtue. On the contrary, let everyone who is a good and true Christian

understand that truth belongs to his Master, wherever it is found.[8]

Literature--even pagan literature--conveys truth and is therefore not to be despised. Unfortunately, the balance is provided by lesser-known treatises such as the Christian Education, leaving the negative impression of the Confessions unchallenged for most readers. Yet even in the Confessions, learning to read is a good thing and even eloquence as such is admitted not to be inherently evil: "I blame not the words, which of themselves are like vessels choice and precious; but that wine of error that is in them."[9] Clearly, the studies Augustine seems to reject have enhanced his ability to write the book in which he seems to reject them. The rationale for their use is worked out in the Christian Education.[10]

How then can Christians make use of the products of an idolatrous culture? In pagan learning, error and superstition are to be rejected. But pagan learning also included the liberal arts, which are servants of truth. "Now we may say that these elements are the pagans' gold and silver, which they did not create for themselves, but dug out of the mines of God's providence." Therefore, it is proper for Christians to "take all this away from them and turn it to its proper use in declaring the Gospel."[11]

Even the infamous art of the rhetorician (we should remember that through the Renaissance poetry was considered a species of rhetoric) is in itself morally neutral and capable of being used in the service of truth; therefore, "we should not blame the practice of eloquence but the perversity of those who put it to a bad use."[12] This being so, Christians have not only a right but also an obligation to learn and employ the art of rhetoric. Since it is "employed either to support truth or falsehood, who would venture to say that truth as represented by its defenders should take its stand unarmed?" The result of

Christians abandoning the field would be that falsehood is expounded "briefly, clearly, and plausibly," but truth "in such a manner that it is boring, . . . difficult to understand, and, in a word, hard to believe."[13]

In spite of eloquently expressed doubts, then, Augustine articulates a defense of Christian appropriation of and production of literature on the model of spoiling the Egyptians (see Ex. 11:2-3, 12:35-36). It is a limited and pragmatic approach: Literature is valued for the truth (probably, for Augustine, propositional truth) it contains, and the arts that produce it are valued for the ways in which they can help us understand the Scriptures and proclaim the Gospel. But it is a place to begin, and it adumbrates possibilities which would be developed later.

When Augustine says, for example, that art makes truth plausible and its absence makes it "hard to believe," it is hard not to hear the phrase resonating with Coleridge's "willing suspension of disbelief which constitutes poetic faith" and see C. S. Lewis' magnificent attempts to make Christian truth believable by making it imaginable looming on the horizon. It would be to consider too curiously (not to mention anachronistically) to consider so, as concerns Augustine's meaning. But perhaps in retrospect we can see the seeds of later developments already embedded here.

MEDIEVAL AND RENAISSANCE PERIODS

Augustine set the terms of the discussion and defined the tension which would characterize much of it down through the years. In the Middle Ages, criticism was mainly practical, focussed on grammar, the classification of tropes, etc.[14] Meanwhile, Christian writers wrestled with the issues in practical terms, embodying their Christian vision of the world in concrete images and moving stories. The Beowulf poet struggled with the relationship between his Christian faith and his Teutonic heritage and made a grand synthesis in which the heroic ideal was enlisted in a cosmic war of good and evil.[15] Dante, Langland, and the Pearl poet created concrete images that incarnated Christian doctrines allegorically so that they could bid their readers to "come and behold, / To see with eye that erst in thought I roll'd."[16] Anonymous lyricists captured the emotion of their faith in musical lines of beauty and simplicity.[17] Chaucer gave us a humane and sympathetic portrait of "God's plenty" and then felt obliged to retract most of it before his death in a passage which still embarrasses his admirers and shows the Augustinian tension to be yet unresolved.[18] By the time of the Reformation, some serious polarization had set in.

Luther said that Reason was the Devil's whore, but he also asked why the Devil should have all the good music and noted that literary study equips people as nothing else does to deal skillfully with Scripture: Before any new revelation of the word of God, He prepares the way "by the rise and prosperity of languages and letters, as though they were John the Baptists."[19] Calvin applied the new grammatico-historical exegesis to secular writings and Scripture alike and increased the number of quotations from Plato, Seneca, and Cicero in the <u>Institutes</u> proportionally to the size of the work in each edition.[20] Ironically, some of his followers would take Augustine's doubts about the value of secular literature, untempered by his more positive perspectives, and run with them to extreme and sometimes almost hysterical lengths.

These objectors have been characterized, not entirely fairly, as Puritan. While Puritans did take the lead in the drive to close the theaters, for example, not all who were sympathetic to the Puritan cause or the spiritual values they represented were in agreement with these objections. Nor could all who raised them be classified, without anachronism, as Puritans. We find it as early as in that old humanist and gentle pedagogue Roger

Ascham, who even as he praises the virtues of the (Greek and Latin) classics, inveighs against "books of chevalry," warning that "Mo papists be made by your merry books of Italy than by your earnest books of Louvain," and railing particularly against Malory's <u>Morte Arthur</u>; "the whole pleasure of which book standeth in two special points, in open manslaughter and bold bawdry." In Malory, "those be counted the noblest knights that do kill most men without any quarrel and commit foulest advoulteries by subtlest shifts."[21] This in a work the whole point of which is to show how sin (the adultery of Guinnevere and Lancelot) has disastrous consequences that lead to the destruction of the kingdom!

When the Puritans do sound this note, even their later, more moderate spokesmen such as the usually sensible Richard Baxter (Seventeenth Century) can sound extreme. Baxter advises Christian readers to read first the Bible, then books that apply it. If there is any time left, they may turn to history and science. But they must beware of the poison in "vain romances, play-books, and false stories, which may bewitch your fancies and corrupt your hearts." He buttresses such attacks with arguments: "Play-books, romances, and idle tales" keep more important things out of our minds; they divert us from serious thoughts of salvation; they are a waste of valuable time. Finally, he asks in a rhetorical flourish, "whether the greatest lovers of romances and plays, be the greatest lovers of the book of God, and of a holy life?" [22]

We have heard it all before. But now it is Augustine one-sided, without the balance of his more mature reflections. It cannot be called an advance, but such sentiments did perform one useful service: They provoked a reaction. It came from a Puritan who did not fit the caricatures. His name was Sir Philip Sidney,[23] and what he wrote could be called an advance indeed. He called it "The Defense of Poesy." It raised the discussion to heights which have seldom been reached again.

THE RENAISSANCE: SIR PHILIP SIDNEY

Responding in general to such scruples as we have noted and in particular to Stephen Gosson's School of Abuse (1579), Sidney wrote his apologia in the early 1580's, though it was not published until 1595. In it, he not only gives a thorough and brilliant refutation of the enemies of "poesy" (by which he means imaginative literature, whether in prose or verse) but also lays out a comprehensive vision of its place in the larger structure of learning and the Christian life.

He leaves no stone unturned, appealing in luminous and eloquently cadenced prose to Poesy's antiquity, its universality, and its effectiveness as a mnemonic device and as an enticement to and adornment of what many of his opponents consider more "serious" studies. In the process, he makes many of Augustine's positive points, distinguishing the right use from the abuse of literary art. He appeals to the example of Jesus and other biblical writers, who told stories (the parables) and wrote beautiful poetry (the psalms, Canticles, etc.). But Sidney is not content merely to win a grudging admittance for literature to the curriculum; he will not stop until he has won it the highest place of all.

Sidney takes it for granted, along with his opponents, that the purpose of education is the acquisition not of knowledge only but of virtue as well. So then: The moral philosopher tells you the precepts of virtue, what ought to be, but he does it so abstractly that he is "hard of utterance" and "misty to be conceived," so that one must "wade in him until he be old before he shall find sufficient cause to be honest." The historian, on the other hand, tells a concrete story we can relate to; but he is limited to what actually has been and cannot speak of what ought to be. The one gives an ideal but abstract precept, the other a concrete but flawed example. So "both, not having both, do both halt."[24] How then do we get beyond this impasse?

> Now doth the peerless poet perform both: for
> whatsoever the philosopher saith should be done, he
> gives a perfect picture of it by someone by whom he
> presupposeth it was done; so as he coupleth the general
> notion with a particular example. A perfect picture, I
> say, for he yieldeth to the powers of the mind an image
> of that whereof the philosopher bestoweth but a wordish
> description, which doth neither strike, pierce, nor
> possess the sight of the soul as much as the other doth.[25]

By combining the virtues of history and philosophy, the poet
then becomes the "monarch" of the humane sciences, the most
effective at achieving their end, virtuous action. He can give us
better role models--and negative examples too--than can be
supplied by real life in a fallen world. "Disdaining to be tied to
any such subjection [to nature], lifted up by the vigor of his own
invention," he makes in effect another nature.[26]

He has the freedom to do this because he is created in the
image of the Creator. Greek and English rightly agree in calling
the poet (from Greek *poiein*, to make) a maker, for people are
most like God the Maker when they create a world and people it
with significant characters out of their imagination. The very
existence of literature, then, even when it is abused, is a powerful
apology for the Christian doctrine of humanity and its creation in
the image of God. Therefore, we should

> give right honor to the heavenly Maker of that maker,
> who, having made man to his own likeness, set him
> beyond and over all the works of that second nature:
> which in nothing he sheweth so much as in poetry, when
> with the force of a divine breath he bringeth things forth
> surpassing her doings.[27]

Here then is finally a profoundly Christian understanding of literature which does not merely salvage it for Christian use but finds the very ground of its being in explicitly Christian doctrine: creation, the *imago Dei*, the "cultural mandate" to subdue the earth. Christians alone understand why human beings, whether "literary" types or not, are impelled to make, tell, and hear stories. When Christians also do so, they are not so much spoiling the Egyptians as recovering their own patrimony. That is why we not only learn from literature but enjoy it: It delights as it teaches. And it conveys its kind of truth through the creation of concrete images which incarnate or embody ideas which would otherwise remain abstract and nebulous. Hence arises wholeness of vision, as literature helps us internalize the great Realities of the created order. To do it at all requires words; to do it accurately requires words ordered by the central and authoritative Word of Scripture.

Subsequent criticism, both Christian and secular, has confirmed Sidney's emphasis on the significance of the concrete image as an important way literature communicates. And the most profound moments in Christian reflection on literature since have simply followed up on hints Sidney gave us: that the principle of incarnation is why images communicate so well; that the *imago Dei* is the key to our identity as poets as well as human beings. It is no exaggeration to call Sidney's "Defense" the fountainhead of modern Christian poetics. Those who do not begin with it are condemned to reinvent the wheel or drag their load without one.[28]

While Sidney gave us the foundation, there is yet a lot that can be built on it. Seventeenth-Century devotional poets such as Donne explored the ability of unexpected metaphors to express the paradoxical mysteries of Christian truth and experience. George Herbert struggled to reconcile sparkling wit and simplicity in the service of edification, finally bringing his "lovely metaphors" to church "Well dressed and clad" because "My God must have my best--ev'n all I had."[29]   Poets such as Herbert increasingly looked to Scripture to provide both a justification for their writing and a model for how to pursue it, thus overtly pursuing the kind of "biblical consciousness" we have been recommending.[30]   John Milton, following Spenser's example, looked to both biblical and classical models as he created images of truth, virtue, and vice (from Sabrina to the Son, from Comus to Satan) which function in precisely Sidneyan terms.[31]

JOHN MILTON

Milton also buttressed Sidney's case with some powerful arguments of his own. The end of learning, he said, is to "repair the ruins of our first parents by regaining to know God aright, and out of that knowledge to love him, to imitate him, to be like him" by acquiring "true virtue."[32] This reinforces and expands Sidney's point that the end of learning is virtuous action. While we are in the body, our understanding must "found itself on sensible things," and education must follow that method--which helps to explain the importance of concrete images for acquiring both understanding and virtue. The well-rounded Renaissance education Milton recommends then include "a well-continued and judicious conversing among pure authors digested."[33]   The salutary effects of reading then come only from a life-long habit of living with the minds of thoughtful and creative people in their books.

It is because of their connection with the mind of the author that books have such power, Milton explains, in a passage which essentially extends one of Sidney's points: If human beings are the image of a creative God, books are the image of such people.

> For books are not absolutely dead things, but do contain
> a potency of life in them to be as active as that soul
> whose progeny they are; nay, they do preserve as in a

vial the purest efficacy and extraction of that living intellect that bred them. . . . [Hence] as good almost kill a man as kill a good book: who kills a man kills a reasonable creature, God's image; but he who destroys a good book kills reason itself, kills the image of God, as it were, in the eye.[34]

It is the "seasoned life of man" that is "preserved and stored up" in books.[35] Part of what Milton valued in a good book then was contact with the mind of an author rendered otherwise inaccessible by distance or time. Such contact is precisely what much recent criticism insists we cannot have. Perhaps a secular world view inevitably leads to a universe in which a text is merely a playing field for the reader's own intellectual athleticism. Perhaps only a Christian view (such as Milton's) of the *imago* descending from God to author to text can preserve the writing of literature as an act of communication. Perhaps we have too easily accepted the dominance of reader-centered approaches when our own tradition could provide the basis for a more humane alternative. At any rate, Milton's language and its theological grounding may explain one reason why Christians still tend to be more sympathetic than many other readers to author-centered approaches such as that of E. D. Hirsch.[36]

Milton also strengthens the rationale for refusing to ban literature on the grounds of its potential for abuse. His arguments against government censorship of some books tell equally against those who would eschew all books lest they be corrupted by them. Such attempts to bury our heads in the sand backfire in terms of their own goals because virtue that is preserved only thus would be "but a blank virtue, not a pure." In the real world after the Fall, as in the literary worlds which represent it, good and evil are so intertwined that the responsibility of discernment cannot realistically be avoided so easily. As a result,

> What wisdom can there be to choose, what continence to
> forbear, without the knowledge of evil? He that can
> apprehend and consider vice with all her baits and
> seeming pleasures, and yet abstain, and yet distinguish,
> and yet prefer that which is truly better, he is the true
> warfaring Christian.[37]

This is so because we "cannot praise a fugitive and cloistered virtue, unexercised and unbreathed, that never sallies out and sees her adversary, but slinks out of the race." Spenser's Guyon is a positive role model of uncloistered virtue who makes his author a better teacher than Scotus or Aquinas. (Thus Sidney's Poet defeats the Philosopher and the Theologian.) But even when a text promotes error, discernment is better than blindness, and "books promiscuously read" can help prepare us for life-- indeed, are a necessary part of that preparation without which biblical consciousness and wholeness of vision are not to be looked for in their fullness. If they do not produce this fruit, the fault lies not in the book but in the reader. Anyone who tries to avoid corruption by avoiding books only makes himself a citizen of Mark Twain's Hadleyburg.

THE MODERN ERA

The Eighteenth and Nineteenth Centuries saw advances in our understanding of literature, but few of them came from Christians speaking specifically as Christians. Dr. Johnson's observation that staying power--"length of duration and continuance of esteem"--is the ultimate criterion of literary greatness has stood the test of time itself, while his dictum that nothing can achieve this stature but "just representations of *general* nature" (italics added) has not.[38] Wordsworth's attack on poetic diction, Coleridge's insights on the role of the imagination, and Keats' concept of negative capability have enriched our appreciation of the range of possibilities in literature. Arnold showed us how literature and its criticism could help us to see things as in themselves they really are and to discern the best that has been done and thought, but he succumbed to the post-Darwinian skepticism of his age so far as to make Poetry more a substitute for faith than its maidservant.

In the Twentieth Century, the New Criticism focussed constructively on the details of the text and sought to define the kind of knowledge literature offers in contradistinction to that which comes from the sciences, concluding that it was knowledge of human experience.[39] It was a positive influence up to a point; but its imbalanced emphasis on the autonomy of the text ironically opened the door to deconstruction and other essentially anti-literary ways of reading. (Texts are to be explicated without reference to the author's life or intention; therefore we concentrate on the internal structures of the text and how they relate to those in other texts; since language is an arbitrary system, those structures relate *only* to themselves and other texts, not to anything in the outside world; and since all language is arbitrary and equivocal, they do not even relate coherently to themselves but always fall apart. This is the sequence that inevitably takes us from New Criticism to Structuralism to Post-Structuralism to Deconstruction when the positive insights of New Criticism are not balanced by and rooted in the biblical world view.)

Christians participated in, benefited from, reacted against, and were influenced by many of these modern movements, but made few contributions to them that were motivated by their distinctively Christian world view as such.

In the meantime, a number of Christian thinkers from various traditions were profitably pursuing the idea that literature is a form of natural revelation parallel to the cosmos, conscience, etc. Jesuit priest Gerard Manley Hopkins held that Nature is "News of God" and sought in his poetry to embody the "inscape," the inner unity of being which a particular created thing has, for "I know the beauty of our Lord by it."[40] Conservative Protestant theologian A. H. Strong saw art giving testimony to "the fundamental conceptions of natural religion"; neo-Thomism emphasizes art as a form of natural revelation; and liberal Protestant theologian Paul Tillich attempted to correlate "the questions posed by man's existential situation, expressed in his cultural creations," with the answers of the Christian message.[41]

Michael Edwards is the best of the recent writers in this vein. "Literature occurs," he says, "because we inhabit a fallen world. Explicitly or obscurely, it is part of our dispute with that world."[42] If the heavens declare the glory of God (Ps. 19:1) and the invisible things are understood by the things that are made (Rom. 1:20), then the things made by the creative member of that creation--especially the *verbal* artifacts--ought in a special way to bring the truths embodied in creation into focus. An eye that knows where to look should then be able to find in the recurring themes and structures of human literature (whether written by believers or not) an apology for and an elucidation of biblical motifs. As Edwards puts it,

> If the biblical reading of life is in any way true, literature will be strongly drawn towards it. Eden, Fall, Transformation, in whatever guise, will emerge in literature as everywhere else. The dynamics of a literary work will be likely to derive from the Pascalian interplays of greatness and wretchedness, of wretchedness and renewal, of renewal and persisting wretchedness.[43]

INKLINGS AND FRIENDS

The most interesting contributions to Christian poetics in the Twentieth Century came from a group of friends centered in

Oxford, England, in mid-century, who, consciously or not, harked back to Sidney's themes and brought them to their fullest development. Seldom have more biblical consciousness and wholeness of vision been concentrated in one place than when the Inklings (C. S. and Warren Lewis, J. R. R. Tolkien, Charles Williams, Owen Barfield, etc.) met in Lewis's rooms or in the Eagle and Child pub in Oxford. And they were present in like-minded friends such as Dorothy L. Sayers who were not actually members of the Inklings as well.

In 1938, J. R. R. Tolkien gave a lecture at St. Andrews University which was later published as "On Fairy Stories."[44] In it he provides a full critical vocabulary for Sidney's idea of the poet as maker made by the Maker: *sub-creation* for the process, *primary creation* for God's making, *secondary creation* for the poet's created world.

> Although now long estranged,
> Man is not wholly lost, nor wholly changed.
> Dis-graced he may be, yet is not de-throned,
> And keeps the rags of lordship once he owned:
> Man, Sub-creator, the refracted Light
> Through whom is splintered from a single white
> To many hues, and endlessly combined
> In living shapes that move from mind to mind.[45]

While the doctrine of sub-creation was created to explain certain features of fantasy literature, it is applicable to other genres as well. Even in the most "realistic" fiction, the writer creates a world, peoples it with characters whose actions give its history significance, and determines the rules of its nature. And usually there will be a hero, a villain, a conflict, and some sort of resolution (which might approach what Tolkien called *eucatastrophe*[46]), so that the secondary world echoes the primary creation in more ways than one. The hero, at great personal sacrifice, defeats the villain, rescues the damsel in distress, and they ride off into the sunset to life happily ever after: This basic plot we keep coming back to is Salvation History writ small, as it were. As Edwards says, literature is "drawn" towards a biblical reading of life. Tolkien explains why: "We make still by the law in which we're made."[47]

In 1941, Dorothy L. Sayers provided a detailed analysis of that creative process in The Mind of the Maker.[48] She developed the relevance of the *imago Dei* for understanding artistic creation in explicitly Trinitarian terms. In every act of creation there is a controlling *idea* (the Father), the *energy* which incarnates that idea through craftsmanship (the Son), and the *power* (which flows, *filioque*, from the Father and the Son) to elicit a response in the reader (the Spirit). These three, while separate in identity, are yet one act of creation. So the ancient creedal statements about the Trinity are factual claims about the Mind of the Maker which can be shown to be literal truth about the mind of the maker created in his image.

Sayers delves into the ramifications of these ideas for writing and reading, using numerous literary examples, in what is one of the most fascinating accounts ever written both of the nature of literature and of the *imago Dei*. While some readers may think she has a tendency to take a good idea too far, The Mind of the Maker remains an indispensable classic of Christian poetics.

C. S. Lewis never produced a major statement on literary theory from an explicitly Christian standpoint to rival Tolkien's or Sayers',[49] but he gave us a constant stream of practical criticism from an implicitly Christian stance and a number of provocative essays that deal directly with the relationship between Christianity and literature. Probably best known is the essay "Christianity and Culture,"[50] superficial readings of which have given rise to the notion that Lewis had an "anti-cultural bias."[51] Actually, he was making the point that idolization of culture (including literature) corrupts and destroys culture--a point he made more clearly in later essays.[52] In "Christianity and Culture" he was engaged in the Augustinian task of defending the *innocence* of literary pursuits; in later writings he expanded his view of the positive *value* of reading. These essays constitute in effect a fascinating explanation of why and how the right kind of reading nurtures biblical consciousness and wholeness of vision.

In the first place, literature enlarges our world of experience to include both more of the physical world and things not yet imagined, giving the "actual world" a "new dimension of depth."[53] This makes it possible for literature to strip Christian doctrines of their "stained-glass" associations and make them appear in their "real potency,"[54] a possibility Lewis himself realized magnificently in the Narnia series and the Space Trilogy. Then, too, literature can have something of the significance that Lewis denies it in "Christianity and Culture" through the creation of positive role models and the reinforcement of healthy "stock responses": life is sweet, death is bitter, etc.[55] "Since it is likely that [children] will meet cruel enemies, let them at least have heard of brave knights and heroic courage."[56] Finally, literature can cure our chronological snobbery and provincialism and fortify us in the "mere Christianity" that has remained constant through the ages, if we do not limit ourselves to the books of our own age.[57]

That literature will do these things is uncertain. Much depends on the reader himself, and much modern literature tries *not* to. But the literature of the ages *can* accomplish these things if we receive it sympathetically. In An Experiment in Criticism, Lewis shows us how to do just that, in a book that shows the possibility of a sane reader-centered criticism which would not exclude the authority of the author.[58]

OTHER VOICES

No one writer had more influence on modern thinking about literature than T. S. Eliot, whose conversion brought him back from the wasteland of modernity to dance at the still point of the turning world. Two major themes from his criticism compel our attention here. The first was a constant in both his modernist and Christian periods, though it makes best sense when grounded in the Christian world view: the importance of rootedness in the literary *tradition* of the West for both intelligent reading and original writing. Many modernists and post-modernists tend to dismiss the "dead writers" (today, dead white European male writers)--or at least their ideas--as irrelevant because "we know so much more than they did." "Precisely," Eliot replied, "and they are what we know."[59] And their writings, starting with Homer, form the context within which all new writings must take their place and without which no writings can be fully understood.

The second theme is the relation of *content* and *literary value*. Here, Eliot gradually moved from an early aestheticism in which he tended rigorously to separate the two toward an appreciation of the fact that ultimately literary greatness is inseparable from the value of the ideas expressed or implied. In 1927 he said that, from the standpoint of poetry, Dante's system of thought was "an irrelevant accident."[60] Just two years later, he recognized that Dante's "His will is our peace" was "literally true," and that "it has more beauty for me now, when my own experience has deepened its meaning, than it did when I first read it," concluding that appreciation of poetry could not in practice be separated from personal belief after all.[61] By 1935 he was calling for literary criticism to be "completed by criticism from a definite ethical and theological standpoint,"[62] and for Christians to produce both such criticism and also literary works themselves whose content was "unconsciously Christian."

A final important voice for twentieth-century Christian poetics belonged to an American local-color writer, the self-styled "hillbilly Thomist" Flannery O'Connor. Like Tillich and Edwards, she believed that great literature deals with ultimate concerns which are essentially theological; like Lewis, but in a totally different manner, she removed stained-glass associations so that the "action of grace" could be seen in new contexts with power. In a small but powerful body of fiction she made the American South an image of the human condition seen in profoundly Christian terms. Her letters and critical writings are loaded with practical wisdom on how to embody the anagogical vision in concrete images which can speak to the modern reader.[63]

CONCLUSION

Where, then, has this brief history of Christian thinking about literature brought us? Cary rightly notes that "the modern critic who wants to deal with literature from a Christian standpoint has not found direct precedent in the literary criticism of the past 150 years, which constitutes what is inevitably the critical milieu for him."[64] The Christian giants we have surveyed in the Twentieth Century definitely stood outside the mainstream. They all had roots sunk deep in a venerable and humane tradition which goes back to the Ancients through Milton and Sidney, and thus they preserve a way of reading and writing which has been able to resist the ideological fragmentation and de[con]struction which have followed the breakup of the hegemony of New Criticism. They are for that reason indispensable helps in the task of recovering the biblical consciousness and resulting wholeness of vision which the Evangelical world is rapidly loosing.

In the pages of journals such as Christianity and Literature, explicitly Christian wrestling with literary questions continues.

It ranges from futile attempts to accommodate modernist and post-modernist perspectives to virile and living heirs of what we have presented as the right Evangelical tradition descending from Sir Philip Sidney. By grounding literary activity in a specifically Christian understanding of human nature, that tradition gives a coherent explanation of why people make worlds out of words and of the ways in which those worlds are valuable.

Perhaps being reminded that there is a unique and distinctively Christian tradition of poetics can help us tap into its power once agin. In America, Evangelicals produce too many cheap imitations of Lewis and Tolkien on the one hand and too many saccharine historical romances on the other. While writers such as Walter Wangerin, Jr., Donna Fletcher Crow, and Calvin Miller have produced some interesting creative work, and writers such as Leland Ryken, Gene Edward Veith, and Michael Bauman have produced some incisive criticism, there is no one on the scene with the power of a Lewis, a Tolkien, a Sayers, or an O'Connor--much less a Milton. But the tradition which gave us those writers can give us more--and perhaps the first step towards that end is for it to give us *readers* worthy of the name, in whom biblical consciousness is being reborn. As Francis Schaeffer reminded us, "The Christian is the one whose imagination should fly beyond the stars.[65]

Notes to Chapter 2

[1.] See H. Richard Niebuhr, <u>Christ and Culture</u> (N.Y.: Harper & Row, 1951), Henry R. Van Til, <u>The Calvinistic Concept of Culture</u> (Philadelphia: Presbyterian & Reformed, 1959), and Leland Ryken, <u>Culture in Christian Perspective</u> (Portland: Multnomah, 1986).

2. Augustine, <u>Confessions</u>, w. Eng. trans. by William Watts. The Loeb Classical Library. 2 vol. (Cambridge: Harvard Univ. Pr., 1946), I.xvii (1:51).

3. Ibid., I.xiii (1:39-40).

4. Ibid., III.ii (1:103).

5. Ibid., III.ii (1:101).

6. Ibid., III.iv (1:109).

7. Ibid., III.iv (1:109f).

8. Augustine, <u>Christian Education</u> II.xxviii-xxxii, in George Howie, ed. & trans., <u>St. Augustine: On Education</u> (Chicago: Regnery, 1969), pp. 350-51.

9. Augustine, <u>Confessions</u>, op. cit., I.xvi (1:149).

10. Cf. also <u>Confessions</u> XI.xxvi (2:267) for a discussion of how a knowledge of scansion helps us understand the concept of time.

11. Augustine, <u>Christian Education</u>, op. cit., II.lvi-lxi (p. 364).

12. Ibid., II.liv (p. 360).

13. Ibid., IV.ii-xi (p. 369); cf. Henry Chadwick, <u>Augustine</u> (N.Y.: Oxford Univ. Pr., 1986), who notes that "Cicero's prose and Virgil's poetry were so profoundly stamped on Augustine's mind" that he could not write without a reminiscence or allusion (p. 4), and that in his old age he was still quoting Cicero (p. 10).

14. Alex Preminger, et. al., eds., <u>Classical and Medieval Literary Criticism: Translations and Interpretations</u> (N.Y.: Ungar, 1974), pp. 285-86.

15. See J. R. R. Tolkien, "<u>Beowulf</u>: The Monsters and the Critics" and Marie Padgett Hamilton, "The Religious Principle in <u>Beowulf</u>," both reprinted in Lewis F. Nicholson, ed., <u>An Anthology of Beowulf Criticism</u> (South Bend, Ind.: Univ. of Notre Dame Pr., 1963), pp. 51-103 & 105-135. The standard edition of the text is Fr. Klaeber, ed., <u>Beowulf and the Fight at Finnsburg</u>, 3rd ed. (Lexington, Mass.: D. C. Heath, 1950); good modern translations include E. Talbot Donaldson's prose, in Joseph E. Tuso, ed., <u>Beowulf: The Donaldson Translation, Backgrounds and Sources, Criticism</u> (N.Y.: Norton, 1975), and Charles W. Kennedy, <u>Beowulf: The Oldest English Epic, Translated into Alliterative Verse with a Critical Introduction</u> (N.Y.: Oxford Univ. Pr., 1978).

16. William Langland's work is available in paperback in Thomas A. Knott and David C. Fowler, eds., <u>Piers The Plowman: A Critical Edition of the A-Version</u> (Baltimore: Johns Hopkins Pr., 1952), Elizabeth Salter and Derek Pearsall, eds., <u>Piers Plowman</u> (Evanston: Northwestern Univ. Pr., 1969), and in a prose translation by J. F. Goodridge, <u>Piers The Plowman</u> (Baltimore: Penguin, 1966). The best edition of <u>The Divine Comedy</u> in English is Dorothy L. Sayers' translation with its wonderful introductions and notes (Baltimore: Penguin, 1949-62); see also her <u>Introductory Papers on Dante</u> (N.Y.: Harper &

Brothers, 1954) and Charles Williams, <u>The Figure of Beatrice:</u> <u>A Study in Dante</u> (N.Y.: Farrar, Strauss, & Cudahy, 1961); the Pearl poet's works are found in E. V. Gordon, ed., <u>Pearl</u> (Oxford: Clarendon, 1953) and J. R. R. Tolkien, E. V. Gordon, & Norman Davis, eds., <u>Sir Gawain and the Green Knight</u>, 2nd ed. (Oxford: Clarendon, 1967); a fine modern English translation is J. R. R. Tolkien, <u>Sir Gawain the Green Knight, Pearl, Sir Orpheo</u> (Boston: Houghton Mifflin, 1975). The definition of allegory used here is from Thomas Sackville's "Induction" to <u>The Mirror</u> <u>for Magistrates</u>, in Hyder E. Rollins & Herschel Baker, eds., <u>The</u> <u>Renaissance in England</u> (Lexington, Mass.: D. C. Heath, 1954), p. 273.

17. Accessible collections include Robert D. Stevick, ed., <u>One</u> <u>Hundred Middle English Lyrics</u> (Indianapolis: Bobbs-Merrill, 1964) and Henry A. Person, ed., <u>Cambridge Middle English</u> <u>Lyrics</u>, rev. ed. (N. Y.: Greenwood Pr., 1969).

18. F. N. Robinson, ed., <u>The Works of Geoffrey Chaucer</u>, 2nd ed. (Boston: Houghton Mifflin, 1961), p. 265.

19. Qtd. in Wallace K. Ferguson, <u>The Renaissance in Historical</u> <u>Thought: Five Centuries of Interpretation</u> (N. Y.: Houghton Mifflin, 1948), p. 54.

20. See chapter 3 below for further treatment.

21. Roger Ascham, <u>The Schoolmaster</u>, in Rollins & Baker, op. cit., p. 833. For Malory, see Eugene Vinaver, ed., <u>King Arthur</u> <u>and his Knights: Selected Tales by Sir Thomas Malory</u> (Boston: Houghton Mifflin, 1968).

22. Richard Baxter, <u>The Practical Works of Richard Baxter</u>, vol. 1, <u>The Christian Directory</u> (London: George Virtue, 1838), pp.

56-57. Apparently the Puritans *had* biblical consciousness, but some of them had a truncated version of it. Yet even their incompletely developed vision (compared to that of Sidney, for example) made them spiritual giants in many areas (compared to us). See David Martyn Lloyd-Jones, The Puritans: Their Origins and Successors (Edinburgh: Banner of Truth, 1987), J. I. Packer, A Quest for Godliness: The Puritan Vision of the Christian Life (Wheaton: Crossway, 1990), and Leland Ryken, Worldly Saints: The Puritans as They Really Were (Grand Rapids: Zondervan, 1986) for excellent perspectives on the more positive contributions of the Puritan movement. And we should remember that people such as Sidney, Spenser, and Milton showed it was possible to have all the Puritan virtues without their typical shortcomings.

23. For an excellent overview of Sidney's life and evaluation of him as a Christian thinker and statesman, see David S. Gordon, "Sir Philip Sidney: The Faith and Practice of an Elizabethan Christian" (M.A. Thesis, Trinity Evangelical Divinity School, 1995).

24. Sir Philip Sidney, The Defense of Poesy, in Rollins & Baker, op. cit., p. 610.

25. Ibid.

26. Ibid., p. 607.

27. Ibid., p. 608.

28. S. K. Heninger, Jr., Sidney and Spenser: The Poet as Maker (University Park: Pennsylvania State Univ. Pr., 1989), p. 225, notes that the Defense was "*the* major event in the development of literary theory in England."

29. F. E. Hutchinson, ed., The Works of George Herbert (Oxford: Clarendon Pr., 1941), p. 176. See the chapter on Herbert here for further treatment of his "poetics of edification."

30. For a masterful treatment of this point, see Barbara Kiefer Lewalski, Protestant Poetics and the Seventeenth-Century Religious Lyric (Princeton: Princeton Univ. Pr., 1979).

31. See Milton's own statements to this effect in "Areopagetica," in Merritt Y. Hughes, ed., John Milton: Complete Poems and Major Prose (Indianapolis: Bobbs-Merrill, 1957), pp. 728-29.

32. Milton, "Of Education," in Hughes, op. cit., p. 631.

33. Ibid.

34. Milton, "Areopagetica," op. cit., p. 720.

35. Ibid.

36. E. D. Hirsch, Validity in Interpretation (New Haven: Yale Univ. Pr., 1967).

37. Milton, "Areopagetica," op. cit., p. 728.

38. Samuel Johnson, "Preface to the Plays of William Shakespeare," in Geoffrey Tillotson et al., eds., Eighteenth-Century English Literature (N.Y.: Harcourt, Brace, & World, 1969), pp. 1066-67.

39. Important statements include Cleanth Brooks and Robert Penn Warren, Understanding Poetry, 3rd ed. (N.Y.: Holt, Rinehart, & Wilson, 1960), Cleanth Brooks, The Well-Wrought Urn (N.Y.: Harcourt, Brace, & World, 1947), and other works

by John Crowe Ransom, Allan Tate, etc.

40. W. H. Gardner & N. H. MacKenzie, eds., The Poems of Gerard Manley Hopkins, 4th ed. (London: Oxford Univ. Pr., 1967), pp. xx-xxi.

41. Norman Reed Cary, Christian Criticism in the Twentieth Century (Port Washington, N.Y.: Kennicat Pr., 1975), pp. 35, 27. For a useful critique of Tillich's thought on art, see Jeremy S. Begbie, Voicing Creation's Praise: Towards a Theology of the Arts (Edinburgh: T. & T. Clark, 1991).

42. Michael Edwards, Towards a Christian Poetics (Grand Rapids: Eerdmans, 1984), p. 12.

43. Ibid.

44. J. R. R. Tolkien, "On Fairy Stories" (1938); rpt. in C. S. Lewis, ed., Essays Presented to Charles Williams (Oxford: Oxford Univ. Pr., 1947 & Grand Rapids: Eerdmans, 1966), pp. 38-89; and in The Tolkien Reader (N.Y.: Ballantine, 1966), pp. 26-84. See also his fictional symbolisation of the same ideas, "Leaf by Niggle," in The Tolkien Reader, pp. 85-112. Both essay and story are also to be found in Tree and Leaf (London: Allen & Unwin, 1964). Citations here are from The Tolkien Reader.

45. Ibid., p. 54. Superficial resemblances to Coleridge's language in Biographia Literaria chp. xiii should not blind us to the fact that the conception here is fundamentally different. Coleridge speaks of "primary" and "secondary" *imagination*, but they are not parallel to Tolkien's primary and secondary *creation*. Coleridge's primary imagination is a "repetition" of God's act of creation; Tolkien's primary creation *is* God's act of creation.

Tolkien's exposition is more simple and direct, and closer in spirit to Sidney than to the Romantics. Cf. Coleridge, Biographia Literaria, ed. by George Watson for Everyman's Library (London: J. M. Dent & N. Y.: E. P. Dutton, 1960), p. 167.

46. Ibid., p. 68.

47. Tolkien, op. cit., p. 54.

48. Dorothy L. Sayers, The Mind of the Maker (London, Methuen, 1941; rpt. San Francisco: Harper & Row, 1968); see also the many stimulating essays reprinted in A Matter of Eternity (Grand Rapids: Eerdmans, 1973) and Christian Letters to a Post-Christian World (Grand Rapids: Eerdmans, 1969); see also her Creed or Chaos? (London: The Religious Book Club, 1947).

49. See Margaret L. Carter, "Sub-Creation and Lewis's Theory of Literature," in Bruce L. Edwards, ed., The Taste of the Pineapple: Essays on C. S. Lewis as Reader, Critic, and Imaginative Writer (Bowling Green, Ohio: Bowling Green State Univ. Pr., 1988), pp. 129-37, for an interesting comparison of Lewis and Tolkien as theorists.

50. C. S. Lewis, "Christianity and Culture," in Walter Hooper, ed., Christian Reflections (London: Geoffrey Bles & Grand Rapids: Eerdmans, 1967), pp. 12-36; cf. Leland Ryken's excellent summary and evaluation of the argument in Triumphs of the Imagination: Literature in Christian Perspective (Downers Grove, Ill.: Inter-Varsity, 1979), pp. 225-27. For examples of Lewis' practical criticism, see A Preface to Paradise Lost (N. Y.: Oxford Univ. Pr., 1942), or Walter Hooper, ed., Selected Literary Essays (Cambridge: Cambridge Univ. Pr., 1969).

51. Cary, op. cit., p. 16.

52. C. S. Lewis, "First and Second Things," in Walter Hooper, ed., God in the Dock (Grand Rapids: Eerdmans, 1970), pp. 278-81; in England, it is in Undeceptions (London: Geoffrey Bles, 1971; rpt. as First and Second Things, London: Collins Fount, 1985); and "Lilies that Fester," in The World's Last Night and Other Essays (N. Y.: Harcourt, Brace, & World, 1960), pp. 31-49, or in They Asked for a Paper (London: Geoffrey Bles, 1962), pp. 105-19.

53. C. S. Lewis, "On Three Ways of Writing for Children," in Walter Hooper, ed., Of Other Worlds (N. Y.: Harcourt, Brace, Jovanovich, 1964), p. 29, or in Hooper, ed., Of This and Other Worlds (London: Collins, 1982), p. 65; cf. "The Language of Religions," in Christian Reflections, op. cit., p. 333; "An Expostulation Against Too Many Writers of Science Fiction," in Walter Hooper, ed., C. S. Lewis: Poems (London & N. Y.: Harcourt, Brace, Jovanovich, 1964), p. 58; and C. S. Lewis, An Experiment in Criticism (Cambridge: Cambridge Univ. Pr., 1969), p. 40.

54. C. S. Lewis, "Sometimes Fairy Stories Say Best What's to be Said," in Of Other Worlds, op. cit., p. 37, or in Of This and Other Worlds, op. cit., p. 71.

55. C. S. Lewis, "A Confession," in Poems, op. cit., p. 1. See chapter 7, on Lewis and T. S. Eliot, for further discussion of this point.

56. C. S. Lewis, "On Three Ways of Writing for Children," in Of Other Worlds, op. cit., p. 31.

57. C. S. Lewis, "On the Reading of Old Books," in God in the Dock, op. cit., pp. 200-207, or in Walter Hooper, ed., The Grand Miracle (N. Y.: Ballantine, 1970), pp. 122-28; cf. "Is English Doomed?" in Hooper, ed., Present Concerns: Essays by C. S. Lewis (San Diego: Harcourt, Brace, Jovanovich, 1986), pp. 27-31.

58. Op. cit. Lewis argues that a book should be judged by the quality of reading it encourages over time, not that its *meaning* is a wax nose to be twisted into whatever shape the readers (or "interpretive community"), in their ignorance, prefer.

59. T. S. Eliot, "Tradition and the Individual Talent" (1919), in Selected Essays of T. S. Eliot (N. Y.: Harcourt, Brace, & World, 1964), p. 6.

60. T. S. Eliot, "Shakespeare and the Stoicism of Seneca" (1927), in Selected Essays, op. cit., p. 116.

61. T. S. Eliot, "Dante" (1929), in Selected Essays, op. cit., p. 231.

62. T. S. Eliot, "Religion and Literature" (1935), in Selected Essays, op. cit., p.354.

63. Flannery O'Connor, Mystery and Manners: Occasional Prose, ed. Sally & Robert Fitzgerald (N. Y.: Farrar, Strauss, & Giroux, 1961 & London: Faber, 1972); cf. Sally Fitzgerald, ed., The Habit of Being: Letters of Flannery O'Connor (N. Y.: Farrar, Straus, & Giroux, 1974 & London: Faber, 1979); Her fiction can be found in Flannery O'Connor: The Complete Stories (N. Y.: Farrar, Strauss, & Giroux, 1974 & London: Faber, 1990); for several of the short stories with two novelettes, see Three by Flannery O'Connor (N. Y.: Signet, n.d.).

64. Cary, op. cit., pp. 3-4.

65. Francis A. Schaeffer, <u>Art and the Bible: Two Essays</u> (Downers Grove, Ill.: Inter-Varsity Pr., & London: Hodder & Stoughton, 1973), p. 5. Schaeffer is known for his incisive discussions of the ways in which art reflects the world-view of the artist. This little pamphlet contains much sane discussion which would surprise readers who know Schaeffer only by reputation and caricature.

INTERLUDE

DEFINITIONS

Tending to Show that Theology is Indeed
The Queen of the Sciences

I

Philosopher: a man who tries to shave
With Ockham's Razor by the flickering light
That shines behind his back in Plato's Cave.
He'll know that's what he's doing if he's bright;
He may take Pascal's Wager if he's brave
(*Fides quaerens intellectum*), and he might
Thus feel his chains fall off and leave that place
And feel the Sonlight full upon his face.

II

Historian: he deals in documents,
And what he cannot find there he invents.
As long as it fits in with and makes sense
Of what he has of solid evidence,
It's called "interpretation," and he prints
It up. In this there is no vain pretense,
As long as we can tell the difference.

III

The ***Poet*** is a wielder of that word
That clothes the unformed thought and makes it seen,
That sings the silent thought and makes it heard,
That tells us how to say the thing we mean.
Sir Philip Sidney said it long ago
In his book the Defense of Poesy:
Philosophy's business is to seek to know
Not just what is, but that which ought to be,
Truth in its very essence, plain and bare
(Though he may leave it hanging in the air);
History can tell us how, below,
The truth has fared and still is apt to fare;
The ***Poet's*** language teaches us to care.

IV

The ***Theologian*** has to be all three:
The *Logos*, the divine *philosophy*
Which was incarnate in our *history*
Must still be fleshed with *words* to make men see.
The ***Theologian*** simply has to be
All three.

--D.T.W.

Chapter 3

JOHN CALVIN: HUMANIST AND REFORMER
Renaissance, Reformation, and Biblical Consciousness

"Now when their weary limbs with kindly rest,
And bodies were refreshed with due repast,
Fair Una gan Fidelia fair request
To have her knight into her schoolhouse placed,
That of her heavenly wisdom he might taste,
And hear the wisdom of her words divine.
She granted him, and that knight so agraced
That she him taught celestial discipline,
And opened his dull eyes, that light mote in them shine."
--Edmund Spenser, Faerie Queene, I.xviii.

The end of the Middle Ages was a time like our own in which biblical consciousness was in eclipse. It was not so much the fact that relatively few could read, or that only certain kinds of books were read by many of the literate, as *how* things were read, in ways that effectively insulated many readers from the power of the texts.

That reform in doctrine and life was desperately needed in the Church was acknowledged by many. But before that reform could be deep and lasting, a new way of reading would have to be found which would allow biblical consciousness to be restored.

And for that--ironically, given the bad name the original humanists have acquired in the Church from their secular heirs--the Renaissance would have to come first.

One of the most fascinating aspects of historical study is the question of the relationship between the Renaissance and the Reformation.[1] While the precise nature of this relationship

remains a matter of debate,[2] one generally recognized conclusion
has been that many reformers used for their own purposes the
critical methods of scholarship developed by the Renaissance
humanists. To this John Calvin added a genuine love for the
texts of pagan antiquity which were dear to humanist hearts. In
this chapter we will try to cast some light on the impact Calvin's
humanism had on his work as a Reformer and Theologian, for
nothing provides more insight into the kind of reading that leads
to biblical consciousness.[3]

We must begin with a careful definition of the kind of
"humanism" we are talking about. Then, after surveying some
background information which can set Calvin's use of this
humanism in its context, we will proceed to an analysis of its
function in the Institutes.

RENAISSANCE HUMANISM

Humanism is one of those words which have so many
definitions as to be almost meaningless. Its modern connotation
of "theological anthropocentrism" is not necessarily applicable to
the original humanists of the Renaissance. Even within the
Renaissance period it is helpful to avoid confusion by following
Linder, Breen, et al. in distinguishing "general" and "particular"
humanism.[4] General humanism is a philosophical concern for
man and his place in the universe, in the search for the "true
man." While Pico's Oration on the Dignity of Man may be taken
as a representative example, general humanism as a whole should
not be seen as consisting of any coherent body of doctrines about
man or his place in the created order.[5] Unlike modern secular
humanism, Renaissance humanism did not commit its adherents
to an ideology so much as to a program of reading.

In this chapter we will be dealing with particular humanism,
a concept whose definition is more concrete and hence more
easily isolated in the work of a man such as Calvin. In its

particular or narrow sense, *humanism* denoted *a concern for the study of Greek and Roman antiquity from the standpoint of philology and rhetoric.* Though he does not use the term himself, Kristeller gives the classic definition of particular humanism:

> The term *humanista*, coined at the height of the Renaissance period, was in turn derived from an older term, that is, from the "humanities," or *studia humanitatis.* This term was apparently used in the general sense of a liberal or literary education by such ancient Roman authors as Cicero and Gellius, and this use was resumed by the Italian scholars of the late Fourteenth Century. By the first half of the Fifteenth Century, the *studia humanitatis* came to stand for a clearly defined cycle of scholarly disciplines, namely grammar, rhetoric, history, poetry, and moral philosophy, and the study of these subjects was understood to include the reading and interpretation of their standard ancient writers in Latin, and, to a lesser extent, in Greek.[6]

To be a humanist in this sense would not commit a person to any set of philosophical ideas, but rather to a "cultural and educational program which emphasized and developed an important but limited area of studies," which "might be roughly described a literature."[7] The humanist must not merely be in favor of, but must in some sense be involved in, such a program. Thus, the word *humanist* was "commonly used in the Sixteenth Century for the professor or teacher or student of the humanities."[8] However, as Kristeller points out, it is inadequate to define humanism simply as an interest in ancient authors as such. Otherwise, Thomas Aquinas, for example, would have to be classified as a humanist because of his deep indebtedness to

Aristotle. What set the humanist apart from the scholastic was his strong interest in the classical writers *from the standpoint of grammar and rhetoric*, rather than that of *dialectic*, which characterized the schoolmen.[9]

Professionally, the humanists were the descendants of the *dictatores* of the late Middle Ages in Italy. These men were professional secretaries whose business was to write letters, speeches, etc. Humanism arose when they realized that "in order to write and speak well, it was necessary to study and to imitate the ancients."[10]

That is, if you want to write an effective political speech, and you think that because Cicero used to do it so well he might be able to help you, you will not only read Cicero (instead of just the Church Fathers, say) but read Cicero asking a new set of questions: What was the historical situation in which he wrote his orations? What was the goal he was trying to achieve in terms of that situation? Why did he write the way he did in order to achieve that goal? What, then, would this oration have meant to the original audience for which it was written? And how can I apply those same techniques to be effective in *my* situation? You cannot answer the last question until you have understood something about the answers to the prior ones--and they were not the questions that the typical medieval reader was prone to ask.

The implications of this new attitude for the methodology of scholarship were profound. Harbison compares the older and newer approaches to reading brilliantly:

> The classical revival brought with it a fundamental change in scholars' minds as to the nature and objectives of scholarship. While Abelard culled passages to support or destroy propositions, Petrarch read (and became enthusiastic about) whole works of ancient writers. Abelard subordinated grammar and rhetoric to dialectic; Petrarch and his followers subordinated

dialectic to grammar or rhetoric. The study of words and of style, the analysis of how a language is put together and what it may be made to do, the examination of an author in relation to his audience and the whole purpose of his work--these became increasingly the preoccupations of scholars.[11]

It was Renaissance humanists such as Erasmus, Lorenzo Valla, and John Colet, in other words, who pioneered what today we would call "grammatico-historical exegesis." Their battle cry was "*Ad fontes*," "back to the sources!" But what was significant was not only what they were reading--ancient secular authors-- but how they were reading them. What humanism had made possible was, as Bousma puts it, "an imaginative reconstruction of the ancient world through its literature."[12]

When some of those humanists began applying their new way of reading to the Bible, among other ancient sources, the Reformation became a possibility. Before Luther had ever been heard of, John Colet was already sending shock waves across Europe by expounding the Book of Romans, not as a starting place for allegory, but as a real book written by a real Apostle to a real audience with particular needs in a particular historical situation. As a result, unlike Wycliffe and Hus, Luther and Calvin could appeal to the original text of Scripture *and* do it in such a fashion that scholars across Europe could see for themselves, on the basis of what was now becoming common sense, whether this allegedly "new" Gospel was in the Text or not. For "a major novelty of humanistic reading, based on seeing classical authors as human beings rather than vehicles of transcendent wisdom, was insistence that an interpreter of a text faithfully respect its author's intention."[13] (Of course, the invention of the printing press, which allowed both these newly recovered texts and the new ideas they were spawning to be rapidly disseminated across the continent, didn't hurt either.)

A divine conjunction of dates brings the whole relationship into focus: In 1516 Erasmus the Renaissance humanist published the first printed edition of the Greek New Testament; in 1517 Martin Luther nailed his Ninety-Five Theses to the Wittenberg Church door. The *Reformation* exploded across Europe because the *Renaissance*, recovering grammatico-historical exegesis for reasons of its own, had unwittingly unleashed the power of biblical consciousness once again. As Luther himself observed, "There has never been a great revelation of the word of God unless He has first prepared the way by the rise and prosperity of languages and letters, as though they were John the Baptists."[14] It even became a proverb: "Erasmus laid the egg, and Luther hatched it."

CALVIN AND HUMANISM

John Calvin studied under the best humanist scholars France had to offer, at Orleans, Bourges, and Paris, where he distinguished himself by industry and self-discipline. He was so proficient in his studies that as a student of only nineteen years of age he was often called to take the chair of an absent professor. When he left the universities he was, according to Schaff, "the most promising literary man of the age."[15]

Calvin's first literary work, published before his conversion when he was only in his twenties, was a commentary on Seneca's *De Clementia*. While it was not a great seller, it did establish his reputation as a classical scholar.

> It moves in the circle of classical philology and moral philosophy, and reveals a characteristic love for the nobler type of stoicism, great familiarity with Greek and Roman literature, masterly Latinity, rare exegetical skill, clear and sound judgment . . . but makes no allusion to Christianity.[16]

The few insignificant biblical references show no real interest in religion at this time.[17] His earliest letters from this period (1530-1532) are also silent on religious subjects, referring to humanistic studies, matters of friendship, and business.[18]

Thus, when Calvin's conversion came, at about the age of twenty-four (it is difficult to know the exact time of his conversion),[19] he was already a seasoned humanist, as proved by the Seneca commentary. Breen argues that by this time Calvin's mind set must have been firmly established, that, "having so thoroughly imbibed the spirit of humanism, his conversion could not possibly negate his acquired habits and attitudes of mind."[20] What "could not possibly happen" is a perilous realm for historical pronouncement, but in this case Breen was right. Calvin did not feel that his conversion required him to jettison the basic intellectual interests and tools with which humanism had equipped him.

In a rare autobiographical moment, Calvin gives us a glimpse of his own early life and training.

> When I was yet a very little boy, my father had destined me for the study of theology. But afterwards, when he considered that the legal profession commonly raised those who followed it to wealth, this prospect induced him suddenly to change his purpose. Thus it came to pass, that I was withdrawn from the study of philosophy, and was put to the study of law. To this purpose I endeavoured faithfully to apply myself.[21]

His conversion was apparently sudden, and did have profound implications for his thinking. He describes it thus:

> And first, since I was too obstinately devoted to the superstitions of Popery to be easily extricated from so profound an abyss of mire, God by a sudden conversion

> subdued and brought my mind to a teachable frame. . .
> . Having thus received some taste and knowledge of true
> godliness, I was immediately inflamed with so intense a
> desire to make progress therein, that although I did not
> altogether leave off other studies, I yet pursued them
> with less ardor.[22]

Thus, unlike Petrarch, Calvin saw no conflict between the pursuit of divine and human learning.[23] It is true that his love for Seneca and Cicero had to take second place now--he pursued them "with less ardor." But he sees no reason to upbraid himself for continuing the relationship with his old friends. It is instructive to compare the wholesome sanity of Calvin's attitude here with the desperate, impassioned inner struggle of Petrarch which comes out in a work such as the Secretum, where he feels compelled to defend human learning against the charge that it is inherently vain and sinful. The defense is not completely successful, and Petrarch is never quite able to reconcile his internal conflict. But Calvin felt he had good precedent for his attitude toward the ancient authors. Even the Apostle Paul, in Titus 1:12, had not disdained to quote the pagan poet Epimenides. Commenting on this passage, Calvin infers that

> those are superstitious who never venture to quote
> anything from profane authors. Since all truth is from
> God, . . . why is it not lawful to turn to his glory
> whatever may be applied to this use?[24]

Calvin's justification for the pursuit of secular learning is referred to by later writers as the doctrine of *common grace*, the idea that God gives some light even to reprobate men who otherwise would not have it, and that Christians may profit from that light if they subject it to Scripture as their final criterion of truth.[25] By this concept Calvin sought to avoid the equal and opposite errors of, on the one hand, despising what can profitably be learned from natural revelation, or, on the other, neglecting the strategic importance of Holy Writ as providing the necessary framework for the proper correlation and interpretation of all data. Thus he hoped to profit from the wisdom of the ancients without repeating their mistakes.

Most studies of humanism in Calvin have concentrated on the theory for the use of classical material, i.e., on the doctrine of common grace. We will look rather at his practice--what use does he actually make of his classical quotations, what purpose do they serve, etc. We will focus our attention on the Institutes, but first let us look at some of the general indications of Calvin's use of his humanist background in his wider ministry.

Calvin's work was influenced by both the methods and interests of Renaissance humanism. Breen cites as evidence of that influence "his zeal for restoring the true text of Scripture . . . and his respectful mention of the critical work of Valla and Erasmus."[26] Like most of the Renaissance humanists, Calvin seems to have been primarily a man of letters, and to have had relatively little interest in the sciences.[27] (We today would tend to look on that lack of interest as a failing, but what should be emphasized about Calvin was the real interest in letters, in which he was ahead of most educators of his time; science as we know it would not form a major part of anybody's curriculum for some time yet.) This emphasis was reflected in the major thrust of the curriculum at the Academy of Geneva.

The Academy of Geneva is one of the clearest examples of the effects of humanism on Calvin's work. Renaissance humanists were united in the belief that the best preparation for a useful life was an education in the classical authors of Greek and Roman antiquity. In this, Calvin was no exception. So, when he founded the Academy, "it was his ideal to have men trained for the professions by grounding them in the arts and letters, that is, he insisted that they know their Latin and Greek."[28]

Perhaps the most fruitful result of Calvin's humanism was its effect on his work as a commentator on Scripture. He thought it important that even laypersons "know how Holy Scripture uses words," for "We cannot at all understand the doctrine of God if we do not know the procedure [Scripture] employs and its style and language."[29] He shared with Petrarch, Erasmus, and John Colet a desire to get to know ancient writers as real men and to understand their writings as real messages to actual historical situations, rather than as take-off points for fanciful allegorization. Eschewing the traditional method of searching for hidden "deeper" meanings, Calvin "affirmed and carried out the sound and hermeneutical principle that the biblical authors, like all sensible writers, wished to convey to their readers one definite thought in words which they could understand." Schaff therefore calls him "the founder of modern grammatico-historical exegesis."[30] While that title might more accurately be applied to Colet, it is undeniable that Calvin was one of the forerunners of the method as applied to Scripture in modern times, that his commentaries alone of those written in his time are still deservedly in wide use today, and that it was the kind of reading he learned from the humanists which formed the foundation of that work.

But though Calvin made good use of his humanist background, he did not slavishly adhere to it in every respect. He shared the humanists' love for the classical languages, but parted from them in their contempt for the "vulgar tongues." Thus, in the first edition of the Institutes, published only a few years after his conversion, "The one-time humanist, ostensibly not interested in the vernacular . . . is in favor of the use of the vulgar tongue in public prayer."[31] And it was Calvin himself who undertook the laborious task of translating the later and bulkier editions of his *magnum opus* from Latin into the vulgar French.

Ganoczy summarizes the general impact of humanism on Calvin's ministry well:

> A good portion of the humanist heritage passed into Calvin's theology: . . . his method of exegesis, the importance attached to the study of the Fathers, the acceptance of a kind of "Christian Philosophy," the respect for several thinkers of pagan antiquity, and the strongly ethical character of his thinking on the Christian life.[32]

HUMANISM IN THE INSTITUTES

Calvin's Institutes of the Christian Religion took twenty-five years to evolve into the form in which we know them today. The first edition was written sometime between 1534-35, and was published in 1536 as a short apologetic tract whose purpose was to defend the persecuted reformed believers of France by presenting a summary of their beliefs to prevent their being confused with the seditious Anabaptists. It had six chapters, one each on the Law, faith, prayer, the sacraments, spurious sacraments, and Christian liberty. By the second edition of 1539 the book had become a systematic theology, with a new format and a doubled size. The Institutes underwent six more revisions until the definitive edition of 1559.[33]

Now five times its original size, the final version had a masterfully symmetrical organization patterned on the Apostle's Creed. So balanced is the architecture that the work must almost be viewed as a work of art. Warfield quotes Peter Bayne, who describes the final Institutes in glowing, though perhaps somewhat exaggerated terms, as

> in all, save material form, a great religious poem. . . . Calvin treats, in four successive books, of Christ the

Creator, Christ the Redeemer, Christ the Inspirer, and Christ the King; if he had written in verse, avoided argumentative discussion, and called his work The Christiad, it would have been the most symmetrical epic in existence.[34]

It is interesting to note that Calvin might not have been metrically incapable of such an epic as Bayne suggests; he did write the *Epicinion Christo Cantatum* in sixty-one distichs in Worms in 1541, "for his private solace, not for publication."[35]

Undoubtedly one of the most fascinating facts about the history of the composition of the Institutes for our purposes is that, as the work grew, the number of classical quotations *increased* from edition to edition in proportion to the size of the whole,[36] suggesting that Calvin's interest in humanist learning was not just a memory of past training, but rather continued throughout his life. Tracing these additions of references to the classics as the Institutes grew might provide a profitable task for some future study.[37] In this chapter, however, we will concentrate on the use Calvin made of these references in the definitive edition of 1559.

A total of fifty-nine different non-biblical authors are cited throughout the body of the Institutes. Of these, thirty are early Church Fathers or Medieval Christian writers (mostly early Fathers), twenty-seven are classical pagan philosophers, historians, or poets, one is a Jewish father (Josephus), and one, Lorenzo Valla, is a contemporary humanist. Thus, almost half (45.8%) of the authors cited are from classical antiquity, and were it not for Augustine, who alone is cited over three hundred times, the proportion of total references would not be greatly dissimilar.[38]

Between them, the twenty-seven classical authors account for a total of fifty-two citations, according to the author index in Beveridge. We may roughly divide these references into three categories: positive citations, in which the author cited agrees with or supports the point Calvin is making; negative citations, in which the author cited represents a position from which Calvin dissents; and neutral citations, in which the author is cited for illustrative purposes and no clear-cut positive or negative value can be readily assigned. I suspect that in reading through these quotations in context, most readers will classify about nineteen as positive, nineteen as negative, and eleven as neutral.[39] While some degree of subjectivity is necessarily involved in assigning texts to such categories, it is clear that the number of positive and negative citations is roughly equal.

It is therefore apparent that Calvin does not draw uncritically upon his classical sources for their content. Nor does Calvin seem to have any favorite authors, as far as content is concerned. Most frequently quoted is Cicero; in eight citations, Calvin dissents from him four times and agrees thrice.[40] Calvin calls Plato "the soberest and most religious" of all the philosophers," yet in seven references he disagrees with him three times.[41] The reformer refers to Seneca, object of his earlier studies, three times, twice negatively.[42]

Let's look at some examples of these citations, both positive and negative. Calvin agrees with Cicero that man has a universal belief in some kind of deity. "As a heathen tells us, there is no nation so barbarous, no race so brutish, as not to be imbued with the conviction that there is a God."[43] Yet he does not follow him in drawing an optimistic conclusion from that fact. "I do not say, with Cicero, that errors wear out by age, and that religion increases and grows better day by day."[44] For Calvin, man *ought* to proceed from knowledge of a god to knowledge of God, but cannot because of the noetic effects of sin.

Calvin most often brings in the pagans, almost as an afterthought, in connection with some point he has already established on other grounds than their testimony. For example, after a long argument from universal human experience that knowledge of God is man's *summum bonum*, Calvin mentions that "This did not escape the observation even of the philosophers. For it is the very thing which Plato . . . taught."[45] This can happen negatively as well. After employing a lengthy scriptural exposition to prove that Christ is the only mediator between God and man, Calvin suddenly strikes home with the following bolt of polemic lightning:

> Away then with that Platonic philosophy of seeking access to God by means of angels . . . a philosophy which presumptuous and superstitious men attempted at first to introduce into our religion, and which they persist in even to this day.[46]

Calvin's attitude toward the authority of the classical philosophers he quotes is illustrated by a disapproving citation of Xenophon, who has Socrates praise Apollo's edict enjoining every man to "worship the gods according to the rites of his own country, and the particular practice of his own city." Calvin's response to this type of thinking is, "But what right have mortals thus to decide of their own authority in a matter which is far above the world?"[47]

Thus, a much higher authority than man is needed in discussing Calvin's topic, knowledge of God. He does not really use the classical authors to support his conclusions--often he brings them in after having already decided the issue, and when he does agree with them, he often does so in a disparaging manner ("even the philosophers know this," etc.). They are only right about half the time, anyway. By contrast, Holy Scripture, as the word of God, never errs. On the mere possibility that it does so (i.e., that James disagrees with Paul on grace and works) Calvin comments, "This it were impious to suppose."[48] Yet he cares enough about the classical writers to add more quotations from them every time he revises the <u>Institutes</u>.

For Calvin, the primary source of error in the pagan philosophers is their optimistic view of Man, stemming from their ignorance of Scripture and the biblical doctrine of the Fall. They,

> being unacquainted with the corruption of nature, which is the punishment of revolt, erroneously confound two states of man which are very different from each other. ... Hence the great darkness of philosophers who have looked for a complete building in a ruin, and arrangement in disorder. . . . So far, well, had there been no change in man. This being unknown to them, it is not surprising that they throw everything into confusion.[49]

Here we see the true parting of the ways: not between Christianity and Humanism but between *Biblical* and *Secular* humanism. All humanists cared about going back to the sources (*Ad fontes!*); all cared about defining the human condition; all cared about education. Those humanists whose trip back to the sources included the Bible and who gave it first place, and who therefore started from the fact of Man as fallen, became known as Reformers; those who were more secular picked up from the Greeks the idea of Man's perfectibility and the notion that he needs, not redemption, but enlightenment. The assumption that we need only enlightenment, coupled with the hope that the humanist program could provide it, gave birth to what we now know as *Secular Humanism.*

Calvin knew better: the humanist program was an indispensable tool, but could only take us so far without a supernatural regeneration of the human soul by God's sovereign grace. The point we must see now is that the idea that the humanist program *could* be a sufficient end in itself was never the essence of the original humanism of the Renaissance; those humanists who did come to think so have muddied the etymological waters by being the only ones to keep the *name* of humanists.

In his popular film series How Should We Then Live, Francis Schaeffer gets the story almost right. He says that up to a certain point, the Renaissance could have gone one of two ways; had it merely restored nature to its proper place, it would have been a good thing, but it went bad, making Man autonomous. The truth is more like this: Up to a certain point, the Renaissance could have gone two ways--and it did. Renaissance humanism and its way of reading, when protected by Scripture against perfectionism, made the Reformation possible and *became* the Reformation; when it went bad, it gave birth to modern secularism. So the way out of the morasse of secularism is not to abandon humanism (as we have defined it) but to go *back* to it so that Reformation becomes possible once again. The awakening of biblical consciousness in people who are readers must precede the growth of wholeness of vision.

Calvin's understanding of the source of pagan error also warns us to be cautious, by the way, about attempts to show that the Institutes is in places dependent on the classical writers for its content. One instance of this is the alleged dependence of Institutes I.i-v. on Cicero's philosophical treatises, which, according to Battles, is "well known."[50] One of the more important articles that has been done on this matter is that of Grislis, who claims that Calvin "exhibits an impressive agreement with classical thought, as represented by Cicero, and at the same time undertakes a basic reinterpretation of it from the standpoint of biblical revelation."[51] Grislis does well to emphasize the biblical reinterpretation, and he does point out an "impressive agreement" between Cicero and Calvin on the natural theology presented in the opening chapters of the Institutes. But he fails to give sufficient weight to the fact that the natural theology under discussion could just as easily have been derived from the opening chapters of the Book of Romans without Cicero's involvement. In such a case it is difficult to establish dependence beyond doubt, and in the light of our findings above, we must conclude that if Calvin put some of Cicero's ideas into the Institutes, it was because he thought he could also find those ideas in the Bible. The fact that Calvin got his way of reading Cicero from the humanists did not mean that he swallowed everything (or anything) that Cicero said unless it was biblical.

If Calvin had such a low opinion of the reliability of the pagan philosophers in theological matters, why did he include them at all? In the light of our discussion of particular humanism, we may suspect that these classical quotations served some kind of rhetorical purpose. Calvin was certainly interested in effective communication and persuasion. He would have agreed with his contemporary Lorenzo Valla, who said,

> Some people deny that Theology is subject to the rules of grammar, but I say that theologians ought to obey the rules of a language, whether written or spoken. In fact what is more stupid than to corrupt the language you use and make yourself unintelligible to those whom you are addressing![52]

Yet it does not seem that Calvin tried to imitate the ancients in his *style*--at least he is not guilty of the excesses of Ciceronianism. Breen states indeed that he "betrays no anxious care to copy Cicero."[53] If there is any style that really attracted him it seems to have been that of the Bible, for though he does not say that he imitates it, he praises it above all others. Breen captures Calvin's attitude toward the style of the Bible thus:

> There is in it no utter lack of eloquence, for sometimes "speech flows sweet and pleasant (*suavis et iucunda fluit oratio*), as in David and Isaiah." But for the most

part the style is "unpolished and plain (*rudi et crasso stylo*)." But throughout Scripture, even when the form is homely and rustic, there is conspicuous the majesty of the Spirit. Calvin's thrust is to body forth this majesty, so far as it can be done without the inspiration under which he believed the Bible writers had written.[54]

If Calvin's classical references serve a rhetorical function, then, it must be found elsewhere than in their influence on his own style. One more positive citation may give us a clue as to what that function might be.

> Thus Gryllus, also, in Plutarch, reasons most skillfully when he affirms that, if once religion is banished from the lives of men, they not only in no respect excel, but are, in many respects, more wretched than, the brutes.[55]

Gryllus reasons "most skillfully." Here, and in many like places, Calvin uses classical quotations because the ancient writer had stated well or memorably the idea which Calvin is concerned either to propound or to refute. He does not range the ancients against each other in a dialectical pattern as would a medieval scholastic, nor does he use them as models for behavior as would a Machiavelli, nor as sources for hidden meaning as would a Pico Della Mirandola. But he does use them, in so far as they can help him communicate the message that burns within him. Thus, in the service of God, he "turns to his glory whatever may be applied to this use."

This may help explain why the number of classical references increases in a proportion greater than that of the size of the work itself as the Institutes is composed. In the first edition, "he is too much in earnest, and writes too directly, to adorn his pages with classical references."[56] The first edition was composed hurriedly and without much polish, and Calvin professed never really to have been satisfied with his masterpiece until the final edition of 1559.[57] Though in saying that Calvin had in mind primarily the organization of the work, it may be that in preparing this finally polished version of his book he was able to take more care to "adorn" its pages. For the results, we can have nothing but gratitude.

CONCLUSION

In conclusion, we have defined humanism as an interest in the ancients from the standpoint of grammar and rhetoric which could, in a receptive mind, create the conditions in which biblical consciousness could arise and flourish, and hence made possible the Reformation. Calvin's humanism made a positive contribution to his work in providing a methodology of scholarship which thus allowed him to approach ancient writings, including the Bible, with a sound hermeneutic, and also provided him with a broad background in the thought that was influencing his own times.

Calvin's belief in the authority of Scripture, coupled with his doctrine of common grace, enabled him to use the ancient pagan writers while avoiding their errors; other humanists, without these safeguards, showed by becoming the ancestors of modern secular humanism that good reading and writing do not *automatically* produce biblical consciousness. In the Institutes, it is Scripture which determines content, and the classical authors are used for ornamentation, not ostentatiously, but to enhance communication in that they have stated well or memorably some pertinent idea.

The marriage of divine and human letters in John Calvin was a happy one, perhaps because his vision of the majesty of God enabled him to keep things in perspective. He shows that, from a historical perspective at least, the phrase *Christian humanist* does not have to be an oxymoron; it is precisely his Christian humanism that makes him such an excellent role model for believers seeking to recover biblical consciousness and wholeness of vision today. He was able to use all the good things that humanism taught him without succumbing to its excesses, such as Ciceronianism, or its dangers, such as its potential to lead to modernism. Take away either the Christian or the Humanist from his makeup, and the whole theological foundation he provided for Reformation Christianity collapses.

Warfield therefore sums up perfectly not only the man Calvin but precisely why he is still so important for us:

> He did not cease to be a man of letters any more than he ceased to be a man. But all his talents and all his acquisitions were henceforth dedicated purely to the service of God and his Gospel.[58]

Notes to Chapter 3

1. For an excellent overview of both movements, see William R. Estep, <u>Renaissance and Reformation</u> (Grand Rapids: Eerdmans, 1986).

2. For the classic study of that debate, see Wallace K. Ferguson, <u>The Renaissance in Historical Thought: Five Centuries of Interpretation</u> (N. Y.: Houghton Mifflin, 1948), esp. for our purposes chp. 2, "The Humanist Tradition as Altered by Northern Humanism and the Renaissance," pp. 29-58.

3. For excellent overviews of Calvin's life and thought, see Timothy F. George, <u>Theology of the Reformers</u> (Nashville: Broadman, 1988), pp. 163-251, and Alister E. McGrath, <u>A Life of John Calvin</u> (Oxford: Blackwell, 1980).

4. Robert D. Linder, "Calvinism and Humanism: The First Generation," <u>Church History</u> 44 (June, 1975), p. 168.

5. See Andre Bieler, <u>The Social Humanism of Calvin</u>, trans. Paul T. Fuhrmann (Richmond, Va.: John Knox Pr., 1961) for a discussion of general humanism, the search for the "true man," etc. in Calvin.

6. Paul Oskar Kristeller, <u>Renaissance Thought: The Classic, Scholastic, and Humanist Strains</u> (N.Y.: Harper & Row, 1961), pp. 9-10.

7. Ibid., p. 10.

8. Ibid., p. 9.

9. Ibid., p. 11. Basil Hall, <u>John Calvin: Humanist and Theologian</u> (London: The Historical Association, 1956), has a

different categorization of humanist "types," but rightly puts Calvin with the "philologists." Cf. McGrath, op. cit., pp. 52-4.

10. Kristeller, op. cit.., p. 13.

11. E. Harris Harbison, The Christian Scholar in the Age of the Reformation (N. Y.: Scribner's, 1956), p. 35.

12. William J. Bousma, John Calvin: A Sixteenth-Century Portrait (N.Y.: Oxford Univ. Pr., 1988), p. 117.

13. Ibid., p. 118.

14. Qtd. in Ferguson, op. cit., p. 54.

15. Philip Schaff, "Calvin's Life and Labors," The Presbyterian Quarterly and Princeton Review 4 (1875), p. 256.

16. Ibid., p. 257.

17. See Ford Lewis Battles, "The Sources of Calvin's Seneca Commentary," in G. E. Duffield, ed., John Calvin: A Collection of Essays, Courtenay Studies in Reformation Theology, vol. 1 (Grand Rapids: Eerdmans, 1966), pp. 38-66, for a discussion of Calvin's use of the classics before his conversion.

18. Schaff, op. cit., p. 257.

19. Ibid.

20. Quirinus Breen, John Calvin: A Study in French Humanism, 2nd ed. (Archon Books, 1968), p. 146.

21. John Calvin, "The Author's Preface to the Commentary on the Book of Psalms," in John Dillenberger, ed., <u>John Calvin: Selections from his Writings</u> (N. Y.: Anchor Books, 1971), p. 26. Interestingly, Thomas F. Torrance, <u>The Hermeneutics of John Calvin</u> (Edinburgh: Scottish Academic Pr., 1988), pp. 100-111, thinks it was particularly the rhetorical tradition of humanist legal training that led to the "sanity" of Calvin's approach to Scripture.

22. Dillenberger, op. cit., p. 26..

23. For an English translation, see W. H. Draper, <u>Petrarch's Secret</u> (London, 1911); for an abstract of the <u>Secretum</u> and a good, concise discussion, see Morris Bishop, <u>Petrarch and His World</u> (Bloomington, Ind.: Indiana Univ. Pr., 1963), pp. 192-214.

24. qtd. in Breen, op. cit., p. 465.

25. See Herman Bavinck, "Calvin and Common Grace," trans. Geerhardus Vos, in William Park Armstrong, ed., <u>Calvin and the Reformation</u> (N. Y.: Revell, 1909), pp. 99-130, for an excellent discussion of Calvin's doctrine of common grace in relation to his theology as a whole; see also Kenneth Sealer Kantzer, "John Calvin's Theory of the Knowledge of God and the Word of God" (Diss. Harvard, 1950), pp. 313-395, for a thorough treatment of the doctrine and a survey of its interpretation in secondary literature.

26. Breen, op. cit., p. 148.

27. Ibid., p. 155.

28. Ibid., p. 157.

29. Qtd. in Bousma, op. cit., p. 118.

30. Philip Schaff, "Calvin as a Commentator," Presbyterian and Reformed Review 3 (July, 1892), p. 466. Cf. T. H. L. Parker, Calvin's Preaching (Louisville, Ky.: Westminster/John Knox Pr., 1992), for a thorough analysis of Calvin's expository method.

31. Breen, op. cit., p. 163.

32. Alexandre Ganoczy, The Young Calvin (Philadelphia: Westminster Pr., 1987), p. 181; cf. Hall, op. cit., pp. 32f.

33. Benjamin Breckenridge Warfield, "The Literary History of Calvin's Institutes," The Presbyterian and Reformed Review 10 (April, 1899), pp. 200f.

34. Ibid., p. 205.

35. Ibid., p. 205n.

36. Linder, op. cit., p. 173.

37. Ibid., p. 174n. According to Linder, "The critical apparatus in the most recent scholarly edition of Calvin's Institutes in English (ed. John T. McNeill, 2 vols., Phil., 1960) will enable any interested person to check these facts." See also Harbison, op. cit., p. 145 and Sir H. W. Ward, et al., eds., The Cambridge Modern History, vol. 2, The Reformation (Cambridge: Cambridge Univ. Pr., 1934), p. 357.

38. John Calvin, The Institutes of the Christian Religion, 2 vols., trans. Henry Beveridge, with intro. by John Murray (Grand Rapids: Eerdmans, 1975), pp. xxi-xxiv. This famous translation of the definitive edition of 1559, with its useful author index, will

be the basis of our study. Some minor inaccuracies have been noted in the index, which account for any discrepancies noted in the figures we will cite. As the figures fall out into clearly recognizable blocks, these small discrepancies will not appreciably affect our conclusions.

39. Ibid. See subsequent notes for details.

40. Ibid., 1:143, 45, 59, 60, 104, 168, 225 (Inst. I.iii.1, 3; I.v.11, 12; I.xii.1; I.xv.6; II.ii.3).

41. Ibid., 1:54, 150, 159, 168, 224; 2:183, 227 (Inst. I.v.5, 11; I.xiv.12; I.xv.7; I.ii.2; III.xx.34; III.xxiii.2).

42. Ibid., 1:60, 109; 2:19 (Inst. I.v.12; I.xiii.1; III.viii.4).

43. Ibid., 1:43 (Inst. I.iii.1).

44. Ibid., 1:45 (Inst. I.iii.3).

45. Ibid.

46. Ibid., 1:150 (Inst. I.xiv.12).

47. Ibid., 1:61 (Inst. I.v.13).

48. Ibid., 2:115 (Inst. III.xvii.12).

49. Ibid., 1:168-69 (Inst. I.xv.7).

50. Battles, op. cit., p. 38.

51. Egil Grislis, "Calvin's Use of Cicero in the Institutes I.i-v.--A Case Study in Theological Method," Archiv Fur

Reformationsgeschichte 62 (1971), p. 5.

52. Laurentii Vallae, In Novum Testamentum Annotationes (Basel, 1541), fol. 12; qtd in Harbison, op. cit., p. 46. Perhaps modern theologians--who could certainly be accused of being unintelligible--have forgotten who their audience is: the Church first, and the academy only second.

53. Quirinus Breen, "John Calvin and the Rhetorical Tradition," in Nelson Peter Ross. ed., Christianity and Humanism, w. a foreword by Paul Oskar Kristeller and a pref. by Heiko A. Oberman (Grand Rapids: Eerdmans, 1968), p. 112.

54. Ibid. See also Inst. 1:74-83 (I.vii.) and Kantzer, op. cit., pp. 296-301.

55. Calvin, Institutes, op. cit., 1:45 (I.iii.3.).

56. Ward, op. cit., p. 357.

57. Calvin, op. cit., 1:24.

58. Benjamin Breckenridge Warfield, Calvin and Augustine, ed. Samuel G. Craig w. a foreword by J. Marcellus Kik (Phil.: Presbyterian and Reformed, 1956), p. 4.

INTERLUDE

THREE CITIES
A Reformation Tryptich
(Curtal Sonnets 1-3)

Rome

Stained light slanting through the dusty air
Pointed to the alcove in the nave
Where in his silent niche the stone saint stood.
Beneath his cool and quiet marble stare
Passed countless pilgrims marching to the grave;
He never thought to do them any good.

The contrast, sharp as flesh stripped bare to bone:
The bone-white marble, impotent to save;
The flesh, flowing past in hopes it would,
Stained red where in his silent niche the stone
 Saint stood.

Wittenburg

Four nails driven deep into the door:
"The coin into the coffer springs no soul."
Then, "I can do not other; here I stand!"
Because he'd plumbed the Gospel to its core,
The true treasure of the Church, extolled
God's grace--for this he had his doctrine banned,

Himself, too. In the Wartburg hid for fear,
Translated Scripture, preached like thunder, told
Katie he would, the Pope he wouldn't, and
Roared laughing, "I can do no other; here
        I stand!"

Geneva

Luther learned the Gospel in his gut
And taught that Reason was the Devil's whore.
Calvin fed his mind upon the Book
Until, reformed and sanctified, the slut
Walked saved and singing through the Church's door,
Where all her former thoughts she clean forsook.

The Lord repaired the eyes of one born blind
In Scripture, and he did it one time more:
And fearfully the Devil's kingdom shook
When God fixed Luther's heart and Calvin's mind
        Upon the Book.

--D.T.W.

Chapter 4

BIBLICALLY CONSCIOUS MARTYRS:
John Foxe and a Christian Philosophy of History

*"In books lies the soul of the Past Time; the articulate
audible voice of the Past, when the body and material
substance of it has altogether vanished like a dream."*
--Thomas Carlyle, Heroes and Hero Worship.

We need a man that knows the several graces
Of history, and how to apt their places:
Where brevity, where splendour, and where height,
Where sweetness is required, and where weight;
We need a man can speak of the intents,
The counsels, actions, orders, and events
Of state, and censure them; we need his pen
Can write the things, the causes, and the men.
But most we need his faith (and all have you)
That dares nor write things false, nor hide things true.
--Ben Jonson, "To Sir Henry Savile," Epigrams

John Foxe was one of that select group of scholars who have
made history in the act of writing it. The Book of Martyrs (as his
Actes and Monuments of these Latter and Perilous Dayes,
Touching Matters of the Church is more popularly known) is
perhaps surpassed only by the English Bible and equalled only by
Bunyan's Pilgrim's Progress as a book that has shaped the ethos
and sensibility of English-speaking Protestantism. And it was an

ethos and sensibility energized and informed by the same kind of biblical consciousness that had lived in the minds of Foxe's predecessors, such as Erasmus and Calvin.

Yet most modern readers have encountered this book only in a severely truncated form. The eight massive volumes of small print in the latest complete edition[1] are reduced to a smattering of the more sensational anecdotes, leaving the impression that the whole is a mere catalog of cruelties:[2]

> Some slain with the sword; some burnt with fire; some with whips scourged; some stabbed with forks of iron; some fastened to the cross or gibbet; some drowned in the sea; some their skins plucked off; some their tongues cut off; some stoned to death; some killed with cold; some starved with hunger; some their hands cut off alive, or otherwise dismembered; imprisonment, stripes and scourgings, drawings, tearings, stonings, plates of iron laid unto them burning hot, deep dungeons, racks, strangling in prisons, the teeth of wild beasts, gridirons, gibbets and gallows, tossing upon the horns of bulls.[3]

Such scenes do abound in the <u>Acts and Monuments</u> as they have in the history of the Church; but they are not its essence. Rather, Foxe was attempting to vindicate the cause of truth by giving a universal history of God's work in building the Church from the standpoint of the testimony of its martyrs. He "set these stories of recent and remembered figures in what was for his own age a convincing, momentous, historical-scriptural perspective, made meaningful by the unfolding context of immediate events."[4] He strove to see the events of history, in other words, from the standpoint of biblical consciousness. In the process he articulated both a history of theology and a theology of history which are still worth our consideration today. And he also can teach us what the reading of history can contribute to the biblical consciousness we strive to recover.

FOXE'S LIFE

Foxe was born in 1516 at Boston, Lincolnshire.[5] In that year Erasmus produced the first published edition of the Greek New Testament, and the following year Martin Luther nailed his Ninety-Five Theses to the Wittenburg Church door. So Foxe came into the world with the Reformation his writings would seek to vindicate and grew up as it was coming to England; he was eighteen in 1534 when the Act of Supremacy made Henry VIII supreme head of the Church in England. Henry only wanted to change his wife, but his political move gave more spiritual-minded reformers such as Cranmer, Latimer, and Ridley the opportunity they needed to begin the real reformation of the Church.[6]

Foxe's mind was nurtured on the theology of the Reformation and the learning of Renaissance humanism, a happy combination he would use to good effect in his life's work and one, as we have seen in John Calvin, conducive to the development of biblical consciousness. He took his B.A. at Magdalen College, Oxford, in 1537, was elected a fellow in 1539, and took his M.A. in 1543. His friends and correspondents at Oxford included Alexander Nowell, John Cheke, and the reformers Latimer and Tindal.

Reformation was a slow process, even before the setback that occurred under Bloody Mary. In 1545, Foxe felt constrained to resign his fellowship over his objections to the requirement of celibacy. He was to fight a running battle with poverty the rest of his life. He was not a party man; Olsen notes Fuller's distinction between the "fierce and fiery" and the "mild and moderate" Puritan and places Foxe in the latter category.[7] In other words, his Puritan sympathies (against wearing the surplice, for example) were just strong enough to hinder his advancement in the Church, despite the popularity of the <u>Acts and Monuments</u>. In spite of frequently straitened circumstances, though, Foxe had a reputation for generosity to those even poorer than himself.

In the meantime, Foxe was married to Agnes Randall on February 3, 1546-7. In 1548 he was appointed tutor to the orphaned children of Henry Howard, Earl of Surrey. He stayed in that post for five years, publishing Latin theological tracts advocating reform. In 1550 he was ordained deacon by Nicholas Ridley in St. Paul's Cathedral. But this peaceful period of his life was about to end: With the untimely death of the youthful and pious Edward VI, Mary came to the throne in 1553.

What Foxe was to call "these meek and gentle times of King Edward" were over. He would remember with satisfaction that "amongst the whole number of the popish sort, some of whom . . . were crafty dissemblers, some were open and manifest adversaries; yet of all this multitude, there was not one man that lost his life" for his religion.[8] Such was not to be Mary's policy. The reformers hoped that she would listen to reason, but that hope was quickly disappointed. Foxe records that Ridley visited the new queen and offered to preach before her but was sharply rebuffed:

> *Bishop*: Madam, I trust you will not refuse God's Word.
> *Mary*: I cannot tell what ye call God's word: that is not God's word now that was God's word in my Father's days.
> *Bishop*: God's word is all one in all times; but hath better understood and practiced in some ages than others.
> *Mary*: Ye durst not, for your ears, have avowched that for God's word in my father's days, that now you do.

And as for your new books, I thank God I never read any of them: I never did, nor ever will do.[9]

The import of the queen's refusal was not lost on the bishop. After the interview, Ridley was offered a drink by Sir Thomas Warton.

> And after he had drunk, he paused awhile, looking very sadly; and suddenly brake out into these words: "Surely I have done amiss." "Why so?" quoth sir Thomas Warton. "For I have drunk," said he, "in that place where God's word offered hath been refused: whereas, if I had remembered my duty, I ought to have departed immediately, and to have shaken the dust off my shoes for a testimony against this house." These words were by the same bishop spoken with such a vehemency, that some of the hearers afterwards confessed their hair to stand upright on their heads.[10]

In 1554, Mary released the old Duke of Norfolk, grandfather of Foxe's pupils, who fired him as their tutor. The direction from which the wind was now blowing was becoming obvious. That same year, Foxe fled to the continent. He met Grindal--later to become Spenser's ideal bishop, the "Algrind" of the Shepheardes Calendar--in Strasburg in July. Foxe had brought with him a Latin manuscript on the persecutions of reformers from Wycliffe to the present. Grindal was enthusiastic. The book was published in Strasburg, a small octavo of 212 leaves called the *Comentarii Rerum in Ecclesia Gestarum*. It was in effect the first draft of what would become the Acts and Monuments. Grindal would keep encouraging Foxe to expand this account and supply him with many of the documents he would use.

At the end of 1554, Foxe moved to Frankfurt, where he found the exiles split over the forms of worship. John Knox, the pastor, recommended Calvin as an arbiter. Foxe supported this proposal, and Calvin urged a compromise. But in 1555 the controversy broke out anew, with the result that Knox left. Foxe then became the head of the Genevan party, but in November he too left for Basle. Already the reformers were finding it difficult to agree on the precise extent of reform they wanted. It was not a good omen for the future.

At Basle, Foxe worked for the printer Oporinus and continued his writing. In 1556 he published *Christus Triumphans*, a five-act apocalyptic drama in Latin verse. In 1557 came a plea for toleration addressed to the English nobility, *Ad Inclytos ac Praepotentes Anglicae Prioceres . . . Supplicatio*. Foxe wanted them to influence the queen against persecution. "If heretics they were," he argued, "what avail these naked arguments of blood but to confirm them in heresy? Where is the gentleness of Christ?"[11]

The testimony of martyrs weighed so heavily with Foxe in part because of an abhorrence of persecution in which he was far ahead of his time. When his side came to power, he consistently pled for mercy for Jean Boucher, Flemish Anabaptists, even papists. Mozley thinks that the anonymous person in the *Acts and Monuments* (5:860) who pleads for mercy for Joan of Kent was Foxe himself; he was an eyewitness, and the arguments are like those he was known to use.[12] He argued thus to Queen Elizabeth on behalf of the Anabaptists:

> I defend them not: these errors should be repressed. . . . It is the manner of their punishment which shocks me. To burn up with fiery flame . . . the living bodies of wretched men who err through blindness of judgment rather than deliberate will, is a hard thing and belongs more to the spirit of Rome than to the spirit of the Gospel.[13]

Reports of the Marian persecution continued to filter back to Foxe from England. On June 10, 1557, Grindal urged him to complete the history of persecutions through Henry VIII. In 1559, the result was the *Rerum in Ecclesia Gestarum*. The Book of Martyrs had now grown to 732 pages in six books.

Meanwhile, Mary's death and the accession of Elizabeth in 1558 had made possible a return to England. But the need for continuing the history was not over. Mozley remarks that "to us the enthronement of Elizabeth is the beginning of a long period of prosperity and of freedom from the persecutions of Rome."[14] But the people of that day did not yet know this. People still needed to be fortified in the truth against a return of persecution; that is, they needed to see their own circumstances as a part of a history focussed through the lense of Scripture. Or, to put it another way, they needed a particular application of biblical consciousness to their own situation. And Foxe's book would be the medium by which these things were brought into focus for them.

> When Foxe landed in England in October of 1559, the full horror of the Marian persecution must have burst upon him. Men's tongues were loosened at last, and on every hand stories of woe were to be heard. The friends and kinsfolk of the sufferers would be ready enough to tell their tale, and there was nothing now to hinder him from completing his story.[15]

Foxe lost no time in completing it. He was ordained to the priesthood by Grindal on January 25, 1559-60. On March 20, the English version of Actes and Monuments appeared. People continued to send him documents and accounts, and he continued to revise, expand, and incorporate. In 1570 a new edition consisting of two volumes of 934 and 1378 pages came out. On April 3, a convocation at Canterbury resolved to place copies in all cathedral churches. The resolution was never confirmed by parliament, but was widely implemented nevertheless. In 1576 and 1583, further editions were published containing more revisions and additions but no substantial changes.

Posthumous editions based on the 1583 text appeared in 1596, 1610, 1631-2, 1641, and 1648. In 1837, S. R. Cattley edited an eight-volume edition of the 1583 text "slightly bowdlerized and at certain points awkwardly conflated with" the 1563 edition.[16] Josiah Pratt revised Cattley with pagination unchanged in 1870 and 1877; this is the only complete edition available to most scholars today, and it is unfortunately not identical with any of the texts overseen by Foxe himself. Foxe studies continue to be hampered by lack of a first-rate critical edition.

Foxe spent his last years working on his martyrology and developing a reputation for frugality, generosity, and piety. His objections to wearing the surplice denied him the ecclesiastical preferment he had otherwise earned,[17] though at Jewell's suggestion he was made prebend in Salisbury Cathedral. He died in April of 1587, and is buried at St. Giles, Cripplegate.

Foxe has been called "not properly a historian at all," but rather merely a "compiler on a gigantic scale,"[18] and the Acts and Monuments has been called a "jungle" of documents, "horrendous woodcuts," and grossly prejudiced propaganda.[19] The massive size of the work--about five million words by one estimate[20]--may have made it difficult for some readers to perceive its architecture. It is built according to a definite plan nonetheless, and embodies a fully worked out conception of what history is and what the historian's task should be. That conception can teach us much about what the contribution of reading and writing history is to the biblical consciousness we must try to develop as believers.

Helen C. White has rightly called the Acts and Monuments "more than a history. It is, also, an encyclopedia of the

Reformation in England" in which "all the main issues of the English Reformation are fought out before one's eyes."[21] It is essentially historical apologetics in the tradition of Augustine's *De civitate Dei*, whose purpose is to give the common man a biblical framework for understanding his own times. Within that framework, we can analyze Foxe's contributions to Protestant historiography under three main headings: the historian's mission, the historian's method, and the historian's message.

THE HISTORIAN'S MISSION

Foxe was not unaware of the need to justify his labors in imposing such a huge volume upon the world:

> Seeing the world is replenished with such an infinite multitude of books of all kinds of matters, I may seem, perhaps, to take a matter in hand superfluous and needless . . . considering now-a-days the world is so greatly pestered, not only with superfluous plenty thereof, but of all other treatises, so that books now seem rather to lack readers, than readers to lack books.[22]

But his first motive for writing history was that there was a story which deserved to be told. He did not want so many "memorable acts and famous doings" to "lie buried by my default, under darkness and oblivion" when they were worthy to be recorded.[23]

History then helps to preserve cultural memory--and to ensure its accuracy: when Foxe "considered this partial dealing and corrupt handling of histories" on the part of Roman Catholic writers, he thought that nothing was more needed than the "full and complete story."[24] One of the benefits of biblical consciousness, that kind of mentality structured and nourished by texts, with *the* Text of Scripture central, is an outlook informed by a greater awareness of how to read our own present time in the context of the past out of which it flows.

Foxe's readers needed to have the story told and preserved because it was *their* story. Haller reminds us that "it was no new thing in the history of Christianity for an upsurge of the religious spirit to find expression in the writing of history. History was what Christianity was all about." The very essence of Christian faith is the conviction that "at a particular moment in time a particular event had occurred" that focussed the whole meaning of life.[25] Thus part of the Christian historian's task is to enable his readers to "perceive the continuity of the present moment . . . with the whole sequence of providentially directed events since the first day of creation."[26]

Foxe is definitely operating within this framework. "The knowledge of ecclesiastical history" in his mind "ought not to be separate from" the knowledge of God's word, "that like as by one, the people may learn the rules and precepts of doctrine, so by the other, they may have examples of God's mighty working in his church."[27] He wants his readers to connect the Old-Testament history and the Book of Acts with "the acts of Christ's martyrs now," plus "other manifold examples and experiments of God's great mercies and judgments."[28] Knowing the history of the Church helps the believer maintain his connection with sacred history by showing him the continuing unfolding and outworking of the plan and principles revealed in the Bible. In other words, Foxe applied in history the standard Puritan homiletic practice of explicating cases in terms of principles and then applying them to the circumstances of the hearers.[29]

The greatest needs Foxe saw in the recent circumstances of his readers were the ability to discern the true Church, the skill to defend it, and the courage to die for it if necessary. Hence he not only preserves the stories of the martyrs' deaths for which he is famous, but also detailed transcripts of their disputations and trials, asking his readers to note "the full pith and ground of all their arguments."[30] As Thompson points out, this was not just an academic exercise but was designed to give people practical help in understanding the issues and answering attacks if times of persecution should come again.[31]

The main Catholic argument was that Protestants were guilty of innovation: Where was their "Church" just fifty years ago? Foxe responded to this challenge not only by trying to write a new history "so overwhelming in size, scope, and documented sources that it could claim to provide historical legitimacy for a church only fifty years old,"[32] but also by specifically declaring that the purpose of history was to help the faithful to "discern the better between antiquity and novelty. For if the things which be first, after the rule of Tertullian, are to be preferred . . . then is the reading of histories much necessary in the church."[33] Knowledge of history--and nothing else--could show that it was Rome, not the Reformation, which was guilty of innovation. For this reason, an understanding of history was for Foxe an essential part of the biblical consciousness needed by his generation. And while Sidney held that the Poet surpasses the Historian as a teacher of virtue, he would not have disagreed with the very practical necessity of knowing history as well.

Perhaps the thing that most separates Foxe from modern historians is not his partisanship (we simply disguise ours more cleverly) or his lack of rigor in methodology (he was, as we shall see, ahead of his time on that score) but his refusal to see history as a merely academic pursuit. Olsen rightly remarks that Foxe was most basically a theologian and a preacher--that is, a physician of souls--who saw history as a handmaid of those disciplines and became a historian to serve those ends.[34] Wooden notes the many ways in which Foxe's history reaches out to children and the unlearned: using children and simple folk as exemplars, providing woodcuts, pointing out the moral "as explicitly as any in Aesop."[35]

These are certainly emphases which appear on page after page. Foxe apologized to his fellow academics for not writing in Latin, but "the needs of the common people of our land drove me to the vernacular."[36] The ignorant flock has "long been led in ignorance and wrapped in blindness" for lack not only of God's word but also for "wanting the light of history." Seeing this, he "thought pity but that such should be helped."[37] Christ's simple flock, especially the unlearned, have been "miserably abused, and all for ignorance of history, not knowing the course of times and the true descent of the church."[38] Biblical consciousness is not just for scholars but for all believers, for all must meet the challenges of a hostile world.

Foxe was constantly pointing out the moral and indicating the practical application of the past events he narrated. "Nations and realms" should "take example" from those in the past who had rejected God's truth or persecuted his messengers.[39] Any prince who so desires may follow the good example of King Alfred.[40] From the Norman Conquest we may "note and learn" the dangers of princes leaving no "issue or sure succession" and the dangers of foreign marriage with other princes.[41] (These were of course pressing concerns during the reign of the virgin Queen Elizabeth.) But by far the bulk of Foxe's concern is for the lessons of history for the average Christian lay person who, while reading the lives of the martyrs, may "therein, as in a glass," behold his own case. Secular history helps fit us for "warlike affairs"; the history of the Church prepares us for better living. In sum, it can "declare unto the world what true Christian fortitude is, and what is the right way to conquer."[42]

For Foxe, the ultimate benefit of church history is spiritual health in its broadest sense: the understanding, wisdom, character, and fortitude which will enable us to take our place in the continuing line of witnesses, prepared if need be to seal their testimony to the Gospel with their blood, which constitutes the history of the Church. A better definition of biblical consciousness would be hard to find.

"Observing and noting" the acts of God in history, Foxe explains, will

> minister to the readers thereof wholesome admonitions of life, with experience and wisdom both to know God in his works, and to work the thing which is godly; especially to seek unto the Son of God for their salvation, and in his faith only to find what they seek.[43]

He prays that all "true disposed minds" which shall read his book may by the example of the martyrs' life, faith, and doctrine, receive "spiritual fruit to their souls."[44] He exhorts his readers to "draw near the fire" of the martyrs so that "our cold hearts may be warmed thereby."[45] And among the very last of his five million words is a prayer that

> the grace of the Lord Jesus work with thee, gentle reader, in all thy studious readings . . . that by reading thou mayest learn daily to know that which may profit thy soul, may teach thee experience, may arm thee with patience, and instruct thee in spiritual knowledge more and more to thy perpetual comfort and salvation in Jesus Christ our Lord; to whom be glory *in secula seculorum*, Amen.[46]

In sum, Foxe joins to the Renaissance idea that history teaches virtue by example a profoundly Christian concept of what that virtue is and of why it is needed in terms of our place in the ongoing history of redemption. It not only gives us examples to follow but helps teach us who we are, why we are here, and where we are going. Ironically, by making History the handmaid of Theology, by subordinating it to higher values, Foxe gives it as high a place as one can conceive for any human study.

THE HISTORIAN'S METHOD

All these pious intentions, however, count for nothing unless the history *as history* is sound. Biblical consciousness structures the mind according to the truth, and hence it demands that truth be distinguished from error through critical thinking. But it is at precisely this point that Foxe has been sharply attacked, long dismissed--and more recently defended. His whole approach was calculated to produce strong reactions. They began early. In his own life he complained that

> certain evil-disposed persons, of intemperate tongues, adversaries to good proceedings, would not suffer me to rest, fuming and fretting, and raising up such miserable exclamations at the first appearance of the book, as was wonderful to hear.[47]

He was not exaggerating. Thomas Harding, in an aside during his attack on Bishop Jewell, called the Acts and Monuments "that huge dunghill of your stinking martyrs," full of a thousand lies. Foxe had "into that huge volume infarced lies more in number and notabler for vanity than ever were raked together into one heap or book."[48]

A strong partisan must inevitably face the question whether he has doctored or even falsified his data to make it fit his vision of the world, even if unintentionally. For years with Foxe studies it was simply partisan versus partisan, until beginning in 1837 S. R. Maitland published the first detailed scholarly analysis of Foxe's use of his sources.[49] The seeming thoroughness of Maitland's work created the illusion that Foxe's honesty and accuracy had indeed been overthrown: "No need henceforward for a reader to rebut any story which he found unpalatable; it was quite enough to murmur something about the proven untrustworthiness of Foxe and pass on."[50] These views were reported as simple fact in the 1929 Encyclopedia Britannica and in Sidney Lee's piece on Foxe in the Dictionary of National Biography, and thus influenced a whole generation of scholars.

Lee, for example, states that Foxe was "too zealous a partisan to write with historical precision," as if the equation were self-evident. Foxe's history is valuable only in that it illustrates the "tone of thought" of Elizabethan Protestantism; its "mistakes" are the result of both haste and "wilfull exaggeration."[51] In the same vein, others have called the Acts and Monuments an "imaginative and credulous book" which has "all the qualities that will delight the partisan and that must torment the historian."[52]

Perhaps. But when we read that, "Supremely sure of himself, Foxe believed that truth could be conveyed without taking the reader through the sources, although he did occasionally incorporate a document in the text,"[53] we must wonder what is going on. For that last statement could only have been made by a person who has never actually read the Acts and Monuments, which is a veritable library of transcriptions of every original source Foxe could lay his hands on.

Indeed, the most remarkable feature of Foxe's historiography is the diligence with which he sought to collect and preserve original accounts of significant events. Mozley's description is accurate:

> First-hand documents jostle one another, that never would have been preserved but for his zeal, documents written by simple folk straight from the heart, giving us the most lifelike and vivid pictures of the manners and

feelings of the day, full of details that could never have been invented by a forger.[54]

The eye-witness accounts of recent martyrdoms for which Foxe is chiefly known are only the tip of the iceberg. He "ransacked documents of all kinds, ancient and modern, printed and unprinted."[55] He took pride in these labors: "I have an old worn copy of the said sermon [preached at Paul's Cross in 1388], written in very old English, and almost half consumed with age."[56] Readers must sometimes make up their own minds about the truth reported in these documents; but if they reject it, "yet I have shown them my author."[57] Fussner indeed credits Foxe with making "a distinct contribution to historiography" by printing original sources for the benefit of the common reader, thus extending the Renaissance humanist emphasis on evidence (as in Lorenzo Valla's exposure of the forgery of the Donation of Constantine) to a larger audience.[58]

The question remains as to the use Foxe made of his sources: Did he check them for accuracy, did he force their interpretation to fit his partisan bias? Probably the most important event in the history of Foxe studies was the publication of J. F. Mozley's John Foxe and his Book in 1940.[59] His defense of Foxe's accuracy and integrity rescued us from the caricature of Foxe the mere Protestant mythmaker created by Maitland and perpetuated by Lee, and made possible a balanced appraisal of Foxe's work once again.

Foxe himself certainly gives evidence of caring about accuracy, and his handling of his sources is often demonstrably anything but uncritical. His partisanship is unquestionable, but he was not so biased that he could not include facts damaging to his thesis that the sufferings of her martyrs give moral testimony to the truth of the Church's message and help to distinguish the true Church from the false. Along with the accounts of the heroes he also records stories of potential martyrs whose courage failed them,[60] and he quotes Cyprian to the effect that some persecutions come upon the Church for its sins rather than as attacks of the Enemy.[61]

Neither did Foxe believe everything he read. He is skeptical of miracle stories, not only when they involve Roman Catholic saints, but even when they enhance the memory of heroes he considers to be in the line of true witnesses. Yet he never rejects such accounts simply because of the supernatural element they contain, but conscientiously subjects them to the canons of historical evidence.

Abdias reports that when Paul's head was struck off, white milk came out instead of blood; but, "this being found in no other history," Foxe rejects it as Abdias' own invention.[62] He reports the martyrdom of Clement of Rome, but notes that there is "no firm relation in the ancient authors, but only in such new writers of later times, which are wont to paint out the lives and histories of good men with feigned additions," and therefore gives it "less credit."[63] He would like to believe the various miracles reported of Alexander, but "as I deny not but they may be true, so, because I cannot avouch them by any grave testimony of ancient writers, therefore I dare not affirm them."[64] In other words, he asks for corroboration from other sources and weighs testimony in terms of its proximity to the event and the reliability of the reporter to see if it is "able to abide the touch of history."[65]

Foxe is also apt to question the authenticity of a source if its style or matter seem out of keeping with the times it purports to represent.[66] Here he is consciously carrying on the tradition of Renaissance humanist critical scholarship which descends from Lorenzo Valla, More, and Erasmus.[67] His judgment in such cases is not infallible: He speculates that Cranmer's recantation was faked by the bishops to confuse the people, in a passage which contradicts his own later report of Cranmer's dramatic gesture of holding first into the fire the offending hand which had signed the recantation.[68] Nevertheless, most scholars who have checked him find him to be "well up to the average of historical accuracy in his day,"[69] indeed unusually fair, balanced, and sympathetic for his times,[70] more scrupulous in his use of sources and in verifying their authenticity than his contemporaries,[71] and in fact a pioneer of the "incipient scientific methodology" of history who "aspires to the kind of plainness and truthfulness he sees in the Biblical record."[72]

If the old charge of "willful falsification of evidence" will not stick,[73] Foxe's strong loyalty to the Protestant cause is still a stumbling block for many. Mozley comments perceptively,

> At the very word partizan scientific historians begin always to look uncomfortable. The partizan hardly plays the game of history as they understand it. Not that they are hard men or severe in their judgments. . . . They can forgive much: they can bear any amount of dullness, particularly when buttressed by terrific arrays of footnotes. . . . But partizanship--to have strong feelings and opinions and to show them--this comes near to putting a man outside the pale.[74]

But, he argues, open and honest partisanship is to be preferred to the veiled variety which masquerades as objectivity. And Foxe certainly makes no effort to hide his feelings. He

> had no use for "impartiality." He has passed through the fire, and learnt to dread it. . . . He writes with a purpose. . . . He must honor the dead and warn and encourage the living. His book is a blow in the battle against cruelty: and Foxe hated cruelty with all his heart.[75]

Foxe, in other words, believed that truth matters and that historical truth ought to make a difference. He strives to give us not just a collection of documents and facts but also a vision of life which emerges from them, a vision which is profoundly and particularly Christian. As Thompson puts it, he "merges his Reformed bias with the facts." There is no necessary tension between the two, and the end result is "a harmonious synthesis of supernatural and human causality, of the biblical version of history with actual events."[76] Or, to put it another way, he achieved a wholeness of vision which flowed from the fact that his historical consciousness was rooted in biblical consciousness. What Christian historian could ask for more--or offer less?

THE HISTORIAN'S MESSAGE

Foxe's interpretation of history is solidly within the Augustinian two-cities tradition as mediated to Sixteenth-Century Protestants by John Bale.[77] Foxe's contributions to that framework involve the superimposition upon it of a rather idiosyncratic eschatological scheme, an influential perspective on the role of England in salvation history, and an abidingly significant view, conveyed by his incomparable skill for simple, straightforward, and vivid narration, of the role of the testimony of Christ's martyrs in the ongoing struggle between the forces of darkness and light.

In the earlier pages of the Acts and Monuments, Foxe labors to establish a correlation between the progress of Church history and a preterist interpretation of the Book of Revelation.[78] After an initial period of "tribulation" (Rev. chp. 13), Satan is bound for a thousand years. This millennium corresponds roughly to the time between Constantine and Wycliffe, a time in which there was no major widespread persecution, but the Roman church was gradually becoming corrupt. With the persecution of Wycliffe and the Lollards, the Pope is revealed as Antichrist and Satan is unleashed for a season; in other words, the Church reenters a period of widespread persecution of true believers by the false

Church. This conflict comes to a head with the Reformation, and especially with the Marian persecutions, which vindicate the true Church and will eventually usher in the Second Coming and the Kingdom of God on earth.[79]

The attempt to read prophecy as history is a perilous undertaking, if in a sense a necessary one for people who look to its fulfillment as indeed the climax of history. Only one such attempt (at most) will be correct, and by the time we know which one it is, it will be too late to argue about it. Foxe's laudable desire to integrate his interpretation of history with his faith and his natural desire to buttress his view of the centrality of martyrdom to the unfolding of history with every means at his disposal led him to read the history he knew into John's prophecy. But the Reformation, important to the story of the Church as it was, did not bring in the Kingdom. Foxe did not in fact live in the Last Days (though we might), and his eschatology now seems forced and naive (as ours someday might). He shows that biblical consciousness, even when it is real and runs deep, does not guarantee infallibility.

Fortunately, Foxe himself seems to have realized that the details of his reading of Revelation were not central to his interpretation of history. McNeill reminds us that it is possible to over stress the importance of "all this apocalyptical apparatus for Foxe himself." He "respects" dates, facts, and sequence and refuses to "juggle" them to force them to fit his scheme. And in the last half of the work it recedes almost completely from view.[80] The attempt at prophetic interpretation remains a weakness, but one which can serve as a warning to us without detracting from more important facets of Foxe's vision.

What was supremely important to Foxe was that history—however periodized or related to prophecy—be understood as the record of the ongoing conflict between Truth and Error, Good and Evil, Christ and Satan. "Always," says White, "it is the battle between light and darkness that is the main standard of values, the focus of all issues for Foxe."[81] The protagonists in this struggle have founded *two communities* reminiscent of Augustine's two cities: Foxe calls them "this world" and "the kingdom of Christ," and warns his readers early on that the difference between them is what is "most requisite and necessary for every Christian man to observe and note" in his history.[82]

They must note them carefully because the struggle is not a simple matter of the Church versus the World. The World now appears wearing the face of the Church, which is precisely what makes the study of history crucial:

> Now forasmuch as the true church of God goeth not . . . alone, but is accompanied with some other church or chapel of the devil to deface and malign the same, necessary it is therefore the difference between them to be seen, and the descent of the right church to be described from the apostles' time: which hitherto, in most part of histories, has been lacking.[83]

The two Cities become increasingly focussed as the two Churches, and history describes the descent of the right one in two ways. First is by the comparison of doctrine and practice which shows the continuity between the Reformation and the primitive Church. If we think of ordinance and doctrine rather than ecclesiastical organization, history shows that "our church was, when this [Roman Catholic] church of theirs was not yet hatched out of the shell."[84] This is why so much more space is given to examinations, trials, and disputations than to actual martyrdoms, because it gives Foxe an opportunity to deal with *ideas* which are ultimately important.[85]

But the second way is the one for which Foxe is uniquely remembered. The moral force of the testimony of her martyrs creates its own continuity which helps to identify the true Church and bring into focus the power of her message.

If the possession of a central theme be one of the prerequisites for a great view of human history, then it cannot be denied that Foxe has it. He goes through past history, garnering up every rebel against Rome that he can find whose position can be reasonably interpreted as involving a return to the position of the Primitive Church, and out of these figures and movements of the past he establishes what he regards to be a continuing tradition of striving for the restoration of the Church to the purity of its first days.[86]

In a telling summation, Foxe contrasts the "primitive" and the "latter" church of Rome: a "persecuted church" versus a "persecuting church," a church whose bishops "were made martyrs" versus one whose bishops "make martyrs."[87] Thus the Reformers' martyrdoms at Rome's hands identify them effectively with the primitive Church, and the church of Rome with the pre-Constantinian persecuting Empire. The graphic stories of suffering are present not for the love of gore but because they reveal the true character of both sides with its powerful moral testimony to the truth of the one and the diabolical falsity of the other. "For Foxe, his martyrs are people whose characters and behavior may be taken as arguments for the truth of the position they have taken up. The character of their adversaries is clearly the opposite."[88] This Foxe labors unceasingly to bring out: again and again, his martyrs

> humbly offered themselves to the hands of their tormentors; and so took their death both Christianly and constantly, with such patience as might well testify the goodness of their cause. Wherein is to be noted how mightily the Lord worketh with his grace and fortitude in the hearts of his servants.[89]

For Foxe, then, the blood of the martyrs is not only the *seed* of the Church but also its *sign*. Persecuted or persecuting: Between the active and passive participles lies the clearest difference history shows between the Spirit of Christ and that of AntiChrist. This principle the fires of Smithfield burned indelibly into the mind of Foxe, and through his, into the minds of succeeding generations of Protestant believers.

An important subplot to this story for Foxe is the role of England in the historic struggle between the Two Churches. He sees for his own people a pivotal role in God's plan for the history of the Church. It was Constantine, a "Britayne born" through his mother Helena, who brought an end to the first wave of persecution;[90] it was the Englishman Wycliffe and his Lollards who recovered the Gospel in its purity and became the firstfruits of the new harvest of martyrs in modern times leading to the Reformation;[91] and it is the English Elizabeth who, as the new Constantine, has restored peace and the true Church once again.[92]

In general, the conflict of Christ and AntiChrist is represented on the temporal level by the (usually English) king versus the Pope.[93] When English monarchs (even Mary) support Pope and persecution, it tends to get blamed on evil counselors such as Gardiner.[94] On the whole, as Haller summarizes it,

> Every examination, as Foxe reports it, tended to wind up in a dramatic scene in which an honest believer was shown pitting the plain truth of the Word against the super-subtle sophistries of hypocritical churchmen and a loyal subject of the Crown was shown asserting his rights as an Englishman against a popish prelate.[95]

England is, in Haller's phrase, the "elect nation" intended by God to lead mankind to righteousness and freedom for true worship. But this is not mere national chauvinism; rather, the

English king and the English people are judged as they fail or succeed in living up to that role. There is, nevertheless, great hope for success under Elizabeth to match the egregious failure under Mary.

We should not dismiss this element of Foxe's vision as mere Eurocentric Anglophilia in a misguided passion for political correctness. The English-speaking peoples have indeed played a major role in the propagation of the Gospel across the world and the creation of the Church's literature--and a larger role than even Foxe could have foreseen in bringing religious freedom to the world through the American Experiment. Therefore, while few would follow him in the details (seeing the king as the bulwark of the true faith, for example), the major thrust of his vision here seems almost prophetic. It may indeed have helped to sow the seeds of its own fulfillment by creating a sense of destiny in such terms for the nation and its progeny. And we should remember that scholars such as Haller who see this theme as the central one of the Acts and Monuments are probably guilty of imbalance. The nationalistic element is certainly there, but as Olsen rightly recognizes, it is subordinate to the Gospel which is for *all* nations.[96] *That* is what ultimately receives its credibility from the testimony of the English martyrs throughout history.

In summary, history as Foxe wrote it had the power of bringing key events from the past into focus in such a way as to give an individual or a people a sense of identity, purpose, and destiny--no small contribution to the full-orbed biblical consciousness Christian readers strive to gain. "History, as he wrote it," says Haller, "always came back to the story of an individual . . . yet every individual case was charged with the whole meaning of history as he conceived it."[97] Hence that biblical consciousness led to wholeness of vision. Thompson describes it as a "cosmic vision" which always looms in the background, "lending a ritual quality to actions and words." Everything is defined by the struggle of AntiChrist versus Christ, the Mass versus the Word, the Sacrifice of the Mass versus the Sacrifice of the Martyrs.[98] If subsequent history has rendered obsolete his way of meshing history with eschatology, it has refined while confirming his high view of the role of England in church history and done nothing to alter his sense of the significance of her martyrs in the proclamation of the Church's message, as the Auca martyrs and others have amply demonstrated in our own generation.

CONCLUSION:

The taunt, "You're history!" seeks to cut its verbal victim down to size by relegating him to the irremedial irrelevance of the irretrievable past. The final thing to be said about John Foxe is that, for all his faults, he does at times succeed in reversing that commonly accepted meaning. In his book the past lives in the present and charges it with meaning. No one who has met them can ever forget Foxe's martyrs: Anne Askew, who had received from Wriothesly letters offering the king's pardon if she would recant, and who, "refusing once to look upon them, made this answer again, that she came not thither to deny her Lord and Master";[99] Cranmer holding his offending right hand into the flame;[100] and Latimer, saying on his way to the stake, "Be of good cheer, Master Ridley, and play the man. We shall this day light such a candle, by God's grace, in England, as I trust shall never be put out."[101] They, being dead, yet speak, and so their cause, as Foxe intended, lives on.

But note: they, being dead, yet speak--but only to *readers*. They speak because Foxe was a reader and a writer whose biblical consciousness and wholeness of vision enabled him to transmit their meaning to us in his account of history. Is not one of the reasons for the spiritual impoverishment even of believers in our generation the fact that they can no longer hear these voices? Surely one of the great motives for striving for a revival of biblical consciousness is so that the labors of men such as Foxe shall not have been in vain, that Hugh Latimer's final words may not finally be given the lie.

Follow me in your imagination to Oxford, England, where the University Church of St. Mary the Virgin, near the Bodleian Library at the heart of the University, has a column with a section chipped out to make room for the platform that held Latimer, Ridley, and Cranmer when they were tried for heresy. What must have been going through their minds?

THE OXFORD MARTYRS
Sonnet LXXIII

St. Mary the Virgin has a pillar defaced,
    A ledge chipped in the stone on which to rest
    The beam that held the platform where they placed
    The men they meant to martyr. Who'd have guessed
The way the Faith they stubbornly confessed
    Would rise up like a Phoenix from the flames?
    (A few blocks down, a cross still marks its nest.)
    And when those stalwarts stood to hear their names
Read out as heretics, their mortal frames
    Consigned to fiery death, could they have known?
    Did they by faith then hear the Lord proclaim
    Their place among the martyrs 'round his throne?
Latimer and Ridley played the man,
    And Cranmer clasped the fire by the hand.

--D.T.W.

The Book of Martyrs' biggest fault is its sheer size, which daunts all but the most obsessive readers and obscures its structure and theses. Most of the abridgements, which are legion, focus on the dramatic anecdotes and slight the historiographical context which gives them their meaning. A good critical edition for scholars is a desperate need--and then a popular abridgement, based on it, which could bring its sprawling bulk into focus, might even rekindle the light of Latimer's candle once again.

Notes to Chapter 4

1. John Foxe, <u>Actes and Monuments of the Latter and Perilous Dayes, Touching Matters of the Church</u>, ed. George Townsend, 8 vols. (London: Sedley & Burnside, 1841; rpt. N. Y.: AMS Pr., 1965).

2. See William Haller, <u>Foxe's Book of Martyrs and the Elect Nation</u> (London: Ebenezer Baylis & Sons, Ltd., 1967), p. 252-3 for a description of typical abridgements.

3. Foxe, op. cit., 1:99, 109-110.

4. Haller, op.cit., p. 57.

5. Sidney Lee, "Foxe, John," <u>Dictionary of National Biography</u> (Oxford: Oxford Univ. Pr., 1917), 7:581-90. Though biased, Lee's biography is still the most useful collection of the basic facts about Foxe's life, and will be the source of those facts otherwise undocumented here.

6. See Donald T. Williams, "Dossier: Thomas Cranmer," <u>Eternity</u> (Sept., 1986), p. 17, for a brief review of the English Reformation. The best general history of the Reformation in England is A. G. Dickens, <u>The English Reformation</u> (N. Y.: Schocken Books, 1964); see also Philip Edgcumbe Hughes, <u>Theology of the English Reformers</u>, new ed. (Grand Rapids: Baker, 1980).

7. V. Norskov Olsen, <u>John Foxe and the Elizabethan Church</u> (Berkeley: Univ. of Cal. Pr., 1973), p. 9.

8. Foxe, op. cit., 5:704.

9. Ibid., 6:354.

10. Ibid., 6:355.

11. Qtd. in J. F. Mozley, John Foxe and his Book (London: SPCK, 1940), p. 54.

12. Ibid., p. 35; cf. Neville Williams, John Foxe the Martyrologist: His Life and Times (London: Dr. Williams' Trust, 1975), p. 22.

13. Mozley, op. cit., pp. 86-7.

14. Ibid., p. 126.

15. Ibid., p. 128.

16. Haller, op. cit., p. 9; cf. Leslie M. Oliver, "The Acts and Monuments of John Foxe: A Study of the Growth and Influence of a Book," Diss. Harvard, 1945, which, according to Haller, "John Foxe and the Puritan Revolution," in The Seventeenth Century: Studies in the History of English Thought and Literature from Bacon to Pope (ed. Richard Foster Jones; Stanford: Stanford Univ. Pr., 1951), is the fullest account of the bibliographical history of the Acts and Monuments. Mozley, op. cit., p. 25, says that while most of the valuable material from the Latin work was carried over into the English editions, "the Latin book must not for this reason be neglected: for in translating it Foxe and his assistants would often omit some point of interest, sacrifice some graphic touch, or even drastically curtail a narrative." Hence, it is still "always worthwhile" to consult the Basel edition.

17. On March 26, 1566, Foxe was summoned to Lambeth to answer for his refusal to wear vestments. When Archbishop Parker required him to subscribe, he "produced a New Testament in Greek. 'To this,' saith he, 'will I subscribe'" (Mozley, op. cit., p. 74).

18. Mozley, op. cit., p. 153.

19. Hyder E. Rollins and Herschel Baker, eds., The Renaissance in England: Non-Dramatic Prose and Verse of the Sixteenth Century (Lexington, Mass.: D. C. Heath, 1954), p. 174.

20. John T. McNeill, "John Foxe: Historiographer, Disciplinarian, Tolerationist," Church History 43 (1974), p. 225.

21. Helen C. White, Tudor Books of Saints and Martyrs (Madison: Univ. of Wisconsin Pr., 1963), p. 179.

22. Foxe, op. cit., 1:xxv.

23. Ibid. Cf. Spenser, The Faerie Queene, Proem to Book I, where he sets out to sing of gentle deeds whose praises, "having slept in silence long" in antique rolls, must now be blazoned abroad.

24. Foxe, op. cit., 1:xviii.

25. Haller, Elect Nation, op. cit., p. 130.

26. Ibid., p. 145.

27. Foxe, op. cit., 1:viii.

28. Ibid.

29. Haller, Elect Nation, op. cit., p. 153.

30. Foxe, op. cit., 6:511.

31. Geraldine Vina Thompson, "Foxe's Book of Martyrs: A Literary Study" (Diss. Oregon, 1974), p. 191.

32. Mark Breitenberg, "The Flesh made Word: Foxe's Acts and Monuments," Renaissance and Reformation 25 (1989), p. 397.

33. Foxe, op. cit., 1:xix,

34. Olsen, op. cit., p. 49.

35. Warren W. Wooden, "From Caxton to Comenius: The Origins of Children's Literature," Fifteenth-Century Studies 6 (1983), pp. 307f.

36. Qtd. in Mozley, op. cit., p. 136.

37. Foxe, op. cit., 1:viii.

38. Ibid., 1:xviii.

39. Ibid., 1:91.

40. Ibid., 2:26.

41. Ibid., 2:108.

42. Ibid., 1:xxvi.

43.Ibid., 1:viii.

44. Ibid., 1:xvii.

45. Ibid., 1:207.

46. Ibid., 8:754.

47. Ibid., 1:vi.

48. Qtd. in Mozley, op. cit., p. 138-39; see also Thomas H. Clancy, S.J., Papist Pamphleteers: The Allen-Persons Party and the Political Thought of the Counter Reformation in England, 1512-1615 (Chicago: Loyola Univ. Pr., 1964), who gives a number of contemporary reactions to Foxe.

49. Olsen, op. cit., p. 91.

50. Mozley, op. cit., p. 183.

51. Lee, op. cit., 7:588.

52. Philip Hughes, The Reformation in England, 3 vol. (London: Hollis & Carter, 1951-54), 2:257-58; cf. Thompson, op. cit., pp. 59-61 and Stefan J. Smart, "John Foxe and 'The Story of Richard Hun, Martyr,'" Journal of Ecclesiastical History 37 (1986), p. 14 for similar reactions.

53. Joseph H. Preston, "English Ecclesiastical Historians and the Problem of Bias," Journal of the History of Ideas 32 (1971), pp. 203-20.

54. Mozley, op. cit., p. 168.

55. Ibid., p. 130.

56. Foxe, op. cit., 3:292.

57. Ibid., 1:217.

58. F. Smith Fussner, <u>Tudor History and the Historians</u> (N. Y.: Basic Books, 1970), p. 27.

59. Op. cit. C. S. Lewis, <u>English Literature in the Sixteenth Century, Excluding Drama</u>, vol. 3 of <u>The Oxford History of English Literature</u> (Oxford: Oxford Univ. Pr., 1954), pp. 299-300, judges Mozley's defense of Foxe's integrity to be a "complete success": "For the Marian persecution his sources are usually the narratives of eyewitnesses . . . Men who have seen their friends die in torture are not always inspired by that coolly scientific spirit which the academic researcher so properly demands. But there seems no evidence that Foxe ever accepted what he himself did not believe or ever refused to correct what he had written in the light of fresh evidence."

60. Foxe, op. cit., 1:184-85.

61. Ibid., 1:196-97.

62. Ibid., 1:103.

63. Ibid., 1:111.

64. Ibid., 1:113.

65. Ibid., 1:273.

66. Ibid., 1:149; cf. 1:193.

67. Cf. White, op. cit., pp. 180-81.

68. Foxe, op. cit., 3:340.

69. M. M. Knappen, <u>Tudor Puritanism: A Chapter in the History of Idealism</u> (Chicago: Univ. of Chicago Pr., 1939), p. 495.

70. McNeill, op. cit., p. 228.

71. J. W. Martin, "A Sidelight on Foxe's Account of the Marian Martyrs," <u>Bulletin of the Institute for HIstorical Research</u> 58 (1985), p. 51.

72. Thompson, op. cit., pp. 250-51.

73. Warren W. Wooden, "Recent Studies in Foxe," <u>English Literary Renaissance</u> 11 (1981), p. 228; cf. Neville Williams, op. cit., pp. 17-18: "modern research has done much to confirm the details" of Foxe on Lollardy; Mozley, op. cit., pp. 159-73: Foxe's errors are "small blemishes" compared to the "solid merit" of the whole, and that we know "what manner of man Tyndale was" is due more to Foxe than anyone else, while the same could be said of many other figures he portrays; Haller, <u>Elect Nation</u>, op. cit., p. 124, etc., who adds that Foxe's information on Elizabeth probably came from her old tutor Roger Ascham; and John Fines, "A Note on the Reliability of Foxe," Appendix II of "Heresy Trials in Coventry and Lichfield," <u>Journal of Ecclesiastical History</u> 14 (1963), pp. 173-4, who reports that considering his difficulties, Foxe's accuracy is "amazing."

74. Mozley, op. cit., p. 156.

75. Ibid.

76. Thompson, op. cit., pp. 250-51.

77. Haller, <u>Elect Nation</u>, op. cit., pp. 62-67, pursues this connection profitably; cf. Paul Christianson, <u>Reformers and</u>

<u>Babylon: English Apocalyptic Visions from the Reformation to the Eve of the Civil War</u> (Toronto: Univ. of Toronto Pr., 1978), pp. 39f.

78. Foxe, op. cit., 1:289ff.

79. Ibid., 2:724-26; cf. Olsen, op. cit., p. 71.

80. McNeill, op. cit., pp. 224-5.

81. White, op. cit., p. 146; cf. Haller, <u>Elect Nation</u>, op. cit., p. 187.

82. Foxe, op. cit., 1:88.

83. Ibid., 1:xix.

84. Ibid., 1:9.

85. White, op. cit., pp. 157-8; for a thorough study of the theology of the English Reformation, see Philip Edgcumbe Hughes, <u>Theology of the English Reformers</u> (Grand Rapids: Baker, 1980); for a more concise treatment see the first chapter of Donald T. Williams, "The Depth of Rightful Doom: The English Reformers' Concept of Justice and Book V of Spenser's <u>Faerie Queene</u>" (Diss. Georgia, 1985).

86. White, op. cit., p. 179.

87. Foxe, op. cit., 1:12.

88. White, op. cit., p. 152.

89. Foxe, op. cit., 5:438.

90. Thompson, op. cit., pp. 26f.

91. Foxe, op. cit., 2:791; cf. 3:311.

92. Francis A Yates, "Queen Elizabeth I as Astraea," in <u>Astraea: The Imperial Theme in the Sixteenth Century</u> (London: Routledge & Kegan Paul, 1975), pp. 29-87, sees the Elizabeth/Constantine analogy as the key to Foxe's whole book; cf. Thompson, op. cit., pp. 54f.

93. Thompson, op. cit., 22-23.

94. White, op. cit., p. 178; cf. Thompson, op. cit., pp. 46-49.

95. Haller, <u>Elect Nation</u>, op. cit., p. 183.

96. Olsen, op. cit., pp. 36-37.

97. Haller, "Puritan Revolution," op. cit., p. 217.

98. Thompson, op. cit., p. 5.

99. Foxe, op. cit., 5:550.

100. Ibid., 8:90.

101. Ibid., 7:550.

INTERLUDE

THE RADCLIFFE CAMERA
(Part of the Bodleian Library, Oxford;
Theology and Literature are Housed in the Basement)

The lamp of learning never shone so bright
As there beneath that artificial sky,
The dome of the Radcliffe Camera, graced with light.
That soaring weightlessness of blue and white
Shot through with gold from skylights lifted high:
The lamp of learning never shone so bright.
Not truly weightless, all that stony height:
In the crypt, squat, hunkering arches underlie
The dome of the Radcliffe Camera, graced with light.
There rooted firm, those arches ground their might:
Theology and letters; that is why
The lamp of learning never shone so bright.
That weight of learning buried out of sight
Was what allowed the mind to soar and fly
In the dome of the Radcliffe Camera, filled with light.
Here one might mount a search for what is right,
To extricate he true thought from the lie.
The lamp of learning never shone so bright:
The dome of the Radcliffe Camera, graced with light.

--D.T.W.

Chapter 5

THE EXCELLENCIES OF GOD
Christian Motivation and Themes in Puritan Poetry

*"Conceive of this duty of praising God according to its
superlative excellencies, as the highest service that the
tongue of men or angels can perform."*

--Richard Baxter

*When thou hast told the world of all these things
Then turn about, my book, and touch those strings
Which, if but touched, will such a music make,
They'll make a cripple dance, a giant quake."*

--John Bunyan

One of the notions most difficult to dislodge from the popular mind is the picture of the Puritan as a person characterized by a negative attitude toward pleasure in general and the arts in particular. While scholars have long known better,[1] popular associations of the word are still aptly characterized by H. L. Mencken's crack, "Puritanism is the haunting fear that someone, somewhere, may be happy."[2] Indeed, the Puritans--or at least some of them--have already appeared as villains of a sort in chapter two, where their negative attitudes toward fiction and drama became the foil for Sidney's magnificent apologia for creative writing. But we have already seen that the simple identification of such attitudes with the Puritan movement is too simple.[3] So who were these people anyway, and why do they deserve a chapter in a book on the Christian view of reading?

The Puritans were people who wanted to "purify" the English church further than the English Reformation had already done. The Elizabethan settlement had been a politically brilliant compromise, giving the Protestant faction what it cared about most--the nicely balanced Reformed *doctrine* of the Thirty-Nine Articles--but leaving the old familiar Catholic *style of worship* largely untouched, save for having the service in English. But it wasn't going to satisfy everybody forever, and the Puritans--the more zealously Protestant wing of the Church--wanted further reform in three basic areas. First, they wanted a less liturgical service with more emphasis on preaching, and preaching that was a practical exposition of Scripture aimed at the common people. Second, they wanted to do away with priestly vestments and view the clergy as ministers rather than priests, as being more faithful to the New-Testament principle of the universal priesthood of believers. Third, they wanted a change in church government, from episcopal to (depending on the faction) a presbyterian or congregational form.

However much we may agree or disagree with the Puritans on these three issues which defined their movement, what is interesting to us here is that they tended to be the most serious and untiring practical expositors of the Bible in the Sixteenth and Seventeenth Centuries. They emphasized practical, personal, experiential, reformed spirituality based on exposition of and meditation on the text of Scripture. The zeal with which they pursued these goals made many of them spiritual giants. What Lloyd-Jones perceptively observes of one applies to many of them: "You cannot read a page of Jonathan Edwards without feeling very small indeed."[4]   They were, in sum, people very much concerned with the nurture of biblical consciousness, and as such they are very much a concern of this book.

But they were also a very diverse group. The great names at the center of the movement--John Bunyan, John Owen, Richard Sibbes, Richard Baxter, Jonathan Edwards--are still part of the rich black theological soil in which the Evangelical movement grows when it is most healthy. On the fringes in one direction were genuinely anti-cultural zealots; on the other hand, people such as John Milton were part of the movement, and people such as Edmund Spenser and even Sir Philip Sidney himself were sympathetic to at least some of the values it represented.

How then did a movement that cared so much about the written Word and included people like John Milton get such a reputation for an anti-literary and obscurantist mentality? Its very diversity helped; some members deserved the characterization and others who decidedly did not could sometimes sound as if they did. Caricatures are still sometimes in circulation from older scholars who ought to have know better. Percy Scholes documented this phenomenon in the area of music history, concluding that it was a result of Cavalier misrepresentations of the Puritans having crept into general histories, supplying them with "a wide statement as to Puritan gloom and fanaticism, which they uncritically absorbed and reproduced over and over again with mere changes of wording."[5]

These views have not been without their influence in the field of literary criticism, though no scholar can now go back behind the work of Haller, Miller, etc. Yet it is commonly assumed that loyal churchmen were by nature poetic, while Puritan literature can be expected to be prosaic. We are told, for example, that the doctrinal Puritans "flattened the poetry of the Hebrew Bible into Prose."[6] Somehow a need for an explanation is felt when good poetry is written by men with Puritan beliefs or sympathies, such as Milton, Andrew Marvell, or George Wither.

The Puritan version of biblical consciousness was not as broad as Sidney's or Milton's, but it ran just as deep in the more limited channels it flowed in. And it did produce a characteristic attitude to poetry that may be surprising. In this chapter we want to find its positive elements by asking what it meant to be a Puritan and a Poet in Seventeenth-Century England.

There are passages in Puritan writings which, on a surface reading, seem to support the popular caricature of the Puritan mind. In his Christian Directory, Richard Baxter advises Christian readers to read first the Bible, then books that apply it. Then, if they still have time, they may turn to history, the sciences, and finally the arts. Above all they must beware of the poison in false teachers, "and of vain romances, play-books, and false stories, which may bewitch your fantasies and corrupt your hearts."[7] This sounds suspiciously like an outright condemnation of fiction.

The theater comes in for special denunciation:

> And how much profaneness, or abuse of others, is in many of your stage plays! How much wantonness and amorous folly, and representing sin in a manner to entice men to it, rather than make it odious.[8]

As we have seen, Baxter is not without weighty arguments against these heinous "playbooks, romances, and idle tales." In the first place, they keep more important things out of our minds. Moreover, they divert us from serious thoughts of salvation, and are a waste of valuable time. Finally, he asks us to consider "whether the greatest lovers of romances and plays, be the greatest lovers of the book of God, and of a holy life."[9]

To understand the vehemence of Baxter's denunciation, we must understand the thing he is denouncing. When we think of the theater, for example, we tend to think of Shakespeare's sublime tragedies, and we are incensed to think of Baxter as condemning as "unspiritual" our enjoyment of such art. We may be tempted to grouse at it as hypocritical as well as inconsistent, as Ben Jonson did:

> I cannot think there's that antipathy
> 'Twixt Puritans and players as some cry;

> Though Lippe, at Paul's, ran from his text away
> To inveigh 'gainst plays, what did he then but play?[10]

But we must remember that, while he may well have uncritically lumped in much good literature with the bad, the theater of Baxter's day was not the theater of Shakespeare, and his description of its debauchery is not wholly inaccurate. Later Jacobean drama had attained what Chapman and Grant call the "complete secularization" of the medieval and Elizabethan world views.[11]

Having said this, we are still not sure exactly what Baxter meant to include in his denunciation of "romances and idle tales." Surely he would not have disapproved of Bunyan's Pilgrim's Progress, which, as Lewis has observed, sends Pilgrim on a "journey as enchanting as any in romance."[12] And what of Spenser's Faerie Queene, which is in form and style a medieval romance, but which contains such a statement of classical Puritan piety as

> What man is he, that boasts of fleshly might,
>   And vaine assurance of mortality,
>   Which all so soone, as it doth come to fight
>   Against spiritual foes, yields by and by,
>   Or from the field most cowardly doth fly?
>   Ne let the man ascribe it to his skill,
>   That thorough grace hath gained victory.
>   If any strength we have, it is to ill,
> But all the good is God's, both power and eke will.[13]

Baxter gives no direct answer to these questions. But it is certain that there is more to his view of poetry than meets the eye in the passages we have quoted so far.

The fact that Baxter and his fellow Puritan divines and laymen were not opposed to all poetry is infallibly proved by the fact that they wrote quite a lot of it; and not all of their work was directly "religious" in nature. One of the most popular genres of the Sixteenth and Seventeenth Centuries was the paraphrasing of biblical poetry into English Metrical idioms.[14] In this the Puritans played a large role. As Bush reminds us,

> The widespread impulse to paraphrase the psalms, which had touched poets like Marot, Wyatt, Surrey, and Buchanan, was greatly stimulated by the growth of Puritanism and the influx of Protestant refugees.[15]

This movement ranged from the popular common-meter doggerel of Sternhold and Hopkins to the diverse and complex metrical elegance of Sir Philip Sidney and his sister Mary the Countess of Pembroke.[16]

The great theologian John Owen wrote Latin epigrams and miscellaneous verse.[17] Pithy preacher John Dod made a metrical paraphrase of the Song of Solomon.[18] Poets of no less note than Andrew Marvell and George Wither (in later life) were devout Puritans.[19] Marvell's "To His Coy Mistress[20]" should be an iconoclast sufficient to destroy our preconceptions of Puritan prudery. And many who have benefitted from Baxter's Reformed Pastor would be interested to know that he himself published three books of verse.[21]

The titles of Baxter's three books of poetry are themselves indicative of the peculiar emphases of mainstream Puritans in poetry. The first was Heart Employment with God and Itself: The Concordant Discord of a Broken-Healed Heart (London: 1681). This was followed by Additions to the Poetical Fragments of Richard Baxter (London: 1683), which was described as "written for himself, and communicated to such as are more for serious verse than smooth." Finally came A Paraphrase on the Psalms, with other Hymns left fitted for the Press, published the year after Baxter's death, in 1692.[22]

Interesting light is shed on Baxter's own poetic tastes by the comments he makes about other contemporary poets. He speaks favorably of several, and it is significant that not all who receive his commendation are Puritans themselves. He says that "Honest George Wither, though a Rustick Poet, hath been very acceptable to some for his prophecies, so to others for his plain country-honesty."[23] Francis Quarles "outwent" Wither in "mixing competent Wit with Piety."[24] But Baxter's highest praise is reserved for George Herbert, a loyal Anglican. Baxter quotes one of Herbert's poems from The Temple in The Saint's Everlasting Rest[25] and says elsewhere that "Herbert speaks to God like one that really believeth a God, and whose business in the world is most with God."[26]

What then did it mean to be a Puritan and a poet? In order to deal with this question we will have to limit the scope of this study. Milton, the greatest poet of the age, was a Puritan, albeit an eccentric one. (Fisch remarks that Milton's thinking started from Genesis and went from there to Judges and the Gospels, the books around which he wrote his three major poems. He never wrote a full-length poem on the crucifixion. The doctrinal Puritans, however, started to a man from the book of Romans.[27]) Both his eccentricity and his greatness exclude him from this chapter; the one he deserves to himself has already been written by C. S. Lewis[28] (though see the major role he plays here in chapter two). We will concentrate here on the great divines in the mainstream of Puritan thinking. How did the ones who wrote verse conceive of their task as poets, and what kind of poetry did they write? Our two great examples are Richard Baxter and John Bunyan.

RICHARD BAXTER

For Baxter, the motivation for writing poetry was the same as the motivation for everything else that he did:

> Be sure you intend this end in all, even the everlasting
> sight and love of God, and the promoting his glory, and
> pleasing his holy will; and that you never meddle with
> any studies separated from this end, but as means
> thereto, and as animated thereby.[29]

All of life revolves around the duty to glorify God. The most important aspect of that duty is *praising God*. "Conceive of this duty of praising God according to its superlative excellencies, as being the highest service that the tongue of men or angels can perform."[30] Praising God with the tongue is a joyful act in itself; but it is also excellent by virtue of its effect on other people:

> To be much employed in the praises of God, will
> acquaint the world with the nature of true religion, and
> remove their prejudice, and confute their dishonourable
> thoughts and accusations of it, and recover the honour of
> Christ. . . . Many are averse to a holy life, because they
> think that it consisteth but of melancholy fears or
> scrupulosity: but who dare open his mouth against the
> joyful praises of his Maker?[31]

One of the best means of praising God with the tongue is through poetry and song. Baxter admonishes the Christian to "Be much in singing psalms of praise, and that with the most heart-raising cheerfulness and melody."[32] So Christians may--indeed, should--offer to God the praise of their voices, and, by implication, their pens.

Thus far the poets of the established church would agree. But there are stylistic qualities which mark off Puritan poetry from that of high-church divines such as Donne, though the doctrinal and spiritual content was much the same. The Puritan poet could never see his work as simply an intellectual exercise, or as directed only to God, or to the intelligentsia. The Puritan poets we are considering were first ministers of the Gospel, and literati only secondarily. If their poetry was going to promote God's glory, it must be able to edify the common man.

Thus, the same philosophy which caused the Puritan divines to espouse "spiritual" as opposed to "witty" preaching applied to their poetry as well. This view was based on what the Puritans understood to be the example of the Divine Poet Himself. John Downame tells us that God,

> In the profundity of wisdome could have written in such a loftie stile as would have filled even the most learned with admiration, yet he useth a simple easie stile fit for the capacity of all, because it was for the use of all, and necessarie to salvation to be understood of all sorts and conditions.[33]

Thus the poetry of the Puritan divines was marked by stylistic simplicity, with a general avoidance of the metaphysical conceit so popular among their contemporaries.

The pursuit of simplicity is not necessarily, of course, a renunciation of beauty or of art. Baxter advises that one third of one's commonplace book be devoted to "what is useful for ornamentation and oratory."[34] And one of his directions for praising God with the tongue is that we "speak not so unskillfully and foolishly of God or holy things, as may tempt the hearers to turn it into a matter of scorn or laughter."[35]

There was then, in Puritan poetry, a desire for beauty and ornament that would avoid ostentatious erudition. It is not always easy for men of the intellect, as the Puritans were, to achieve such a balance. George Herbert, whose poetry Baxter so greatly admired, was at one with them in the quest for that balance, though his success in achieving it was greater than theirs (see chapter six). He gives us some insight into what that struggle was like. In "Jordan (2)" he recalls his first attempts:

> When first my lines of heavenly thoughts made mention,
> Such was their luster, they did so excel,
> That I sought out quaint words and trim invention;
> My thoughts began to burnish, sprout, and swell . . .

This seeking was motivated by the thought that, "Nothing could be too rich to clothe the sun." But Herbert was not yet satisfied with the results. He finally realized that,

> While I bustled, I might hear a friend
> Whisper, "How wide is all this long pretense!
> There is in love a sweetness ready penned,
> Copy out only that, and save expense.[36]

Herbert finally achieved a synthesis reminiscent of Luther's famous question, "Why should the Devil have all the good music?" He expresses it brilliantly in "The Forerunners," which is both a statement and example of how "sweet phrases, lovely metaphors" can be enlisted in the service of God. Looking back on his lovely metaphors, Herbert recalls that,

> . . . when ye before
> Of stews and brothels only knew the doors,
> Then did I wash you with my tears, and more,
> Brought you to church well dressed and clad:
> My God must have my best, ev'n all I had.[37]

For Herbert also, but especially for the Puritans, the way to ensure that their poetry would be edifying was to base it on the patterns for poetic communication given by God in Scripture.[38] Another of Baxter's directions for praising God with the tongue is that we

Read much those Scriptures which speak of the praises
of God; especially the Psalms: and furnish your
memories with store of those holy expressions of the
excellencies of God which he himself hath taught you in
his word.[39]

Thus Puritan poetry--or Puritan praise--was the direct fruit
of Puritan biblical consciousness. In a fascinating recent study,
Jeffrey Hammond captures well the way Puritans typically related
to the biblical text:

To internalize the Word this fully was to rewrite the text
within one's heart--to experience the self as an inner
expression of biblical pattern. Whenever readers
appropriated the text as an expression of felt belief, the
result was not a mere aping of biblical language, but
heartfelt empathy with the biblical speaker as
representative saint.[40]

In writing and reading poetry, then, the Puritans tried to
identify themselves with these previously absorbed biblical
patterns. Poetry offered an opportunity "for Puritan writers and
readers to create themselves through language." The result was
an "unconscious aligning of private voice with saintly
paradigm."[41] Hammond has captured not only the Puritan
psychology of reading but also the process by which the biblical
text is transformed into biblical consciousness in receptive
readers, through both the text itself and their own words (or the
poet's appropriated as their own) interacting with the text.

The fruit of such application of Baxter's exhortation can
readily be seen in the history of English hymnody.

The real cradle of English hymns is the English Bible,
and its power on the mind of England is forcibly

exhibited by their history. The new-found Bible seemed to the Reformers the divinely-given well-spring of praise; large portions of it were actual songs, or rapturous utterances of the saints; and in the Bible words alone they deemed themselves secure from human error. The great illustration of this belief is found in the long series of metrical Psalters, which formed the staple of public praise for Churchman and Non-conformist till the close of the Seventeenth Century.[42]

The Puritans, as we have seen, were great contributors to the metrical paraphrasing of Scripture. But their poetic activity did not stop there. Often they would paraphrase several passages from different parts of the Bible, arranging them topically and freely composing logical connecting passages between them. Even when they wrote non-paraphrastic lyrics, they were pregnant with Scriptural content. Julian accurately captures their approach when he notes that

> That grand note of our greatest hymns, impregnation with Scripture, is in great measure the heritage of the paraphrases. The limitation to Scripture had held its ground so long from dread of error. Hence, if a hymn, not verbally derived from Scripture, was to be accepted, it had to give plain evidence of its ground in Holy Writ. . . . Watts, in the Preface to his hymns, is careful to say that he "might have brought some text . . . and applied it to the margin of every verse."[43]

Baxter not only "might have," he often did supply Scripture texts to the margins of his verse. An excellent example of this type of composition, and a piece typical of Baxter's poetry, is "The Prayer of a Penitent Sinner, Collected out of the Psalms."[44] No mere doggerel translation of the Scripture into meter, the

poem moves with an inner logic of its own from the miserable
state of the sinner to the first ray of hope, to the realization of
that hope, the resultant joy, and finally the redeemed saint's
resolve to live a life of praise and holiness in response to what his
Lord has done for him.

> Lord, from the horrid deep my cries   Psal.cxxx.1.
> Ascend unto thine ear;
>   Do not my mournful cry despise,
>   But my petition hear.
> I do confess that I receiv'd   li.5.
>   My very shape in sin:
> In it my mother me conceiv'd,
>   And brought me forth therein.
>
> Numberless evils compass me   xl.12.
>   My sins do me assail:
> More than my very hairs they be,
>   So that my heart doth fail.
> But there is mercy to be had   cxxx.4.
>   With thee, and pardoning grace,
> That men may be encouraged
>   With fear to seek thy face. . . .
>
> Blessed is he to whom the Lord   xxxii.2.
>   Imputeth not his sin;
> Whose heart hath all deceit abhorr'd
>   And guile's not found therein. . . .
>
> O then let joy and gladness speak,   li.8.
>   And let me hear their voice;
> So that the bones which thou didst break
>   May feelingly rejoice! . . .

> With upright heart I'll speak thy praise   cxix.7,8.
>> When I have learned thy word.
> Fain would I keep thy laws always;
>> Forsake me not, O Lord.

The strong echoes of familiar Bible passages are plain, and it is precisely because of them that the poem is an accurate and eloquent statement of what Baxter as representative Puritan felt about his relationship with God. The goal is not originality or novelty, as in modern poetry, but fidelity to the Divine pattern. This is not great poetry, but perhaps that fidelity is why these simple lines have for those in whom their biblical background resonates a power unmatched by much verse that is technically more polished.

Baxter was also capable of composing verse that does not directly depend on a Scriptural original. "A Psalm of Praise, to the Tune of Psalm cxlviii"[45] is a good example. The poem is an antiphonal conversation with parts for "Angels," "The glorified saints," "The world," "The church," and "My soul." The sprightly, exuberant rhythm of the intricate verse form Baxter chooses for this piece itself expresses the burning joy of the life of service to God, and the challenge of writing in this more difficult form may explain why this poem is more successful as a poem than the last one:

> Though sin and death aspire
>> To rob thee of thy praise,
> Still towards thee I'll aspire;
>> And thou dull hearts canst raise.
>>> Open thy door;
>>> And when grim death
>>> Shall stop this breath,
>>>> I'll praise thee more.

Probably Baxter's most well known poem is the hymn "Lord, it Belongs not to my Care."[46] Its clear, deceptively effortless lines are charged with all the submission, trust, and comfort that flow from a devout love of the God of grace.

> Lord, it belongs not to my care
>   Whether I die or live;
> To love and serve Thee is my share,
>   And this Thy grace must give.
>
> If life be long, I will be glad
>   That I may long obey;
> If short--yet why should I be sad
>   To soar to endless day?
>
> Christ leads me through no darker rooms
>   Than he went through before;
> He that unto God's kingdom comes,
>   Must enter by this door. . . .
>
> My knowledge of that life is small,
>   The eye of faith is dim;
> But 'tis enough that CHRIST knows all,
>   And I shall be with Him.

It is clear that this poem is strongly related to biblical passages such as 2 Cor. 5:1-10 and Phil. 1:21-24. Yet it cannot be said to be merely a metrical paraphrase of either of them. Rather, it is something along the lines of a lyrical commentary which brings out, as nothing else could, the full meaning of the Pauline passages which directly or indirectly inspired it. Thus it also indicates the strength of the biblical consciousness in Richard Baxter's mind as applied to his own spiritual condition.

JOHN BUNYAN

The other Puritan poet we shall briefly consider is John Bunyan. His Pilgrim's Progress is universally admired as a classic of English prose. But we may not remember that the book also contains much verse that is not unworthy of praise. Bunyan's pilgrims, like Tolkien's, love to sing, and their songs are indicative of the place of verse in Puritan life.

In 1686, Bunyan published a book devoted solely to poetry, called A Book for Boys and Girls: Or Country Rhymes for Children. Scholes quotes one piece from this book which reminds one of, and compares very favorably with, the "emblem" verse of Quarles:

> Suppose a Viol, Cittern, Lute, or Harp
> Committed unto him that wanteth skill;
> Can he by strokes, suppose them flat or sharp,
> The Ear of him that hears with Musick fill?
>
> No, no, he can do little else than scrape
> Or put all out of tune, or break a string;
> Or make thereon a muttering like an ape,
> Or like one which can neither say nor sing.

COMPARISON

> The unlearned Novices in Things Divine
> With this unskilled Musician I compare,
> For such, instead of making Truth to shine,
> Abuse the Bible and unsavory are.

Bunyan, tinker though he was, proved neither an unskilled musician nor a novice in the things of God. His analogy here, like so many of the images from Pilgrim's Progress, can only be described as *apt*. One thinks not, "Oh, how clever!" or "I could never have thought of that" as when reading the metaphysical poets, but rather it seems as if the idea has always been in the mind, just waiting for Bunyan to bring it out. Again, this is not great poetry, but it achieves its purpose of stimulating useful thoughts, much as the allegorical images of Bunyan's fiction have done for so many.

It is apparent that some Puritans were suspicious of allegory or metaphor in poetry or prose, for Bunyan felt the need to defend his allegorical method in the Pilgrim's Progress. Thus he prefaces the book with a verse apology. His defense is in line with Baxter's dictum that the Puritan poet should follow the pattern of Scripture, but it is a different aspect of the Scriptural style that Bunyan stresses:

> . . . Were not God's laws,
> His gospel laws, in olden times held forth
> By types, shadows, and metaphors? Yet loath
> Will any sober man be to find fault
> With them, lest he be found for to assault
> The highest wisdom. No, he rather stoops
> And seek to find out what by pins and loops,
> By calves and sheep, by heifers and by rams,
> By birds and herbs, and by the blood of lambs,
> God speaketh to him; and happy is he
> That finds the light and grace that in them be.[47]

The regular but not *too* regular iambic pentameter and the deft use of enjambment reveal a competent versifier who has moved far beyond the technical skill of Sternhold and Hopkins or even most of Baxter, and the concrete catalog of biblical examples is a powerful argument. But not all the cavilers are apparently silenced by it, so Bunyan finds it necessary to prefix another apology to the second installment dealing with

Christiana. Some, perhaps having read Baxter's warnings quoted above, object to the Pilgrim as "romance." Whether such an objection rightly understands Baxter's meaning is at least open to question; but at any rate, Bunyan is willing to treat this as simply a matter of taste, and let it pass.

> Some love no cheese, some love no fish, and some
> Love not their friends, nor their own house or home;
> Some start at pig, slight chicken, love not fowl,
> More than they love a cuckoo or an owl.
> Leave such, my Christiana, to their choice,
> And seek those who to find thee will rejoice;
> By no means strive, but in humble-wise
> Present thee to them in thy Pilgrim guise.[48]

Perhaps his response is the best that can be made after all; the Poor we have always with us, intellectually as well as financially, and the mentally impoverished are sometimes that way because they are willfully unteachable. One hopes not so much to convert them by defending good letters as to fortify the tender of conscience against their abuse.

Bunyan's use of allegory is not out of keeping with the general Puritan emphasis that poetry should be understandable and edifying to the common person (and allegory as a hindrance to biblical consciousness of course refers not to allegory as a method of composition but to the school of interpretation that tended to force all of Scripture into an allegorical mold whether it had been written that way or not). His figures are taken straight from the Bible and common experience, not from erudite learning, and they were concocted to represent trials and temptations with which all people are familiar. Hence, Bunyan's very use of allegory was designed to foster understanding.

> . . . a dark similitude
> Will on the fancy more itself intrude,
> And will stick faster in the heart and head,
> Than things from similes not borrowed.[49]

These prologues are interesting for the light they shed on Bunyan's own thoughts about his work. But more typical of Puritan poetry in general are the numerous short lyrics which are interspersed throughout the text of <u>Pilgrim's Progress</u>. Bunyan's pilgrims are great lovers of music, and their typical response to any important event is to break into song. These songs have two basic purposes: to drive home and summarize the ethical or spiritual point of what has just occurred, and to praise God for his mercy or deliverance. We will look at one of the better examples of each.

The pilgrims wander by the "river of life" and are refreshed by its waters and by the goodly fruit trees that grow along its banks. These fruits provide spiritual as well as physical refreshment, and in the context of the rough journey they have had, the experience is an important one for the pilgrims at that time. To drive home the point of the great value of this living water, they sing (as much to solidify the experience for themselves as for the reader):

> Behold ye how these crystal streams do glide,
> To comfort pilgrims by the highwayside.
> The meadows green, besides their fragrant smell,
> Yield dainties for them; and he who can tell
> What pleasant fruit, yea leaves, these trees do yield,
> Will soon sell all, that he may buy this field.[50]

The poem conflates imagery from Eden and Revelation and transplants it into the Parable of the Field, which speaks of the surpassing value of the Kingdom of Heaven and hence the urgency of conversion. Its richness derives from the complex interaction of the various strands of biblical imagery it weaves together, and its potency from the rhetorical strategy of delaying the recognition of the primary one (the parable) until the last line. As a result, the ending explodes with the surprise and pleasure of recognition while effectively driving home the practical point. The effect is not to create for Bunyan's (original) readers a new idea but to enrich and empower a familiar one. As a result, he feeds their biblical consciousness, allowing it to grow and deepen.

One of the most moving scenes in the Pilgrim's Progress is that in which Christian comes to the cross and the burden of sin falls off his back. There he "gave three leaps for joy, and went on singing" this highly appropriate song of praise:

> Thus far did I come laden with my sin,
> Nor could aught ease the grief that I was in,
> Till I came hither. What a place is this!
> Must here be the beginning of my bliss?
> Must here the burden fall off from my back?
> Must here the strings that bound me to it crack?
> Blest Cross! blest Sepulchre! blest, rather, be
> The Man that here was put to shame for me![51]

The Christian's awe at the mode of his redemption is here set forth quite accurately by a man who had experienced it himself. The triple variation on the rhetorical question leads up to a triple blessing which climactically leaves us with the Man Jesus, the Christological center of Christian worship and biblical consciousness.

CONCLUSION

The leading Puritan pastors were not typically great poets, though Edward Taylor is an exception to that generalization, and Baxter at his best and Bunyan more often are not bad ones. (And Sidney, Spenser, and Milton, connected at various levels with the movement, are Olympians who make us all look small.) The purpose of this chapter is not to claim that they were great poets, but to see the effect that their highly developed biblical consciousness had on their approach to writing. Herbert did what they did better, and Spenser and Milton showed that a lot more can profitably be done. But the major positive emphases they did have will be ours as well to the extent that biblical consciousness has truly taken root in our minds.

The Puritans excelled at the practical application of biblical consciousness to the spiritual state of the individual soul, and their poetry models those applications. The motivation behind their poetry was the same as the motivation behind everything else they did: the glory of God and the spread of his Kingdom through the proclamation of the Word.

Puritan poetry began in the paraphrase of Scriptural poetry into English verse and hence into personal consciousness. It moved on into more creative expressions of praise without sacrificing its characteristic dependence on the content of Scripture. It sought to express the excellencies of God in a manner appropriately beautiful, but tended to avoid "dark figures" understandable only by intellectuals. Its themes are the themes of Puritan preaching: the drama of redemption, the triumph of sovereign grace in the soul, and the response of the redeemed heart to its Lord.

If there is a dominant note in Puritan poetry, it is not one of "Puritan gloom" but of joyful praise. It is the poetry of people who "conceived of this duty of praising God according to its superlative excellencies, as being the highest service that the tongue of men or angels can perform."

We could do worse than recapture those emphases in Christian writing and reading today.

Notes to Chapter 5

1. Some of the most important works in the rehabilitation of the Puritan image include William Haller, The Rise of Puritanism (N. Y.: Columbia Univ. Pr., 1938), M. M. Knappen, Tudor Puritanism: A Chapter in the History of Idealism (Chicago: Univ. Of Chicago Pr., 1939), Perry Miller, The New England Mind: The Seventeenth Century (Cambridge: Harvard Univ. Pr., 1967), and Patrick Collinson, The Elizabethan Puritan Movement (Berkeley: Univ. of California Pr., 1967); two fine recent works by Evangelical scholars that give a spiritually sensitive portrayal of the movement are Leland Ryken, Worldly Saints: The Puritans as They Really Were (Grand Rapids: Zondervan, 1986) and J. I. Packer, A Quest for Godliness: The Puritan Vision of the Christian Life (Wheaton: Crossway, 1990). A fascinating collection of essays on the practical application of Puritan wisdom today is D. Martyn Lloyd-Jones, The Puritans: Their Origins and Successors (Edinburgh: Banner of Truth, 1987).

2. Qtd. in Ryken, op. cit., p. 1.

3. See the brilliant brief characterization of Puritanism in C. S. Lewis, English Literature in the Sixteenth Century, Excluding Drama, Vol. 3 of The Oxford History of English Literature (Oxford: Oxford Univ. Pr., 1954), pp. 32-35.

4. Lloyd-Jones, op. cit., p. 44.

5. Percy Scholes, The Puritans and Music in England and New England (1934; rpt. N. Y.: Russell & Russell, 1962), p. 91.

6. Harold Fisch, <u>Jerusalem and Albion: The Hebraic Factor in Seventeenth-Century Literature</u> (N. Y.: Schocken Books, 1964), p. 57.

7. Richard Baxter, <u>The Christian Directory</u>, vol. 1 of <u>The Practical Works of Richard Baxter</u>, 4 vols. (London: George Virtue, 1838), p. 56.

8. Ibid., p. 388.

9. Ibid., p. 57.

10. Ben Jonson, "On Lippe, the Teacher," in Ian Donaldson, ed., <u>Ben Jonson: A Selection of his Finest Poems</u> (Oxford: Oxford Univ. Pr., 1995), p. 30.

11. Robin Chapman and Allan Grant, <u>The City and the Court: Five Seventeenth-Century Comedies of London Life</u> (San Francisco: Chandler Publishing Co., 1968), p. viii.

12. C. S. Lewis, <u>The Allegory of Love</u> (Oxford: Oxford Univ. Pr., 1936), p. 268.

13. Spenser, <u>Faerie Queene</u>, I.x.1-9.

14. For an excellent survey of the metrical Psalm tradition and its influence on other English poetry, see Coburn Freer, <u>Music for a King: George Herbert's Style and the Metrical Psalms</u> (Baltimore: Johns Hopkins Univ. Pr., 1972).

15. Douglas Bush, <u>English Literature in the Earlier Seventeenth Century</u>, vol. 5 of <u>The Oxford History of English Literature</u> (Oxford: Oxford Univ. Pr., 1945), p. 72.

16. See J. C. A. Rathnell, ed., <u>The Psalms of Sir Philip Sidney and the Countess of Pembroke</u> (N. Y.: New York Univ. Pr., 1963).

17. Bush, op. cit., p. 26.

18. "Dod, John," in John Julian, ed., <u>A Dictionary of Hymnology</u> (N. Y.: Dover publications, 1907), 1:345.

19. Scholes, op. cit., pp. 153, 156.

20. In Witherspoon and Warnke, eds. <u>Seventeenth Century Prose and Poetry</u>, 2nd ed. (N. Y.: Harcourt, Brace, & World, 1963), p. 966.

21. "Baxter, Richard," in Julian, op. cit., 1:118.

22. Ibid.

23. Qtd. in Bush, op. cit., p. 82.

24. Ibid., p. 89.

25. Baxter, <u>Works</u>, op. cit., 3:349.

26. Bush, op. cit., p. 137.

27. Fisch, op. cit., p. 5).

28. C. S. Lewis, <u>A Preface to Paradise Lost</u> (London: Oxford Univ. pr., 1961).

29. Baxter, <u>Christian Directory</u>, in <u>Works</u>, op. cit., 1:268.

30. Ibid., 1:147.

31. Ibid., 1:149.

32. Ibid., 1:150.

33. Qtd. in Haller, op. cit., p. 130.

34. Baxter, Directory, op. cit., 1:268.

35. Ibid., 1:150.

36. George Herbert, "Jordan (2)," in F. E. Hutchinson, ed., The Works of George Herbert (Oxford: Clarendon pr., 1941), p. 102.

37. Ibid., p. 176.

38. See Barbara Kiefer Lewalski, Protestant Poetics and the Seventeenth-Century Religious Lyric (Princeton: Princeton Univ. Pr., 1979) for a masterful treatment of this point.

39. Baxter, op. cit., 1:150.

40. Jeffrey A. Hammond, Sinful Self, Saintly Self: The Puritan Experience of Poetry (Athens, Ga.: The Univ. of Georgia Pr., 1993), p. 17.

41. Ibid., p. 23.

42. Julian, op. cit., 1:345.

43. Ibid., 1:346.

44. Baxter, op. cit., 4:286.

45. Ibid., 4:288.

46. Richard Baxter, "Lord, It Belongs not to my Care," in The Oxford Book of Christian Verse (London: Oxford Univ. Pr., 1940), p. 217. Note that this is a modernized version.

47. John Bunyan, The Pilgrim's Progress (N. Y.: Peebles Press, 1968), p. vii.

48. Ibid., p. 158

49. Ibid.

50. Ibid., p. 102.

51. Ibid., p. 31.

INTERLUDE:

THE SOCRATIC METHOD AT WORK
(Michael Bauman Teaching Milton)
Villanelle no. 6

"The first rule: Don't trust anything I say
(I might be speaking for the Enemy),
But when *Truth* calls to you, you must obey."
The student body shuddered in dismay
With pens arrested in mid-note, to see
The first rule: "Don't trust anything I say."
"For there is Truth, though narrow is the Way,
And few that find it." (But they will be free
If, when Truth calls to them, they just obey.)
"Do *you* think so, or is it just O.K.
Because I said it?" This, persistently.
The first rule: "Don't trust anything I say."
"And what *is* Truth? And what the Good? To play
The game you have to know the rules--the key--
So when Truth calls to you, you can obey."
His every wink and word was to convey
The simple skill of doubting faithfully.
The first rule: "Don't trust anything I say,
But when Truth calls to you, you must obey."

--D.T.W.

Chapter 6

"THOU ART STILL MY GOD":
George Herbert and the Poetics of Edification

"My God must have my best, ev'n all I had."
--George Herbert, "The Forerunners"

Though he was not a Puritan, George Herbert was like the great Puritan divines in the depth of his biblical consciousness and in the ways it defined for him the aims of devotional poetry. And Herbert was not only a devout believer but a poetic genius of the first order. Furthermore, no Christian has ever thought harder about what it means to be a Christian and a poet. Consequently, there is no voice which more desperately needs to be recovered for our own conversation about what it means to be a Christian reader.

For we live in an age in which serious poetry and Christian devotion seldom meet--perhaps because they have become estranged, perhaps simply because there are so few healthy examples of either species in circulation. From the standpoint of poetry, the chasm is deep, wide, and growing. Only a few popular Evangelical magazines--mostly small denominational house organs--now print any original verse at all, and when they do the results are depressingly predictable: "sing-songy" lines, sickeningly "sweet" and sentimental subject matter, and stale, trite imagery and diction mercifully tucked away in some obscure corner as mere filler.

No popular Evangelical journal of any substantial circulation offers any alternative to this pattern. Christianity Today and Eternity once were outlets for serious Christian poets, but both have closed their doors to verse in recent years. (Eternity has since--one would like to think as a result--come, in an event supremely ironic given her name and laden with at least poetic if not divine justice, to an end.) So, now effectively shut off from any wider audience, serious Christian poets write only for each other in obscure, specialized journals. And most of what they write would be unintelligible to most intelligent lay readers in any case. Never before have the aims of *excellence* and *edification* seemed more incompatible than they do today. Viewed from a historical perspective, this must surely be one evidence of the drying up of biblical consciousness and wholeness of vision in the Church.

If we view this situation as an impoverishment of both religion and culture and wish to find a remedy, we can do no better than to look closely at an age in which both devotion and poetry not only flourished, but often lived in an intimate and mutually enriching alliance: the age of Donne, Herbert, and Vaughan. Most especially we should examine the work of Herbert, a man who thought deeply and wrote extensively about the nature and purpose of devotional poetry. Not only in The Temple but also in The Country Parson, the Latin poems, and in numerous letters, he wrestles with what it means to be a Christian and a poet, particularly with how the aims of excellence and edification can be reconciled in the ministry of the devotional and meditative poet.

In this chapter, therefore, we have attempted to bring together in a systematic way every statement from his poetry and surviving prose which is relevant to that topic. We will then present a detailed analysis of Herbert's statements concerning the practice of devotional poetry, considered in relation to some contemporary currents of thought on pastoral theology and homiletics, and attempt some brief suggestions about their relevance not only for our understanding of his great work The Temple but also for our ability to construct poetic temples of our own in the present--temples in which Excellence and Edification can serve God together once again. (And while Herbert was specifically a devotional poet, many of the principles he worked by are equally relevant to other types of writing in which we try to communicate the Christian world view.) We will discover that, not only is <u>The Temple</u> a worthy monument of poetic devotion which merits our study for its own sake, but that Herbert can also serve as an alternative role model for present-day Christian writers who wish to find a way out of the current impasse.

BACKGROUND

Poetry is one form that writing about God can take; an even more prominent form in the Seventeenth Century, and one in which Herbert was also a practitioner, was the sermon. Lewalski notes the relevance of contemporary *ars praedicandi* for questions such as Herbert raises about the propriety of sinful man writing about divine truth. These questions, she says, "were explored in greater depth" in Protestant "debates about the framing of sermons than anywhere else."[1] It may therefore be useful to examine these debates as an interesting backdrop to the issues Herbert raises. On its simplest level, the debate was between Puritan plain or "spiritual" preaching and the ornate or "witty" Anglican style. Webber characterizes the two attitudes thus:

> The style of Scripture, it would seem, is in the eye of the beholder. Seventeenth-Century Anglican writers . . . [spoke] of its beauty and elegance and justified their own style by saying that as God comes to us, we must come to him. . . . Puritans, on the other hand, praised the simplicity and clarity of Scripture, and again on that basis justified their own style, as on which neither played games with words nor made darkness out of light.[2]

Already the terms of the discussion sound strangely familiar to one who has read Herbert's "Jordan" poems, where both approaches seem to be presented: the witty ("Nothing could be too rich to clothe the Sunne") and the spiritual ("Copie out only that [i.e. the simple and unadorned sweetness inherent in love] and save expense").[3] His ambiguous--or perhaps more accurately complex--attitude toward these two orientations will play a major role in this study.

Though Herbert was a loyal Anglican, it is not impossible to see him as influenced by the homiletic debate and as having a certain sympathy for the values the Puritans represented in that discussion. More recent scholarship has tended to complicate the once-neat equation of Puritan with spiritual, Anglicanism with witty preaching. In Herr's analysis, there were really *three* styles: the plain (spiritual), the florid (Ciceronian), and the witty (Senecan). Though most Puritans would be plain and most Anglicans witty (Andrewes) or florid (Hooker), some high churchmen, such as John Bridges, used the plain style.[4] Sherwin emphasizes the fact that both Anglicans and Puritans shared the same rhetorical (i.e., humanist--see chapter three on John Calvin) education which made the various witty or learned styles possible.[5] But some men on both sides used that learning in a subdued way in the interests of edification.

Lewalski describes three characteristic attitudes within Anglicanism toward the relationship between preaching and eloquence. The view of the first group was that the secular arts and wit are the *ancillae theologiae*, the handmaids of theology, and may validly be used as long as they remain servants and do not become the masters. The second group, including Donne, saw eloquence and wit not as extraneous servants brought in, but as present in the scriptural model itself. The third group, which included Herbert and many moderate Anglicans and Puritans, were like Donne in seeing the Bible itself as the model for style, but disagreed by seeing it as not "characterized by witty and eloquent figures but by much simpler and more direct rhetorical strategies conveying its powerful message to audiences of all kinds and capacities."[6] This was precisely the Puritan emphasis. John Downame said that the Lord

> In the profunditie of wisdome could have written in such a loftye stile as would have filled even the most learned with admiration, yet he useth a simple easie stile fit for the capacity of all, because it was for the use of all, and necessarie to salvation to bee understood of all sorts and conditions.[7]

The spiritual sermon then seeks simplicity, not because it despises wit or rhetoric (it makes liberal use of both in its own way), but because of its larger goal of being able to edify all kinds of people. That this was Herbert's position is clear from many passages in his writings, of which we shall now mention only two. In a polemic against Puritanism, he analyzes the Puritan position into three points, two of which he agrees with:

> *Ritibus una sacris opponitur; alter Sanctos*
> *Praedicat autores; tertia plena Deo est.*
> *Postremis ambebus idem sentimus.[8]*

"First, he is opposed to the holy rites; second, he preaches the sacred authors; third, he is full of God. On the last two, we feel the same way." It is interesting that preaching is one stated area of agreement. But even more specifically, Herbert says of his country parson that "The character of his Sermon is Holinesse; he is not witty, or learned, or eloquent, but Holy."[9]

Morgan gives one of the best summaries of the Puritan homiletic: The spiritual preachers eschewed literary and cultivated allusions, classical quotations, scholastic or metaphysical arguments, choosing rather to speak in homely language spiced with illustrations culled from the farm, market-place, or home. They became experts in analyzing sin in all its manifestations in the human hearts, often making vivid use of parables and exemplae to drive home their lessons. They found in the Bible all they needed of excitement and adventure in soul-searching, and all framed within the great Biblical epic of man's fall and his redemption in Christ.[10]

Has anyone ever written a better one-paragraph description of The Temple?

A second Puritan--or, rather, Protestant--theme that may have influenced Herbert was the centrality of praising God to the idea of the Christian life. Richard Baxter, as we have seen, gives the following "directions for praising God with the tongue": "Be much in singing psalms of praise, and that with the most heart-raising cheerfulness and melody." The Christian is to "conceive of this duty of praising God according to its superlative excellencies, as being the highest service that the tongue of men or angels can perform."[11]

But how can sinful man hope to praise God aright? Baxter's answer to this question has great relevance for our study of Herbert:

> Read much those Scriptures which speak of the praises of God; especially the Psalms; and furnish your memories with store of those holy expressions of the excellencies of God, which he himself hath taught you in his word.[12]

The currency of this advice lends support to Lewalski's thesis that Protestant poets such as Herbert looked to the Bible as providing them with "a literary model which they can imitate in such literary matters as genre, language, and symbolism, confident that in this model at least, the difficult problems of art and truth are perfectly resolved."[13] And Herbert does seem to be moving in this direction. The frequency of allusions to the Psalms in The Temple is a critical commonplace,[14] and Lewalski also quite plausibly suggests that Herbert "seems to have attempted to provide in 'The Church' just such a compendium of lyric kinds as the Book of Psalms was thought to contain."[15] The above material forms an illuminating part of the context from within which Herbert spoke. It is time now to turn to his words themselves.

POETRY AS VOCATION

The primary fact about divine poetry for George Herbert is that it was his calling. It was a calling to which he dedicated himself early, and to which he never wavered in his devotion; and our interpretation of his struggles with that calling must begin with this basic fact.[16]

First, like Baxter, Herbert holds that the duty of praising God is a calling which is special to man, and is indeed definitive of man's position in the created order. In "Providence," we find that

> Of all the creatures both in sea and land
> Onely to Man thou hast made known thy wayes,
> And put the pen alone into his hand,
> And made him Secretarie of thy praise
> (Hutchinson, p. 117).

This calling is man's generally, but Herbert also very early felt it to be his particularly. Walton preserves a letter from the poet to his mother, dated "New year, 1609/10," in which Herbert includes two sonnets and the following comment upon them: "For my own part, my meaning . . . is in these sonnets to declare my resolution to be, that my poor abilities in Poetry, shall be all, and ever consecrated to God's glory" (Hutchinson, p. 363).[17] This affirmation is particularly significant in the light of the fact that on March 18, 1617, Herbert wrote to Sir John Danvers requesting money for books, since "I am now setting foot into Divinity, to lay the platform of my future life" (Hutchinson, p. 364). This request comes seven or eight years *after* Herbert's vow to pursue divine poetry in the letter to his mother, at which time he was still apparently pursuing a secular career. Thus, Herbert's vocation as a devotional poet is both earlier and more basic even than his calling to the ministry.

The two sonnets enclosed in the letter are related as question to answer. In the first Herbert asks, "Doth poetry / Wear Venus' livery? onely serve her turn? / Why are not sonnets made of thee?" In the second he answers, "Sure, Lord, there is enough in thee to dry / Oceans of ink" (Hutchinson, p. 206). When he revised them as "Love I and "Love II" for The Temple, the idea of vocation was made even stronger:

> . . . then shall our brain
> All her invention on thy altar lay,
> And there in hymns send back thy fire again (p. 54).

Secular poems are "dust blown by wit" and obscure the vision of God; but in Herbert's divine poetry God will "recover all his goods in kind," with the result that

> All knees shall bow to thee; all wits shall rise
> And praise him who shall make and mend our eyes.

It is highly significant that, in this poem which so clearly speaks of divine poetry as vocation, Herbert is also quite clearly concerned with the effect his poems will have on other people. Herbert's poems are certainly devotional. They are expressions of contemplative piety expressed by the soul to God (or, as in "The Collar," contemplative *impiety* addressed to God and thereby corrected). But when Herbert thus speaks with God, he intends his colloquy to be overheard, and he writes, with this end in mind, that not only his own but *all* knees will bow as a result.

POETRY AS SERMON

There is in Herbert's poetry then always a dual audience in mind. The poems are addressed to God, and if he accepts them that is in one sense audience enough. But the other audience--the overhearers--is never forgotten. Summers puts it well when he notes that Herbert's poems are "both 'fruits and flowers' of the Christian life, 'wreaths' of worship for God's altar and the harvest of 'fruits' of edification for others."[18] We might say that each poem of The Temple is simultaneously a sermon and a prayer, and that The Temple as a whole is then simultaneously a body of divinity and a prayer book.

The presence and importance of the aim of edification is not compromised by the fact that "not even so close a friend as Nicholas Ferrar" knew that Herbert wrote English verse until Edmund Drummond showed up at Little Gidding with the manuscript of The Temple.[19] Herbert's famous deathbed request to Ferrar is itself perhaps the most poignant evidence we have of the importance which the parson of Bemerton placed on his second audience:

> Desire him to read it, and then, if he can think it may turn to the advantage of any dejected poor soul, let it be

made public; if not, let him burn it; for I and it are less than the least of God's mercies.[20]

In the light of what we have seen, we must view the advantage which might accrue to dejected poor souls as no afterthought, but as central to Herbert's artistic purpose all along; and it casts no shadow of insincerity on the admirable humility which Herbert expresses to suggest that he was not so naive as to have had any real doubts as to what his friend Ferrar was likely to do with The Temple.

Herbert's approach to work in his literal church at Bemerton was quite consonant with his approach to work in his poetic temple. In The Country Parson he tells us that, in maintaining his church, the parson keeps "the middle way between superstition and slovenliness" by "following the Apostle's two great and admirable Rules: *Let all things be done decently and in order, and Let all things be done to edification*, I Cor. 14" (Hutchinson, p. 246). With reference to catechizing, there are three points of a pastor's duty:"To infuse a competent knowledge of salvation in every one of his flock; the other, to multiply and build up this knowledge to a spiritual Temple; the third, to inflame this knowledge, to presse, and to drive it to practice" (Hutchinson, p. 255). The imagery in these passages is significant, and surely applies to the poetic Temple as well as the one at Bemerton.

From the beginning The Temple asks to be considered as an attempt at edification. The very dedication asks God to

Turn their eyes hither, who shall make a gain:
Theirs, who shall hurt themselves or me, refrain.

And immediately the "Church Porch" beckons the reader to

> Hearken unto a Verser, who may chance
> Ryme thee to good, and make a bait of pleasure.
>   A verse may find him, who a sermon flies,
>   And turn delight into a sacrifice. (pp. 5-6)

Thus the avowed purpose of The Temple is to edify, and its subject is "the whole lifelong process of sanctification, presented under the metaphor of the building of the Temple in the Heart."[21] It is an excellent metaphor also for the building up in the heart of what we have called *biblical consciousness*, as its outlook is structured and formed by the biblical language and Herbert's. Mulder shed a great deal of light on the relationship of the book to the process when he suggests that the most significant biblical text for understanding Herbert's purpose in The Temple is 1 Peter 2:5: "Ye also, as lively stones, are being built up a spiritual house, an holy priesthood, to offer up spiritual sacrifices, acceptable to God by Jesus Christ."[22] And Bloch describes the process and its results beautifully:

> What we find at the heart of Herbert's poetry is not the specter of God cornering the sinner into submission, nor alternatively, that contemporary vision of the spirit freeing itself to untrammeled self-realization, but rather the image of the believer confronting, assimilating, and speaking the Word of God in his human and fallible existence. When "they words" are made "my words," as so often in The Temple, when they are taken off the printed page and admitted to the heart, they do not obliterate the self but rather free it to fulfill its high purpose--as God's own creature.[23]

Thus, paradoxical as it may seem to modern readers, Herbert intends his devotional poetry to be read by others and writes with the goal in view, not so much of communicating his own religious experience (though of course he does) as of doing them good by making a bait of pleasure. And the good he wants to do is the same good that is done by sermons and, as Fish notes, by catechizing. "Herbert's poetry is a strategy . . . the goal is the involvement of the reader in his own edification."[24] Much of what Fish has to say about the poet as catechist applies equally well to the poet as preacher; perhaps applies better, since it is to the preacher that Herbert explicitly compares himself as poet in the passage from "The Church" cited above.

POETRY AS PRAYER

The poems then are sermons addressed to the congregation of readers; but they are also prayers addressed to God. There is no conflict between these two functions, for ultimately the goal of the preacher is to bring his flock to union with God so that they may pray with him. He does this by joining doctrine and life, as in "The Windows" (Hutchinson, p. 67) and in a lesser known, untitled poem (P. 81). This poem is one of many in which Herbert addresses to God a renewal of his vow of dedication to divine poetry, while showing the source of that dedication.

> The shepherds sing; and shall I silent be
>   My God, no hymne for thee?
> My soul's a shepherd too; a flock it feeds
>   Of thoughts, and words, and deeds.
> The pasture is thy word, the streams thy grace,
>   Enriching all the place.
> Shepherd and flock shall sing, and all my powers
>   Out-sing the daylight hours.

When the soul sees itself as a shepherd nourishing the thought life, the speech, and the active life on God's word and his grace, then indeed biblical consciousness will grow and produce the fruit of holy living which tends to active praise. All Christians should do it; the poet is the one who has the gift of modeling the process in words for others. And what he is modeling is his own praiseful communion with the Father.

The soul has primarily two types of prayers to offer up to God: prayers of groaning and prayers of praise. God, in his grace, condescends to delight in both as expressions of devotion on the part of his servants. Thus in "Gratefulnesse," Herbert remarks that it is

> Not that thou hast not still above
> Much better tunes, then grones can make;
> But that these country-airs thy love
> > Did take. (p. 124)

Groans are dear to God because they come from the heart. In "Sion" (p. 106), Herbert compares the pomp and gold of Solomon's temple with the vanity of his own worship at times:

> All Solomon's sea of brasse and world of stone
> Is not so dear to thee as one good grone.
> And truly brasse and stones are heavie things,
> Tombes for the dead, not temples fit for thee:
> But grones are quick, and full of wings,
> And all their motions upward be;
> And ever as they mount, like larks they sing.
> The note is sad, yet musick for a King.

Herbert groans, and his groans are real. But, like Baxter, he puts far the greater emphasis on praise. Praise is demanded as the only response appropriate to the Object of devotion. This is true even on the earthly plane, as Herbert writes of his mother, *"Quin Matris superans carmina poscit honos"* (p. 289).

"Further, my mother's excellence, her honor, deserves a song."
Much more is it true on the spiritual level, as the country parson
prays before his sermon, "Blessed be the God of Heaven and
Earth! who onely doth wondrous things. Awake therefore, my
Lute, and my Viol! Awake all powers to glorify thee!" (p. 289).

Herbert is always ready to break into doxology. In "Praise
II" (p. 146), he lists God's many benefits to him, then gives this
response:

> Wherefore with my utmost art
> I will sing thee,
> And the cream of all my heart
> I will bring thee.

The greatness of God's love and grace demand a corresponding
wholehearted fervor in our praise. There is here no conflict
between artifice and sincerity of heart; indeed, they cannot exist
apart, for the heart has need of the utmost art to express the high
praise which fills it.

At times praise and groaning are combined, as the heart
groans for a greater ability to praise. This occurs in "The
Temper I" (p. 55):

> How should I praise thee, Lord, how should my rymes
> Gladly engrave thy love in steel
> If what my soul doth feel sometimes
> My soul might ever feel!

In "Dulnesse" (p. 115), the poet asks,

> Why do I languish thus, drooping and dull,
> As if I were all earth?
> O give me quickness, that I may with mirth
> Praise thee brim-full!

In fact, the association between poetry and praise is so close for Herbert that he comes close to equating the ability to write with spiritual health. The poems "Grief," The Crosse," and "The Flower" (pp. 164-66) form a mini-sequence within The Temple: grief is the disease, the cross is the cure, and the flower is the restoration to health. In "Grief," Herbert gives up "verses" as a thing "too fine for my rough sorrows." But when restored to normality in "The Flower," he writes, "After so many deaths I live and write; / I once more smell the dew and rain / And relish versing." Thus to write is to live, and because the poetry is prayer, Herbert is most a poet when most a Christian--and *vice versa*. This theme reaches its finest expression in "The Quidditie" (p. 69), where a verse is "that which while I use / I am with thee, *and most take all*." The ability to write well may not be part of spiritual health, but the impulse to praise God surely is, and it is one of the surest signs of a healthy biblical consciousness that such praise find verbal expression in some form. And as textual and biblical consciousness grow, with them the ability to articulate praise will grow as well.

POETRY AS SPECIAL GRACE

Herbert was sensitive to many of the problems raised by the practice of devotional poetry. One of them is, how can man, whose motives and faculties are corrupted by original sin, ever hope to form by his own artifice something which could be an acceptable offering to God? Herbert's answer was simple and profound: God accepts man's offerings as he accepts man, not on the basis of merit but of grace.[25] You simply do your best and trust to his mercy for the rest. As Fish puts it, "Nothing the poet does is wrong, not, however, because he is doing things right, but because in this fortunate universe God turns (indeed has already turned) all to good."[26]

This problem is not peculiar to the poet, for without the intervention of grace *all* human action would be vitiated from the start. In "The Window" (Hutchinson, p. 67), Herbert realizes that the preacher has the same dilemma as the poet: he too is "a brittle crazie glasse." But God in his temple affords him "This glorious and transcendent place / To be a window, through thy grace." Since the poet is also a preacher, as we have seen, he is no doubt afforded the same place by the same grace.

Not only does God accept the poet's offerings by grace, but his grace is also what enables the poet to write in the first place, by giving to the poet his gifts and by sanctifying those gifts to the service of God. In *Musae Responsoriae*, 40 (Hutchinson, p. 403), Herbert speaks to the Holy Spirit and says, "*Quod scribo, et placeo, si placeo, tuum est.*" "That which I write, and by which I please, if I please, is from you." This same theme, in different variations, can be found throughout The Temple. The climax of "Easter" (p. 42) is a prayer that the Holy Spirit will "bear a part / And make up our defects with his sweet art." The poet's dependence on God's grace for the very ability to write is similarly expressed in "Praise I" (p. 61), "Deniall" (p. 70), and "A true Hymne" (p. 168). But perhaps the ultimate expression of the idea of the poem as both result and response to grace is "The Posie" (p. 182), which is simply a commentary ringing the changes on the magnificent statement, "Lesse then the least / Of all thy mercies is my posie still."

POETRY AS COMMON GRACE

The other major problem facing the devotional poet is one of methodology: Granted that by grace it is theoretically possible to write divine poetry, what materials could be appropriate for such a task, and how should they be used? It is very much the same question we saw with reference to sermons at the beginning: Is God more honored by wit or by simplicity? Herbert's answer shows a profound sympathy with the values represented by both sides of that dilemma, and his poetry is certainly one of the greatest syntheses of the two ever achieved.

Herbert's answer to the first question, that of materials, seems to have some affinity with the Calvinistic doctrine of "common grace."[27] The idea is that God gives many good gifts to human beings apart from salvation, gifts from which both the elect and the reprobate receive benefit in common: The rain falls on the just and the unjust, etc. Though these "common" gifts are distinct from special or "saving" grace, they are still good gifts from God, and the Christian may use them for God's glory even though they belong to what some theologians would call the realm of Nature (as opposed to Grace). They are *gracious* gifts in that sinners do not deserve them and they are thus God's unmerited favor; but they are *common* in that they are not limited to the saved.

It is this kind of thinking that allows Herbert to say in "The Church Porch" (Hutchinson, p. 20) that, "The cunning workman never doth refuse / The meanest tool, that he may chance to use." The same idea is present in "Antiphon I" (p. 53): "The earth is not too low, / His praises there may grow." This attitude toward nature is perhaps expressed most clearly in "The Elixir" (p. 184-85):

> Teach me, my God and king,
> In all things thee to see
> And what I do in anything
> To do it as for thee.
> A man that looks on glasse
> On it may stay his eye;
> Or if he pleaseth, through it passe,

> And then the heaven espy.
> All may of thee partake:
> Nothing can be so mean
> Which with his tincture (for thy sake)
> Will not grow bright and clean.
> This is the famous stone
> That turneth all to gold:
> For that which God doth touch and own
> Cannot for lesse be told.

The "glasse" in stanza two is reminiscent of the preacher as "brittle crazie glasse" in "The Window," and since the poet is also a preacher, it is the very images of Herbert's poetry which by common grace are being turned to gold.

Where then may the poet find his images? The answer is the standard answer of metaphysical poetry: anywhere. But because Herbert's aim is edification, he will use Scripture as his model and concentrate first on the images he finds there. We should probably also see this deliberate orientation as at least part of the explanation for the fact that Herbert's imagery tends to be less esoteric than, say, Donne's. This basic attitude of Herbert's toward simile can be interestingly illustrated by a passage from The Country Parson which describes Herbert's practice in catechizing:

> When the answerer sticks, [illustrate] the thing by something else, which he knows, making what he knows to serve him in that which he knows not. . . . This is the skill, and doubtlesse the Holy Scripture intends this much, when it condescends to the naming of a plow, a hatchet, a bushell, leaven, boyes piping and dancing, shewing that things of ordinary use are not only to serve in the way of drudgery, but to be washed and cleansed, and serve for lights even of Heavenly Truth. (p. 257)

The diction is highly reminiscent of Bunyan's defense of Pilgrim's Progress (see chapter five) and of Herbert's "The Forerunners" (p. 176), where "sweet phrases, lovely metaphors" are washed with tears and brought to church "well dressed and clad." There can be no doubt that the parson and the poet are one in their approach.

This brings us then to Herbert's most well-known sequence of poems on poetry: the "Jordan" poems and "The Forerunners." In these poems he deals specifically with the question of what use the poet is to make of his materials, and in "The Forerunners" brings his whole theory to its summary and highest expression.

At first glance, it would seem that the "Jordan" poems are a rejection of the dominant poetic modes current in Herbert's day. "Jordan I" (p. 56) seems a rejection of pastoral and allegorical verse, disparaging "enchanted groves," shepherds, and the necessity of "catching the sense at two removes." And "Jordan II" (p. 102) seems a rejection of metaphysical wit, calling "quaint words and trim invention . . . curling with metaphors a plain intention" nothing more than a "long pretence." This is Joan Bennett's reading: Herbert has eschewed "pastoral affectations" and the "intellectual curiosities of Donne."[28] But a closer reading reveals a fascinating complexity in Herbert's attitudes toward these things. Tuve rightly remarks that to see these poems as a rejection of love, allegory, or wit *simpliciter* is "to stop at the very surface of their meaning."[29]

The first thing to notice is that, if metaphor and other figures are given up in the "Jordan" poems, they are emphatically taken up again in "The Forerunners," and have been liberally used in all the poems in between. They are used in a different way and for different ends, perhaps, but they are used nonetheless. Martz is heading in the right direction when he says that "The 'Jordan' poems speak in the hyperbole of dedication; 'The Forerunners' describes the actual achievement, in terms that show a fervent devotion to all the arts of poetry, properly used."[30]

A closer look at the texts of the poems bears Martz out. In "Jordan I" Herbert asks, "Who says that fictions *onely*, and false hair / Become a verse?" He concludes that "Shepherds [like Sidney and Spenser?] are honest people" and should be allowed to sing, as long as he *also* is allowed to "plainly say, *My God, My King*." Thus, as Tuve says, "'Jordan I' is not a protest against love poetry but against its usurpation of the whole field and very title of poetry."[31]

But what does Herbert mean by the "plainness" mentioned at the end? Martz notes that while "Jordan I" might be taken to imply a "simplicity of bareness," the second "Jordan" poem "considerably qualifies that emphasis."[32] Martz stresses the echoes of Sidney's Astrophel and Stella to support his contention of Herbert's development from the style of Donne toward that of Sidney. But the real importance of these echoes in "Jordan II" is for the interpretation of the poem. When Sidney claims to look in his heart and write *instead* of seeking for invention, the heavy presence of invention in the very context warns us not to take him literally. What he is doing is using a rather clever invention to say, "Indeed, in spite of all the cleverness shot forth here, I really *do* feel this love in my heart; in fact, I feel it so deeply that I actually *have* to use the utmost artifice in order to write accurately about it at all."

Far from being inconsistent with heart-felt sincerity, the ironic artifice is actually the very mode of that sincerity. By climaxing "Jordan I" with a strong allusion to Sidney's sonnet, Herbert is declaring himself to be on the same ground: "There is in love a sweetness ready penn'd: / Copie out onely that, and save expense." Thus, the notion that "Nothing can be too rich to clothe the sunne," far from being rejected, is actually in a sense reaffirmed by the ending of the poem.

This interpretation of "Jordan I" is confirmed by "The Forerunners," where eloquence and metaphor are "brought to church well drest and clad" because "My God must have my best, ev'n all I had." The poet may use all his skill in praising God because this skill is demanded by the subject: "Beauty and beauteous words should go together." It is true that Herbert admits that "*Thou art still my God* is all that ye / Perhaps with more embellishment can say," but as Martz so perceptively notes, "What a world of reservation lies in that one word, so emphatically placed: 'Perhaps.'"[33]

This line of reasoning might now seem to place Herbert in line with the "witty" preachers and thus go counter to much of our argument earlier in this chapter. But we must be careful not to forget the dual audience for which Herbert wrote. The poems must be witty because wit is one of God's good gifts and must, like all his other gifts, be returned to him. But the poems are gifts, not only to God, but also to the Church. Wit must therefore be controlled and thus enrolled in the service of the edification of God's people, including but not limited to the intellectuals. Grace--the opposite of pride--is the ultimate key to all. The bottom line is, as Rosalie Colie puts it, that "Grace solves the problems of art, as it does the problems of life."[34]

CONCLUSION

We have argued than that Herbert saw both sides of the "witty" vs. "spiritual" controversy, and that his special genius lay in the fact that when he wrote that battle was stilled and the antagonists became allies. Surely this view goes a long way toward accounting for that perfect blend of intelligence and simplicity which characterizes his work. As the Puritans themselves recognized, he did better than they did at achieving their own spiritual goals. Accessible without being shallow, edifying without being preachy or predictable, Herbert's poetry has stood the test of time. The product of a deep and rich biblical consciousness, it can *edify*--that is, help to *build* that same biblical consciousness--in others, as his most famous convert, the poet Henry Vaughan, both testified and demonstrated.

What was it then that made George Herbert the greatest devotional poet of all time, as he is widely recognized as being? I would suggest that at least four aspects of Herbert's approach to his calling as we have studied it here contributed to his success and could serve as an inspiration to a new generation of writers who could restore Sacred Poesy to the position of honor it once had in the church. I would also suggest that unless this is done, it will be almost impossible to rebuild a rich and deep biblical consciousness in our current anti-literate generation.

First is the *sense of vocation* with which Herbert approached his work. As clear and as basic as the call to preach was the vocation of praising God and portraying the operations of his grace in the sinful soul in verse as worthy of its subject as Herbert's skill could make it. In a world in which the author of any poetry more advanced than a greeting-card rhyme has no natural channels of access to the general Evangelical public (the drying up of the outlets which existed little more than a decade ago surely constitutes a major betrayal of the arts--and of biblical consciousness--by editors who continue to mouth their support), a world in which the Bible-believing churches place no value on skilled verse outside of hymnology, it is difficult for aspiring Christian poets to feel, much less respond to, such a Call. But in precisely such times it may be a sense of divine vocation alone which can sustain them in their task. The Church impoverishes herself by failing to recognize, encourage, and reward such a sense of vocation. In the meantime, Herbert's sense of such a calling, independent of yet coordinated with his call to the ministry, serves as a bracing and encouraging example for the faithful remnant who would follow in his footsteps today.

Related to that sense of calling was, in the second place, Herbert's *constant awareness of the dual audience* implied in the act of writing: not only the divine Auditor but also the potential human reader, conceived of as a real, flesh-and-blood member of the body of Christ, a "poor dejected reader" to whom the work must minister or face the flames.

I do not for a moment mean that we must surrender to the lowest common denominator of intelligence and attention span that prevails in our anti-intellectual generation. To do that would remove any point from the act of writing. Christian writing should challenge readers to love the Lord their God with all their minds; that which does not is writing in the service of a lesser god. But one notices in modern poetry in general a contempt for all but the most sophisticated of audiences. C. S. Lewis observed that "modern poetry is read by very few who are not themselves poets, professional critics, or teachers of literature," and he also discerned why:

> To read the old poetry involved learning a slightly different language; to read the new involves the unmaking of your mind, the abandonment of all the logical and narrative connections which you must use in reading prose or in conversation. You must achieve a trance-like condition in which images, associations, and sounds operate without any of these. Thus the common ground between poetry and any other use of words is reduced almost to zero.[35]

To sample the writings of most contemporary Christian poets in the specialized journals is to realize why they only appear there: too many of them are indistinguishable from their secular counterparts in the use of these techniques. But the result is that the aim of Edification has to be totally sacrificed in the pursuit of Excellence as our secular culture defines it. Hence the lay reader is fed only greeting-card verse which edifies but in a shallow and insipid manner--which means it cannot really *edify* very much after all, if edification has anything to do with building

biblical consciousness--or free verse which provokes the reaction
Lewis expressed so well:

> I am so dense, the things which poets see
> Are obstinately invisible to me.[36]

Herbert will not let us off the hook so easily. The aims of
Excellence and Edification *must* somehow be held together, else
we do not very well achieve either. Surely a commitment to live
without compromise in the creative tension between those two
poles must be part of the meaning of artistic integrity.

How then *do* we live in that tension? Flowing from Herbert's
first two commitments was, third, a *devotion to craftsmanship*.
The Temple is an impressive array of classical verse forms used
to good effect; surely the modern neglect of this fundamental
source of poetic power is not unrelated to the malaise of
contemporary verse. And here again too few Christian poets
show an inclination to go against the grain. Free verse--which is
usually just arbitrarily fractured prose--is a form appropriate to
a generation which does not believe that the world ultimately
makes sense, that there is any meaningful order in the universe.
Why would poets speaking from within a world view which
begins with the highly articulated *form* of the Trinity then not feel
impelled to express the freedom within form that world view
gives them by breathing new life into the sonnet, say, rather than
merely blindly reflecting the chaos around them? Many of them
can not; they have simply never learned their craft. But they
would not have to go back even as far as Herbert to learn better.
It is no accident that Robert Frost, the last major poet to eschew
free verse (he perceptively referred to it as "Playing tennis
without a net"), was also the last poet able to speak powerfully
to the common man.

Finally, the importance of Herbert's *affinity for images
drawn from biblical story and common experience* is hard to

overestimate. Modern poetry's fascination with privatized and esoteric imagery has inevitably led to the marginalization and trivialization of verse.[37] Here, perhaps, Christian poets do a little better than their peers, but they have not been unaffected by the tendency. Herbert stands as a healthy corrective influence, reminding us where the real source of poetic power lies: We should neither ignore the past nor slavishly repeat it, but rather follow him as he sought in new and creative ways to exploit the common stock of shared meanings accessible to his culture. Poetry is, after all, an act of communication.

The change in orientation suggested here might seem difficult for our generation to achieve. Poets who have grown accustomed to the now-stale combination of free verse with stream of consciousness might feel themselves severely pinched and circumscribed by the discipline and calling implied. But if our generation is to be recalled to biblical consciousness and wholeness of vision, they must at least make a start.[38] And the humble parson of Bemerton could have told them that in his own case it was achieved, if at all, because he had in some measure submitted his heart to the service of his Lord and Master, in whose service he had found perfect freedom.

Notes to Chapter 6

1. Barbara Kiefer Lewalski, Protestant Poetics and the Seventeenth-Century Religious Lyric (Princeton: Princeton Univ. Pr., 1979), p. 11.

2. Joan Webber, The Eloquent "I" (Milwaukee: The Univ. of Wisconsin Pr., 1968), p. 133.

3. F. E. Hutchinson, ed., The Works of George Herbert (Oxford: The Clarendon Pr., 1941). All references to Herbert's writings will be quoted from this edition. All poems not otherwise noted in the text are from "The Church."

4. Alan Fager Herr, The Elizabethan Sermon (N. Y.: Octagon, 1969), p. 89.

5. Wilma Sherwin, "The Rhetorical Structure of the English Sermon in the Sixteenth Century" (Diss. Illinois, 1958), pp. 120f.

6. Lewalski, op. cit., p. 220-22.

7. Qtd. in William Haller, The Rise of Puritanism (Philadelphia: Univ. of Pennsylvania Pr., 1938), p. 130.

8. *Musae Responsoriae*, in Hutchinson, op. cit., p. 386.

9. Herbert, The Country Parson, vii, "The Parson Preaching."

10. Irvonwy Morgan, The Godly Preachers of the Elizabethan Church (London: Epworth, 1965), p. 16; for an excellent recent summary see Leland Ryken, Worldly Saints: The Puritans as

They Really Were (Grand Rapids: Zondervan, 1986), pp. 91ff. See also the fine treatment of these issues with regard to Herbert by William Shullenberger, "*Ars Praedicandi* in George Herbert's Poetry," in Claude J. Summers & Ted-Larry Pebworth, eds., "Bright Shootes of Everlastingnesse": The Seventeenth-Century Religious Lyric (Columbia: Univ. of Missouri Pr., 1987), pp. 96-115.

11. Richard Baxter, The Christian Directory in The Practical Works of Richard Baxter, 4 vols. (London: George Virtue, 1838), 1:147-50.

12. Ibid., 1:150.

13. Lewalski, op. cit., pp. 6-7.

14. For a thorough treatment of Herbert's indebtedness to the Psalms, see Coburn Freer, Music for a King: George Herbert's Style and the Metrical Psalms (Baltimore: Johns Hopkins, 1972).

15. Lewalski, op. cit., p. 51.

16. For a fine book-length treatment of this issue, see Diana Benet, Secretary of Praise: The Poetic Vocation of George Herbert (Columbia: Univ. of Missouri Pr., 1984).

17. Hutchinson states that, "in view of the freedom with which Walton altered and paraphrased some of Donne's letters in the text to the Life (1658), we cannot be sure that we have Herbert's exact words in this reported letter" (op. cit., p. 578n). But there is no reason to doubt the substance of Herbert's avowal.

18. Joseph H. Summers, George Herbert: His Religion and Art (Cambridge: Harvard Univ. Pr., 1954), p. 84.

19. Amy M. Charles, A Life of George Herbert (Ithaca: Cornell Univ. Pr., 1977), p. 78.

20. Isaac Walton, The Life of Mr. George Herbert, in Alexander M. Witherspoon and Frank J. Warnke, eds., Seventeenth-Century Prose and Poetry, 2nd ed. (N. Y.: Harcourt, Brace, and World, 1957), p. 286. Charles (op. cit., p. 179n) notes that "Duncon himself was Walton's source for this famous account, and it is likely therefore to be as accurate as Duncon could make it nearly forty years after the event, albeit an event likely to remain clearly remembered through all subsequent experience."

21. Lewalski, op. cit., p. 25.

22. John R. Mulder, The Temple of the Mind: Education and Literary Taste in Seventeenth-Century England (N. Y.: Pegasus, 1969), p. 140.

23. Chana Bloch, Spelling the Word: George Herbert and the Bible (Berkeley: Univ. of Calif. Pr., 1985), p. 45.

24. Stanley Fish, The Living Temple: George Herbert and Catechizing (Berkeley: Univ. of California Pr., 1978), p. 27.

25. For an outstanding study of Herbert's doctrinal convictions and their impact on his verse, see Richard Strier, Love Known: Theology and Experience in George Herbert's Poetry (Chicago: Univ. of Chicago Pr., 1983. Strier is not only a fine literary critic but also (what is a rare combination today) a profound theologian: "Justification by faith alone is an extraordinarily rich and powerful theological doctrine, one that means to transform

the religious consciousness. Fully accepted, it cannot exist in isolation or as one among many others. It demands a central and commanding role; all other doctrines and positions must derive their energy from it. I believe that Herbert recognized this" (p. xii). He is right on all counts here. Also good is Gene Edward Veith, Reformation Spirituality: The Religion of George Herbert (London: Associated University Presses, 1985). Contrast Terry G. Sherwood, Herbert's Prayerful Art (Toronto: Univ. of Toronto Pr., 1989), who tries to force on Herbert the attempt to break out of an unnatural (and unhistorical) dichotomy between faith and love that never existed in the first place: The Reformers supposedly taught that God loves, but man "responds not in love, but in faith" (p. 33).

26. Fish, op. cit., p. 27.

27. See our discussion of this issue in chapter three and the literature noted there in note 25.

28. Joan Bennett, Five Metaphysical Poets (Cambridge: Cambridge Univ. Pr., 1966), p. 59.

29. Rosemond Tuve, A Reading of George Herbert (Chicago: Univ. of Chicago Pr., 1952), p. 185.

30. Louis L. Martz, The Poetry of Meditation, rev. ed. (New Haven: Yale Univ. Pr., 1962), p. 185.

31. Tuve, op. cit., p. 187.

32. Martz, op. cit., pp. 260-61.

33. Ibid., p. 314.

34. Rosalie Colie, *Paradoxica Epidemica: The Renaissance Tradition of Paradox* (Princeton: Princeton Univ. Pr., 1966), p. 204.

35. C. S. Lewis, An Experiment in Criticism (Cambridge: Cambridge Univ. Pr., 1961), pp. 96-97.

36. C. S. Lewis, "A Confession," in Poems, ed. Walter Hooper (N. Y.: Harcourt Brace Jovanovich, 1964), p. 1.

37. See Donald T. Williams, "The Depth of Rightful Doom: The English Reformers' Concept of Justice and Book V of Spenser's Faerie Queene" (Diss. Georgia, 1985), pp. 169-78, for a more detailed treatment of this point showing the errors which arise when we try to read the same tendencies back into earlier poets. See also Roland M. Kawano, "C. S. Lewis: The Public Poet," Mythlore 9:3 (1982), pp. 20-21, on the contrast between Lewis's approach and the modern tendency toward privatized imagery.

38. Students of Herbert frequently emphasize the fact that the purpose of The Temple was to reproduce itself in that "Temple whose frame and fabric are within the individual heart," as Marion White Singleton puts it in God's Courtier: Configuring a Different Grace in George Herbert's *Temple* (Cambridge: Cambridge Univ. Pr., 1987), p. 202. We *need* devotional poetry (and other types of literature as well) that can structure our inner lives toward biblical consciousness in a life long process; Herbert's poetry models the internalization of Scripture we should all be experiencing. "God's written words work accumatively and progressively, as they are consumed, assimilated in heart and mind and expressed in man's words, thoughts, and deeds" (Sherwood, op. cit., p. 93).

INTERLUDE

BACH'S PHILOSOPHY OF COMPOSITION

Jesu, Juva.

"Jesu, joy of man's desiring,"
Both the words and music say;
Notes and syllables conspiring
Stir the spirit in the clay.

"Come, sweet Death!" How so? Inspiring
Men and women thus to pray?
"*Jesu*, joy of man's desiring,"
Both the words and music say.

"Sheep may safely graze," retiring,
Learn the Shepherd to obey.
Notes and syllables conspiring
Stir the spirit in the clay.

Musicologists enquiring
Cannot brush the thought away:
"Jesu, joy of man's desiring,"
Both the words and music say.

"Jesus, help!" he'd write, requiring
Aid on every page. Today,
Notes and syllables conspiring
Stir the spirit in the clay.

Every page he wrote, aspiring,
"God's alone the glory! May
Jesu, joy of man's desiring
Be what words and music say."

Just aesthetically admiring
Misses what he would convey:
Jesu, joy of man's desiring,
Stirs the spirit in the clay.

"Jesu, joy of man's desiring,"
Both the words and music say;
Notes and syllables conspiring
Stir the spirit in the clay--
Drive the dark of doubt away.

Soli Deo Gloria.

--D.T.W.

Chapter 7

OLD POSSUM'S BOOK OF CHRISTIAN POETS:
Style and Biblical Consciousness in C. S. Lewis and T. S. Eliot

> *Dio kai philosophoteron kai spoudaioteron poiesis historias estin,* "Poetry is something more philosophic and of graver import than history."
>
> --Aristotle, Poetics 9.1451b

> *"It is not meter, but a meter-making argument, that makes a poem,--a thought so passionate and alive that like the spirit of a plant or animal it has an architecture of its own, and adorns nature with a new thing."*
>
> --Emerson, "The Poet"

Two of the most fascinating Christian poets of the Twentieth Century were C. S. Lewis and T. S. Eliot--and they become even more fascinating when looked at together. They made similar spiritual pilgrimages: from the tortured skepticism of the wasteland of unbelief to a rigorous acceptance of the most thoroughly orthodox Christianity as expressed in the Anglican communion. Both men saw life steadily and saw it whole, as a whole defined by their Christian commitment; hence both are case studies of the influence of biblical consciousness. Both sought to express their Christian vision in their poetry; hence both are case studies of the influence of biblical consciousness on artistic creativity. Both are still looked to by Evangelical students as symbols of the possibility of combining orthodox

Christian commitment with a full intellectual life.[1] Yet they had significant differences of opinion on the nature and purpose of poetry, and their practice of poetry found them at opposite poles.[2] Thus a comparative study of their work can shed great light on the relationship of theory to practice, of both to content or message, and of biblical consciousness to all. We will attempt some brief notes toward the definition of these relationships in this chapter.

Lewis is better known for his literary scholarship, his Christian apologetics, and his prose fiction than for his poetry. Yet his chief ambition was to become a great poet; his first two books were a collection of short lyrics and an epic in rhyme royal.[3] Though these books were not successful (they got good reviews but did not sell), Lewis continued to write poems throughout his life.[4] He was aware of the fact that his work was outside the streams in which modern poetry was flowing, but he thought those streams could lead to no good end. Eliot's work became a symbol to Lewis of all that was wrong with modern sensibility.[5] Walter Hooper reports that in 1925, when he was working on the proofs of Dymer, Lewis was

> annoyed at what he called "the hectic theory of poetry as existing in momentary lyrical impressions." Anxious to strike a blow at the new avant-garde poets, he broached to his friends the idea of a literary hoax: "A series of mock-Eliotic poems to be sent up to the Dial and Criterion until sooner or later one of these filthy editors falls into the trap."

None of these poems was ever published.[6]

It should be noted that, characteristically, Lewis' antipathy toward Eliot's poetry did not extend to his person. Hooper recalls that when Lewis and Eliot met at Lambeth Palace in 1959, where they worked together on the revision of the Psalter, they became close friends. "Speaking of this to me afterwards," Hooper remembers, "Lewis said, 'You know that I never cared for Eliot's poetry and criticism, but when we met I loved him at once.'"[7]

Lewis' objection to Eliot's poems was not to their content so much as to their method. Indeed, both poets' work communicate pretty much the same kinds of things: Poems of pessimistic despair before their conversions, and poems of Christian faith and affirmation afterwards convey very similar outlooks on life on the part of both men in both periods. It is instructive, for example, to compare the following stanza from Dymer to the epistemological pessimism of Eliot's more well-known "The Hollow Men":

> Give me the truth! I ask not now for pity.
> When gods call, can the following them be sin?
> Was it false light that lured me from the city?
> Where was the path--without it or within?
> Must it be one blind throw to lose or win?
> Has heaven no voice to help? Must things of dust
> Guess their own way in the dark? She said, "They
> must." (viii.12)

Or compare this "French Noctourne" from Spirits in Bondage (p. 12) with the social pessimism of Eliot's Prufrock:

> There comes a buzzing plane: and now it seems
> Flies straight into the moon. Lo! where he steers

Across the pallid globe, and surely nears
In that white land some harbour of dear dreams!

False, mocking fancy! Once I too could dream,
Who now can only see with vulgar eye
That he's no nearer to the moon than I,
And she's a stone that catches the sun's beam.

What call have I to dream of anything?
I am a wolf. Back to the world again,
And speech of fellow-brutes that once were men.
Our throats can bark for slaughter: cannot sing.

The despair of meaning and communication, the image of the
stone standing for sterility, the dehumanization of the speaker
(Lewis's wolf, Eliot's crab), the interplay of reality and a futile
dream world (as in Prufrock's mermaids) are all the same. Yet
how can two poets with so much in common feel so different?
And the contrast of Eliot's stark, angular *vers libre* with Lewis's
carefully correct traditional forms is only the beginning.

THEORY

The nature and source of these differences can perhaps best
be illuminated by an understanding of the significantly different
ideas of poetry held by these two men. Eliot himself observed,
"People who tell us what poetry ought to do . . . usually have in
mind the particular kind of poetry they would like to write."[8] He
is right, and his statement is certainly applicable to the poetry and
criticism of both Lewis and Eliot.

Let us begin, then, with their most basic ideas concerning what poetic art is for. Eliot states that

> It is ultimately the function of art, in imposing a credible order upon ordinary reality, and thereby eliciting some perceptions of order in reality, to bring us to a condition of serenity, stillness, and reconciliation; and then leave us, as Virgil left Dante, to proceed toward a region where that guide can avail us no further.[9]

With much of this, Lewis would have had no quarrel. Yet in the following statement we can detect a significant difference of emphasis. Reflecting on the New-Testament theme of *mimesis* (imitation) as the basis of the Christian life, Lewis said:

> Applying this principle to literature, in its greatest generality, we should get as the basis of all critical theory the maxim that an author should never conceive himself as bringing into existence beauty or wisdom that did not exist before, but simply and solely as trying to embody in terms of his own art some reflection of eternal beauty and wisdom.[10]

And in another place he said:

> In rhetoric imagination is present for the sake of passion (and therefore, in the long run, for the sake of action), while in poetry passion is present for the sake of imagination and therefore, in the long fun, for the sake of wisdom or spiritual health--the rightness and richness of a man's total response to the world.[11]

Eliot conceives himself as *imposing* order upon a (possibly recalcitrant?) reality; Lewis sees himself *embodying* in his art an order he finds already there in reality. The end result for Eliot is serenity and reconciliation; for Lewis it is wisdom and spiritual health. These aims are not mutually exclusive, but they show the diverging emphases of the poets.

Lewis was strongly committed to the older view which saw poetry, along with rhetoric, grammar, and logic, as the servants of wisdom or truth, things which ultimately come from above. He therefore had little sympathy with the modern notion of poetry as primarily an expression of the self. He thought modern poets, including Eliot, entirely too preoccupied with their own inner lives, in trying to capture the pre-rational mush of emotion that happened to exist in their breasts at any given moment. For Lewis, however, the value of literature was "for me dependent on the moments when, by whatever artifice, [it succeeds] in expressing the great myths"--which, in Lewis's vocabulary, means "the great truths."[12]

For this reason, Lewis would have viewed statements such as the following by Eliot as, in the long run, destructive of poetry by distracting the attention of the poet from the things that really matter: "The duty of the poet, as poet, is only indirectly to his people: his direct duty is to his *language*, first to preserve, and second to extend and improve."[13] "Poetry has primarily to do with the expression of feeling and emotion."[14] It is not that, for Lewis, poetry ought not to do these things, but that they can only really be done when the poet is concentrating on something else: "All the great poems have been made by men who valued something else more than poetry--even if that something else were only cutting down enemies in a cattle-raid or tumbling a girl in a bed."[15]

The modernist tendencies against which Lewis was reacting tended increasingly to make poetry a private phenomenon. Though Eliot realized that "a poem which was a poem only for the author would not be a poem at all,"[16] he was also capable of writing, "The question of communication, of what the reader will get from it, is not paramount: if your poem is right for you, you can only hope that the readers will eventually come to accept it."[17] For Lewis, the emphasis is just the other way around:

> Poetry certainly aims at making the reader's mind what it was not before. The idea of a poetry which exists only for the poet--a poetry which the public rather overhears than hears--is a foolish novelty in criticism. There is nothing specially admirable in talking to oneself. Indeed, it is arguable that Himself is the very audience before whom a man most postures and on whom he practices the most elaborate deceptions.[18]

One of Lewis's most central objections to modern poetry in general is revealed by his reaction to I. A. Richards' denigration of "stock responses":

> By a Stock Response Dr. I. A. Richards means a deliberately organized attitude which is substituted for "the direct free play of experience." In my opinion such deliberate organization is one of the first necessities of human life, and one of the main functions of art is to assist it. All that we describe as constancy in love or friendship, as loyalty, . . . as perseverance--all solid virtue and stable pleasure--depends on organizing chosen attitudes and maintaining them against the

eternal flux (or "direct free play") of mere immediate experience. This Dr. Richards would not perhaps deny. But his school puts the emphasis the other way. They talk as if improvement of our responses was always required in the direction of finer discrimination and greater particularity. To me, on the other hand, it seems that most people's responses are not "stock" enough, and that the play of experience is too free and too direct in most cases for safety or happiness or human dignity.[19]

I have quoted this passage *in extenso* because it is crucial for understanding why Lewis was so passionately opposed to the combination of free verse with stream-of-consciousness which characterizes so much of modern verse, including much of Eliot's. The end of poetry for Lewis has been raised here even above wisdom to virtue, and the function of the poet is not the relatively trivial one of expressing ever finer flavors of sensibility, but the grand one of transmitting the form of virtue received from the past. Virtue is not a finely but a *rightly* organized response of the whole person, including but not limited to the emotions or the feelings. Therefore the predominance in poetry of traditional themes embodied in traditional forms is not for Lewis an issue merely of aesthetics and sensibility but of cultural life and death. Hence to him the triumph of Eliot's brand of poetry was nothing less than calamitous:

> The older poetry, by continually insisting on certain Stock themes--as that love is sweet, death bitter, virtue lovely, and children or gardens delightful--was performing a service not only of moral and civil, but even of biological, importance. . . . Poetry was formerly

> one of the chief means whereby each new generation
> learned, not to copy, but by copying to make, the good
> Stock responses. Since poetry has abandoned that office
> the world has not bettered.[20]

Thus we can see why Eliot was for Lewis a special symbol of what he thought were the unwholesome tendencies of modern verse. For, though Eliot wrote that "One error, in fact, of eccentricity in poetry, is to seek for new human emotions to express,"[21] he could also write that the mind of the mature poet was a "finely perfected medium in which special, or very varied feelings are at liberty to enter into new combinations,"[22] and that "The genuine poet . . . discovers new variations of sensibility which can be appropriated by others."[23] Like Richards' "school," Eliot's tendency was in what Lewis took to be the wrong direction.

Lewis's habit of using Eliot as *the* representative of modernism in poetry and criticism can unfortunately be a source of confusion, making modernism appear to be a more monolithic phenomenon than it actually was. Tetreault notes how in his debate with E. M. W. Tillyard on "the personal heresy" (considering poetry an expression of the self), Lewis "seized upon a sentence in one of Eliot's essays," which was "odd indeed," considering that Eliot's "Tradition and the Individual Talent" "espoused the very position Lewis was arguing."[24] Along the same line, Lewis's complaint with Eliot's verse was not necessarily that of William Carlos Williams, for example--that Eliot had given poetry back to the academy. Lewis' own poetry often depended for its effects on the reader's ability to recognize classical allusions, and thus demanded an educated public. Lewis objected to the needless, self-conscious obscurity (as in The

Wasteland, for example) that turns reading poetry into an exercise in puzzle-solving. He probably would not have approved of W. C. Williams' verse either, for its dependence on momentary imagistic impressions robs poetry of much of its range, and while it can achieve occasional technical brilliance, leaves poetry equally unsuited for the serious cultural task which Lewis called on it to perform.

It is not terribly surprising that Lewis--a medievalist and renaissance scholar by trade--failed to distinguish the finer shades in modernist poetic style and theory. But that failure should not lead us to dismiss the overall thrust of his critique. For it was to the dominance of these tendencies he associated with Eliot in modern poetry as a whole that Lewis attributed the decline in poetry's reading public. Serious verse is now voluntarily read by "very few who are not themselves poets, professional critics, or teachers of literature."[25] Modern poetry was simply too difficult, and unnecessarily so.

> To read the old poetry involved learning a slightly different language; to read the new involves the unmaking of your mind, the abandonment of all the logical and narrative connections which you use in reading prose or in conversation. You must achieve a trance-like condition in which images, associations, and sounds operate without these. Thus the common ground between poetry and any other use of words is reduced almost to zero.[26]

Lewis's quarrel with Eliot and with modern poetry in general is best summed up by his poem "Confession," which rather

obviously uses Eliot's "The Love Song of J. Alfred Prufrock" as
its foil:

> I am so coarse, the things the poets see
> Are obstinately invisible to me.
> For twenty years I've stared my level best
> To see if evening--any evening--would suggest
> A patient etherized upon a table;
> In vain. I simply wasn't able.
> To me each evening looked far more
> Like the departure from a silent, yet a crowded shore
> Of a ship whose freight was everything, leaving behind
> Gracefully, finally, without farewells, marooned mankind.
>
>   * * * * *
>
> I'm . . . one whose doom
> Keeps him forever on the list of dunces
> Compelled to live on stock responses,
> Making the poor best that I can
> Of dull things: peacocks, honey, the Great Wall, Aldebaran,
> Silver weirs, new-cut grass, wave on the beach, hard gem,
> The shapes of horse and woman, Athens, Troy, Jerusalem.[27]

Unfortunately, we have no record of Lewis' reaction to
Eliot's Christian poems such as "Ash Wednesday," the Four
Quartets or Murder in the Cathedral. But Lewis's point was not
that "Prufrock" or The Wasteland was not Christian but that the
kind of esoteric and clinical imagery they employed was good
neither for culture nor poetry. It is quite easy to see the kind of
imagery Lewis preferred. The question he raises is whether it
matters which kind we habitually feed our minds on.

PRACTICE

How then, and to what extent, did Lewis and Eliot realize their ideas of poetry in their practice of the art? In a chapter of this scope we will have time only for a brief look at one of the more mature post-conversion poems of each poet: Lewis's "The Turn of the Tide"(Poems, pp. 49ff.) and Eliot's "Journey of the Magi." Each poem tries, through a series of images and allusions, to get at the meaning of the birth of Christ, and each shows its author at his poetic best.

LEWIS, "THE TURN OF THE TIDE"

Prosodically, Lewis' poem is at a far remove indeed from free verse.[28] It moves in alternating lines of four and three stresses, but it is futile to attempt a more detailed scansion than that. No single foot predominates, for Lewis, like the Anglo-Saxon poets he loved, allows any reasonable number of unstressed syllables between the stresses so long as the natural rhythm of the language is upheld. And indeed, despite the impossibility of their being scanned, the lines read easily, naturally, and well. The rhyme scheme is ABCB.

But what the reader may not notice at first is that this poem has one of the most intricate schemes of *internal* rhyme of any in the language. Its very unobtrusiveness is telling evidence of the skill with which it was executed. In the four-beat lines, the first and third, and the second and fourth stressed syllables rhyme, with Lewis using rhyme to much the same effect as the Anglo-Saxons used alliteration.

The first four lines will serve to illustrate the effect, but the feat of sustaining through a poem of sustaining it through a poem of eighty-four lines can only be appreciated by those who have tried it.

> *Breath*less was the *air* over *Beth*lehem. Black and *bare*
>> Were the fields; hard as granite the clods;
> *Hedg*es stiff with *ice*; the *sedge* in the *vice*
>> Of the pool, like pointed iron rods.

Burying a number of the syllables in the internal rhyme scheme in longer words which couldn't be counted as end-rhymes (*breath*less, *Beth*lehem) contributes to the subtlety of the effect and keeps it from becoming overpowering, even as it creates a richness of word-music rare in the verse of any period. And the evocation of winter almost rivals that in the opening lines of Keats' St. Agnes Eve.

This frozen stillness gradually spreads out from Bethlehem to cover the entire planet, and then radiates out into space. "Great Galactal Lords," worried that entropy is about to catch up with them, stand "back to back with swords / Half-drawn, awaiting the event." Life seems to have ebbed out of the whole universe: "The tide lay motionless at ebb." Then the process repeats itself in reverse; heaven and earth are rejuvenated by "a music, infinitely small." The whole of Creation is caught up in a joyous dance of returning life, from angelic celebrations in the heavenlies to the return of rippling waves to an ocean that had become so still it reflected the stars. The climax is that "In his green Asian dell the Phoenix from his shell / Burst forth and was the Phoenix once more."

In this breathtaking cosmic journey, we have become so caught up in the succession of visual images that we have all but forgotten the place where all the to-do started: Bethlehem. But Lewis suddenly brings us back there with a poignant jerk:

> So death lay in arrest. But at Bethlehem the bless'd
>> Nothing greater could be heard
> Than a dry wind in the thorn, the cry of the One new-born,
>> And cattle in stall as they stirred.

The poem rounds upon itself with a sense of wholeness and completeness: We journey from life to death and back again. We look at the incarnation, not directly, in the vision that has become too familiar to be effective any longer, but indirectly through its effects on the mirroring cosmos. What, going so far down that it passed almost out of existence altogether, would all but make the earth stop spinning on its axis and still the force of the tides? What, re-emerging from the depths of the womb and reasserting its life again, would call forth all the vitality of nature and stimulate the flight of the Phoenix, traditional symbol of rebirth and redemption? The contrast between the vivid cosmic journey and the sudden turn at the end, the simple, natural, night sounds of breeze and cattle and the newborn's cry, reawakens our imaginations to the awesome paradox at the heart of the Christian doctrine of the Incarnation: "Truly God and truly Man"; *Stabulo ponitur qui continet mundum*, "He is placed in a stable who contains the world." The cobwebs are swept away and we are left naked before a flaming sword. If the aim of Lewis' criticism was to argue that powerful poetry can still be written apart from the "liberation" from form to which the Twentieth Century has been enslaved, the final proof and demonstration is surely here.

ELIOT, "THE JOURNEY OF THE MAGI"

In Eliot's "Journey of the Magi," we also begin in winter and are taken on a journey. But while in Lewis's poem the focus is on a change in the external world which is paradoxically tied to a crying baby, and produces as a by-product a change in us (a response of awe and gratitude for the incredible condescension of the Incarnation and at the cosmic issues which depend on it), here the focus is on the change produced in the speaker, which produces a change in the external world: He can no longer be at home there, for his people have become aliens. This contrast is interestingly in keeping with the different orientations of the poets we have seen.

Eliot's poem is in free verse, and thus sacrifices the musical beauty which Lewis achieved. Instead, Eliot seeks a vivid realism of narration as the Magus recounts his story, and this he successfully attains. Like Lewis, he tries to give us a different "take" on the familiar Christmas story. Following the lead of Lancelot Andrewes' famous Christmas sermon from which he took several of his lines, Eliot wants to de-romanticize the Magi while subjecting their experience to theological analysis. But the analysis is carried, not by theological propositions, but by images and diction which sound like things the Magus might easily have said in a mere naturalistic description. Hands playing dice, pieces of silver, wineskins, three trees against the sky: All these images surrounding the Magi's search for the Child point inexorably to his mission and ultimately his death. Cumulatively, they focus the meaning of this birth as having to do with issues of life and death, and life *through* death.

Naturally, scholars have tried to identify the allusions in Eliot's imagery, and have shown some remarkable obtuseness in doing so when their minds do not resonate with Scripture and the Christian tradition as Eliot's had come to do. It was not until 1972 that the Magus' laconic reference to the birth as "satisfactory" was correctly identified as an allusion to the satisfaction theory of the atonement.[29] Despite the rather self-evident character of that identification, subsequent writers have continued to look far afield for other explanations.[30] Nevertheless, a consensus has emerged on enough of the symbols to show the direction the poem is headed: The dice remind us of the soldiers casting lots for Jesus' coat, the silver of Judas' betrayal, the three trees of the crosses, the wineskins of the passing of the old order and the coming of the new.

The cumulative effect of these symbolic images is not only to focus our attention on the purpose of this birth, but also to make it believable when the Magus shakes his head at the connection between this birth and death: "like bitter death, our death." He does not yet understand it all, though his narration has provided all the keys to a proper understanding. But he does know it has changed him: He is no longer at home in this world, "with an alien people clutching their gods." Unlike Lewis's poem, Eliot's does not come to a definite denouement, and deliberately so. The Magus' journey is not over, but points ahead to "another death." Christ's death, our death to self, the death that leads to eternal life, are all here, but not yet fully assimilated. Hence the reader too must participate in the process of assimilation, without glossing over the bitter fact that the path to life leads through death. Neither the Magus' journey nor the readers is then over, and it is to this that the poem owes its haunting effect.

CONCLUSION

What conclusions can we draw from this brief survey? Lewis's idea of poetry was more thoroughly and consistently worked out in terms of the biblical world view and the Christian tradition than Eliot's. Lewis makes the effort to integrate his poetics with biblical motifs such as the *imitatio Christi* (imitation of Christ); his concerns about the direction of modernist techniques resonate with Herbert's concern for the "poor dejected reader"; his view of the importance of "stock responses" reflects an awareness of the effects of the Fall on human nature; he is a throwback in many ways to the biblical humanism of the Renaissance (though as a confirmed medievalist he might have objected to that characterization!). Eliot's poetics moves much more in the orbit of modernism and secular humanism, focussed on aesthetics, self-expression, and sensibility for their own sake, though in his emphasis on the value of tradition he went beyond the normal concerns of modernism. Though he called for literary criticism to be "completed" by ethical and theological criticism and for Christians to produce literature that was implicitly Christian (see chapter two), he did not achieve the synthesis of Lewis, whose statements amount to a systematic doctrine of poetry as related to the moral purpose of human existence. As Daniel puts it,

> One of [Lewis's] primary values as a religious writer has been to champion the objective; to turn us away from the relativism and subjectivism that undermine all values and the very idea of value itself. He is doing the same thing with literature: forcing us to attend to the great reality of the poetry, the vision inherent in so many

works written by so many different persons in different ages of our history.[31]

Many (including the present writer) may feel that Lewis's poetic theory offers a needed corrective to the poetic orthodoxies of our day. But this does not mean that Eliot's verse is without great value. It is obviously not the worthless trivia that Lewis's critique of Eliot's approach would have led us to expect (though that approach has led many of Eliot's successors into the utmost depths of banality). So if we accept Lewis's critique, we must ask why Eliot's poetry can be so powerful and significant.

One of the first things to notice is that, while Eliot's pre-Christian poetry of pessimism is much more effective than Lewis's, the advantage is erased when both have been converted and begun to write verses of Christian affirmation. The Wasteland, "The Love Song of J. Alfred Prufrock," and (my personal favorite) "The Hollow Men" are supremely valuable as the quintessential expressions of the lostness and despair of the modern world, and valuable to Christians for the way they recreate and allow us empathetically to enter into the sensibility of non-Christians who realize where their rejection of traditional religion actually leads. Eliot's verse is the verse of tortured struggle, and even after his conversion he feels, like the Magus of his poem, not quite at ease in the universe. His is thus the authentic voice of the Christian for whom the tension between time and eternity is the stage for a constant struggle. While being a Christian is definitely preferable to the alternatives, Eliot still is not completely comfortable, whereas Lewis' conversion seems to have fit him like a glove once he allowed himself to be dragged kicking and screaming into the kingdom. (This is of course an oversimplification to make a point; it does not mean that Eliot's faith gave no comfort or that Lewis did not have continuing struggles and crises of faith, such as the one chronicled in <u>A Grief Observed</u>.) Thus we may say, to borrow one of Eliot's own metaphors, that Lewis played Lancelot Andrewes to Eliot's John Donne.[32]

Another reason for the felicitous results of Eliot's free verse is that he was a craftsman and a highly disciplined poet who could easily have written in traditional meters had he chosen (as he proves in <u>Old Possum's Book of Practical Cats</u>). The legions of writers of fractured prose whose poems glut the pages of our literary journals would do well to pay close heed to the following statement:

> No verse is free for the man who wants to do a good job. ... A great deal of bad prose has been written under the name of free verse. . . . But only a bad poet could welcome free verse as a liberation from form. It was a revolt against dead form, and *a preparation for new form or for the renewal of the old (*emphasis added).[33]

If only these words could have been as prophetic as they deserve to be!

Both Lewis and Eliot were men of deep biblical consciousness. In Lewis it is seen in both his theory of poetry and his verse itself, in Eliot less in his theory but definitely in the impregnation with biblical and theological imagery one sees in the Christian poems. A final reason for Eliot's significance as a poet may then be the fact that he did become a Christian and therefore had something significant to say. One cannot help but feel that in his later work he moved unconsciously closer to Lewis in both theory and practice; that under the burden of the awesome, paradoxical clarity of the Gospel he became more interested in communication. Much of the unnecessary obscurity drops away, and in "Ash Wednesday," The Four Quartets and Murder in the Cathedral we come finally to as clear a view as one can have of the still point of the turning world.

Notes to Chapter 7

1. See James Tetreault, "Parallel Lives: C. S. Lewis and T. S. Eliot," Renascence: Essays on Value in Literature 38:4 (Summer 1986):, pp. 256-7, for a good summary of the similarities and differences between the two.

2. Tetreault puts this conflict in perspective. Ibid., p. 262.

3. Published under the pseudonym of Clive Hamilton, they are Spirits in Bondage (London: Heineman, 1919; rpt. San Diego: Harcourt, Brace, Jovanovich, 1984), and Dymer (London: J. Dent & Sons, Ltd., 1926).

4. All Lewis poems known to be extant, with the exception of those in Spirits in Bondage, have been collected in two volumes edited by Walter Hooper: Poems (N. Y.: Harcourt Brace Jovanovich, 1964) and Narrative Poems (N. Y.: Harcourt Brace Jovanovich, 1969). Many of the shorter poems appeared in various publications under the pseudonym N. W. Clerk.

5. Tetreault, op. cit., p. 262.

6. Walter Hooper, Preface to Lewis' Selected Literary Essays (Cambridge: Cambridge Univ. Pr., 1969), p. xv.

7. Ibid., p. xvi. Cf. Roger Lancelyn Green & Walter Hooper, C. S. Lewis: A Biography (N. Y.: Harcourt Brace Jovanovich, 1974), pp. 287-88.

8. T. S. Eliot, "The Social Function of Poetry," in On Poetry and Poets (N. Y.: Noonday Pr., 1961), p. 3.

9. T. S. Eliot, "Poetry and Drama," in <u>Poetry and Poets</u>, op. cit., p. 94.

10. C. S. Lewis, "Christianity and Literature," in Walter Hooper, ed., <u>Christian Reflections</u> (Grand Rapids: Eerdmans, 1967), p. 10. This might seem to contradict Sidney's view of the poet as maker; but it is an early passage, and Lewis's views underwent further development, though without losing the emphasis on *mimesis*. See chapter two.

11. C. S. Lewis, <u>A Preface to Paradise Lost</u> (London: Oxford Univ. Pr., 1942), p. 54.

12. Walter Hooper, ed., <u>They Stand Together: The Letters of C. S. Lewis to Arthur Greaves (1914-1963)</u> (N. Y.: MacMillan, 1979), p. 420.

13. Eliot, "Social Function," op. cit., p. 9.

14. Ibid., p. 8.

15. Lewis, "Christianity and Literature," op. cit., p. 10.

16. T. S. Eliot, "The Three Voices of Poetry," in <u>Poetry and Poets</u>, op. cit., p. 109.

17. Eliot, "Poetry and "Drama," ibid., p. 83.

18. Lewis, <u>Preface to Paradise Lost</u>, op. cit., p.54.

19. Ibid., p. 55.

20. Ibid., p. 57.

21. T. S. Eliot, "Tradition and the Individual Talent," in Selected Essays, new ed. (N. Y.: Harcourt, Brace, & Co., 1950), p. 10.

22. Ibid., p. 7.

23. Eliot, "Social Function," op. cit., p. 9.

24. Tetreault, op. cit., p. 259. Cf. Charles A. Huttar, "A Lifelong Love Affair with Language: C. S. Lewis's Poetry," in Peter J. Schackel and Charles A. Huttar, eds., Word and Story in C. S. Lewis (Columbia: Univ. of Missouri Pr., 1991), pp. 97-103.

25. C. S. Lewis, An Experiment in Criticism (Cambridge: Cambridge Univ. Pr., 1961), p. 96.

26. Ibid.

27. Lewis, Poems, op. cit., p. 1; cf. the treatment by Huttar, op. cit., pp. 94-97.

28. See Huttar, op. cit., pp. 87-92, for a good general treatment of Lewis's use of meter, rhyme, etc.

29. R. D. Brown, "Revelation in T. S. Eliot's 'Journey of the Magi,'" Renascence: Essays on Values in Literature 24:3 (Spring, 1972): 136-140. And even Brown thought the wineskins were a reference to communion wine, rather than the much more obvious reference to the old/new wine and wineskins of the parable.

30. E. F. Burgess, vii, "T. S. Eliot's 'The Journey of the Magi,'" The Explicator 42:4 (1984): 36., who takes it as a reference to a Zoroastrian prophecy (!) is an example.

31. Jerry L. Daniel, "The Taste of the Pineapple: A Basis for Literary Criticism," in Bruce L. Edwards, ed., The Taste of the Pineapple: Essays on C. S. Lewis as Reader, Critic, and Imaginative Writer (Bowling Green, Oh.: Bowling Green State Univ. Pr., 1988), p. 25. Cf. also Bruce L. Edwards, "Rehabilitating Reading: C. S. Lewis and Contemporary Critical Theory," in Edwards, Pineapple, op. cit., pp. 28-36.

32. T. S. Eliot, "Lancelot Andrewes," in Selected Essays, op. cit., pp. 299ff.

33. T. S. Eliot, "The Music of Poetry," in Poetry and Poets, op. cit., p. 31.

Interlude

TO MY PREDECESSORS
Sonnet XLV

Their glory has not faded. Though the years
 Have been kind to barbarians, and, worse,
 Have yielded to their hands the realm of verse;
Though students cannot scan; though I have fears
That Keats may cease to be read by my peers
 Except as an assignment and a curse;
 Yet still this melody I will rehearse:
I come to sing the English Sonneteers.

Their glory cannot fade! My tongue repeats
 The words with wonder, hour after hour,
Of Sidney, Spenser, Shakespeare, Milton, Keats,
 Of Wordsworth, Hopkins--tastes within their bower
Rich viands, cates, and soul-sustaining meats:
 Each line a world of wit compressed to power.

        --D.T.W.

Chapter 8

LORD, TEACH US TO NUMBER OUR DAYS:
The Significance of Tolkien's Elves

The Poet's eye, in a fine frenzy rolling,
Doth glance from heaven to earth, from earth to heaven,
And as imagination bodies forth
The forms of things unknown, the poet's pen
Turns them to shapes, and gives to airy nothing
A local habitation and a name.
                    --Shakespeare, <u>A Midsummer Night's Dream</u>

We have examined the concept of biblical consciousness and seen how the right kind of reading of both the Bible, the external world, and other literature is needed to create it. We have looked at the history of Christian thinking about reading and writing, centered on Sir Philip Sidney's recognition that human creativity is rooted in the creative power of God, the Maker of the human maker. We have seen how biblical consciousness manifests itself in and can be fed by the writings of a theologian, a historian, pastors and poets. We now come full circle to the work of a man who not only brought Sidney's insights to their fullest theoretical development but also used the creative power Sidney described to make a world which seems almost as convincing as the world of everyday experience, a world which in fact interprets that world of everyday experience in terms of the most fundamental elements of the biblical vision. The man was John Ronald Reuel Tolkien, and the world he made is Middle Earth.

TOLKIEN AND THE LORD OF THE RINGS

I have often asked myself what it is that makes The Lord of the Rings[1] such a great book. It undoubtedly *is* a great book, arguably the greatest of our time, the one people in the next century will be reading when Vonnegutt and Erica Jong and Rod McKuen are long forgotten and even Hemingway and Faulkner read only by English majors. And unless I am badly wrong, they will not only read it but be profoundly moved by it and come to interpret their own lives, as so many of us have done, in terms borrowed from it.

There is, of course, no simple answer to my question. The values the work embodies, the motif of the Quest, the symbol of the Road, the great dramatic conflict of Darkness and Light, the author's absolute mastery of every appropriate style from the homely to the heroic: All these things are no doubt part of the answer. But other books have had these elements, if not often all at once or in so much abundance. I suspect that the final ingredient which, acting as a catalyst upon the rest, gives the book its peculiar flavor and enables it to catch our hearts in that grasp that can never be shaken off, is the elves.

TOLKIEN AND THE ELVES

The *elves*? What have these pagan, fairy-tale creatures got to do with reality, much less with biblical consciousness? What could be further from a sober biblical view of the world than *those* airy nothings? Well, wait a moment.

The elves. Frosty starlight on a moonless night. The dancing feet and costly love of Luthien Tinuviel. Cities in the treetops, Caras Galadon, the wind in the leaves of Loth Lorien.

Wonder in the eyes of Sam Gamgee. Memories stretching back to days when the world was younger and greener. Wisdom on the brow of Elrond or Galadriel. The last homely house west of the mountains. Ancient blades, wrought with runes, strong for the destruction of evil. Arwen Undomiel, the Evening Star of her people. The fair faces, the grey eyes, the clear voices lifted in song. The songs:

> A! Elbereth Gilthoniel
> Silivren penna miriel
> O menel aglar elenath
> Na chaired palandiriel.

The Three Rings, unsullied by Sauron. And always, heard as from afar, the sound of the sea.

It is significant that the elves are there. Most men and hobbits have never met one (I have not--at least, not for certain), but we know that they are there in the woods. And the world is a stranger, deeper, brighter place for that knowledge. But far more significant than the fact that they are there is the fact that the elves are leaving. They are exiles, wandering with us for a time, but already they are departing, sailing down Anduin to the sea, to be seen no more. Already our paths are sundered, and the reunion, if there is to be one, is beyond the unmaking of the world.

We know the time is coming--we hope it will not be in our lifetime, but we know it is inevitable and may indeed be already upon us--when the Last Ship will set sail from the Grey Havens, and the work of Cirdan the Shipwright will be at an end. With that ship will sail the last living memory of the Elder Days, and so much more that cannot be named any more than it can be recovered. The woods will be empty, the halls of Rivendell silent. The elves will be gone--lost to us--forever. And that will be that.

It is precisely because the time of the elves is passing away that the beauty associated with them--by implication, all beauty--strikes us so deeply when we walk through the imagined countryside of Middle Earth. They thus become a concrete embodiment (or, in Eliot's phrase, an "objective correlative") of that principle which Shakespeare said should make one's love more strong: "To love that well which thou must leave e're long."[2] Their departing presence is a leaven, kneaded thickly through the whole dough of Tolkien's tale, which gives the loaf that same bittersweet flavor which the strongest joys of the waking world have as their inalienable and unmistakable identifying characteristic.

It is a famous cliche that it is better to have loved and lost than never to have loved at all--none the less true for being a cliche. But it is an even more basic truth that, in this present world, to love *is* to lose. We may love for a long time, and perhaps be faithful even unto death. But the shadow of our mortality lies over everything we see, everything we do, everyone we know. The sunset fades, the symphony ends, the book must be put down, the wife or husband dies. Even memories do not last forever. There comes the inevitable parting of paths, the sundering of ways, until, stripped naked, we ourselves fly alone into the Alone.

For it is the simple truth that it is not given to us to possess the beauties of earth. They belong to Another, and we are but allowed to behold them for a moment. We glimpse them out of the corner of our eyes in passing, and gaze longingly after them. But we try too hard to hold them, and they slip from our grasp.

We stumble into the circle of light and the torches vanish, the fire goes up in sparks, the revelers and their feast are gone. Then we hear the singing and see the lights again, off yonder through the trees, leading us we know not whither. We only know that we are doomed to seek and never to possess.

This is the burden of Time the Apostle mentioned, under which we walk. Subject to vanity. The bondage of corruption. And beneath it we groan and travail along with the whole cosmos, awaiting our redemption. The words of the Fisherman: all flesh is grass, and all the glory of man is as the flower of grass. The grass withereth, and the flower thereof falleth away; the elves depart from Middle Earth; only the Word of the Lord abides forever.

The elves remind us of the bondage of corruption, this pathos at the heart of all our most moving tales, in at least three ways. The first way is simply through what they are in themselves: embodiments and partakers of a lofty beauty and goodness which we glimpse, and to which some of us aspire, but to which we can never quite attain. It is significant that the two adjectives most frequently used to describe the elves and things elvish are *high* and *fair*. Only a few Elf-Friends like Bilbo or Aragorn dwell at (or even visit) the Last Homely House West of the Mountains, and even their destiny lies elsewhere. And Lorien is a perilous land which few enter and from which fewer return, and none unchanged--essentially because of its strangely alien *goodness*.

The goodness and beauty of the elves is remote and inaccessible to mortals. It is not something they can attain through effort, and attempts to make contact with the elves in that way always come to grief, as the experience of Bilbo and the dwarves in Mirkwood illustrates. When contact is made, as when Frodo is befriended by Gildor Inglorion, it seems on one level to come by chance of luck, but on a deeper level is perceived as having been *meant* to be; and on the most profound level of all it is an extension of *Grace*. And, like the grace of God, it changes our perception of this world by giving us a foretaste, an earnest, of something we will not ever fully have here. It beckons us onward to a land where the longings stirred in us by this beautiful but fallen and temporal world can really be fulfilled.[3]

The elves remind us of our incompleteness, in the second place, by the fact that even the glimpse of the high and the fair which they offer is being withdrawn. They are themselves exiles in this world, and the longing for Elvenhome across the Western Sea is never quite stilled in them. They, like us, are pilgrims and strangers, but unlike us they are increasingly anachronisms in what is ever more plainly becoming a world of Men. So they simultaneously remind us of our own essential homelessness and refuse to let us forget the fleetingness of earthly beauty.

The ability of the elves to perform these functions for us is intensified by the third thing about them that reminds us of our condition: their immortality within the life of the world. Elves do not die, though they can be killed. Their memories are therefore so long that mere years flit by--a thousand years is as a day. Their experience of time contrasts with ours because of that, which makes the issue of their exile particularly acute for them. For them the years pile up as an ever-increasing burden calling them to rest; for us the pitifully tiny hoard of years is almost immediately exhausted. For both of us the years flow swiftly by, the world changes, and the West calls. The elves cannot forget--and hence will not let us forget--the issue of where our real home lies.

All this is a package of meaning that is present whenever an elf is present, reminding us that all beauty is passing and that we ourselves are exiles with no permanent dwelling here, nothing we can keep safe from the ravages of time and the bondage of corruption. The elves keep laying their finger on the heart of that mystery which makes us Man: the ability to glimpse that which keeps us ever wandering, searching on the Road that goes ever on and on. By translating it into a different mode, they make us keep perceiving this fact of our own exile, our search for our true home, the source of that wanderlust which is to us both a sorrow and an incentive to love well what we e'er long must leave. For though we cannot possess beauty, we do love it from afar, and see its existence as a message of hope which gives meaning to our very emptiness. And because they do embody beauty, even though it is beyond us and we glimpse it only in passing, the elves are also paradoxically beacons of hope, hope that the goal of our quest exists even if we will never live to see it. They demand, in other words, that we ask ourselves afresh what it means to have received from Iluvatar the gift--or doom--of men.

THE ELVES AND MANKIND

For Man does not seem to have been made for the bondage of corruption. The fact that he alone of all creatures feels it as a bondage points in that direction. Robert Frost asks pertinently,

> When to the heart of a man
> Was it ever less than a treason
> To go with the drift of things,
> To yield with a grace to reason,
> And bow and accept the end
> Of love or a season?

This, even though we know in advance that the ending is part of the bargain. So we continue the search:

> The last lone aster is gone,
> The flowers of the witch-hazel wither.
> The heart is still aching to seek
> But the feet question, "Whither?"[4]

The biblical language speaks of an end to the road for believers in Christ: waiting for the adoption, to wit, the redemption of our body; rebirth, not of corruptible but of incorruptible seed. So some--Tolkien and his friend C. S. Lewis among them--have thought that we are denied the final fruition of our deepest longings in this life for a reason: that we might be driven to think of the next life and be prepared for union with that Other to whom we also belong.

Not that they thought the present life was to be despised, or even neglected. It is, after all, the present life, and the future is not yet. It is a necessary place of trial and preparation. It is the arena in which the Quest takes place. It is in it that our redemption will be wrought for us and embraced, here or not at all. Its joys are real joys, its sorrows real sorrows, its good gifts real gifts from above. But it is not All, it is not the End. So with George Herbert they imagined God bestowing all his good gifts on Man, but withholding one: rest, or satisfaction, or possession.

> For if I should (said he)
> Bestow this jewell also on my creature,
> He would adore my gifts instead of me,
> And rest in Nature, not the God of Nature:
> So both would losers be.

> Yet let him keep the rest,
> But keep them with repining restlessness:
> Let him be rich and wearie, that at least
> If goodnesse leade him not, yet wearinesse
> May toss him to my breast.[5]

They asked with Gerard Manley Hopkins if there were *anything* that could keep back beauty, beauty, beauty from vanishing away, and concluded with him in the negative--but with the hope that *elsewhere* the things that really matter are kept for us with fonder a care, far with fonder a care than we could have kept them. Where? "Yonder." "What, high as that?" "Yes yonder, yonder. Yonder." And concluded also with him that "We follow, now we follow."[6] Beauty was to be loved, as a gift and a signpost, a foretaste and earnest beckoning us onward, but it is not ours to possess--yet. And in the meantime, they would not have disagreed with the atheist Housman that,

> Since to look at things in bloom
> Fifty years is little room,
> About the woodlands I will go
> To see the cherry hung with snow.[7]

TOLKIEN AND BIBLICAL CONSCIOUSNESS

Not all Tolkien's readers share with this one his hope in the final Eucatastrophe wrought by Christ, the Faerie Tale Hero who was also History and Fact.[8] Which is to say that not all of them have yet responded in faith to the profoundly biblical vision of the world as fallen but redeemed in Christ which permeates every page of his writing. (This point has frequently been misunderstood because of Tolkien's denial that he had written an allegory.[9] It is true that he does not directly portray specific Christian doctrines the way Lewis does in the Narnia series or the Space Trilogy. But the biblical vision in Tolkien actually goes, in a way, even deeper, ground into the very bones of his imaginary world.) But even those who lack biblical consciousness respond to the bittersweet note of reality sounded so strongly by Tolkien's tale. And it is there precisely because Tolkien's mind was richly imbued with biblical consciousness and hence thought in terms of Creation, Fall, Redemption, Sacrifice, and Grace.[10]

Tolkien's readers live, in other words, in a real world conditioned by the Fall which begins that even greater Story. They live in fact in Middle Earth, *middangeard*, in the Old English sense of the word Tolkien borrowed as the name for his imaginary country. For Middle Earth is that middle kingdom, a land which is neither Heaven nor Hell, but borders on both. It is a land of pilgrimage in which there are many goodly inns but no final dwelling place, in which all paths lead inexorably out across those borders which admit of no return. Not all recognize what lies beyond those borders; but all know instinctively that as yet they have found no home. It is undeniable that in this land it is not given to them to possess, and that Tolkien's elves are among the most powerful symbols ever set down of this note of sadness, paradoxically combined with hope, that enters all our tales. As to whether the tale has a happy ending Yonder, those who believe will discover in time. In the meanwhile, Sauron arises again in new and subtle guise; the elves sail down Anduin to the sea; and the Road goes ever on and on.

Near a place where I once lived there is a road, about half a mile in length, which connects two busy thoroughfares but is itself neglected. It was paved with the expectation that houses would grow up beside it, but they were blighted by high interest rates and never sprouted, leaving the scrubby pines to return with impunity. They stand now ten, some fifteen feet high, and have ceased to worry about competition from houses. They are content to provide a haven for squirrels and cover for rabbits and for the moon, which flits from one to another, stalking me over my left shoulder as I walk on those early autumn nights that push you out of the house with a restlessness that seems to come from nowhere.

In the middle of the road, invisible from either end, there inexplicably stands a single streetlamp, a monument no doubt to the lunacy of some minor city bureaucrat. It gets electricity from somewhere, somehow, and shines, illuminating only me as I take my solitary journeys. It is an annoying intrusion when you stand beneath its bare rays, but I have not complained to the city fathers, for there is a point on the walk which compensates for all. The leaves of an oak surround the light and shield it, filtering its garish whiteness into a soft green which fades imperceptibly into the blackness of the pines. It is not hard to believe at that moment that you are approaching a convocation of Tolkien's elves, or perhaps the Lantern Waste of Narnia. But, as when one is pursuing the elves of Mirkwood, another step destroys the vision and plunges the walker into a glaring darkness.

That night I knew where the restlessness was coming from, though that knowledge availed me nought in my efforts to evade it. It had flown and caught me from half a world away, where the carefully preserved but very dead body of the president of Egypt lay in state. Normally such news would have elicited only a cynical sigh about the prevalence of evil in the world and little more; but tonight was different. Yet the question which drove my feet toward their rendezvous with the elves was precisely my inability to grieve either for Anwar Sadat or for the world that would have to survive without his rare sanity. For my mind would not focus on that one death but was distracted by the Death that touches all. And *that* death is embodied concretely for anyone only in the memory of his own most recent dead. Mine was a beagle dog.

I was ashamed of myself for mourning more for a dog months dead than for a man fresh killed, but there it was. She had not even been especially devoted or obedient. But her musical voice had seen me off in the mornings and greeted me coming home. I had shared my sleeping bag with her on nights too cold for any sensible man to be sleeping out of doors. I had held her head in my hands when she groaned in the birth of her puppies. I had watched her front paws drum on the ground in joyous anticipation of supper. And now the physician had told Sadat's wife that "Only Allah is immortal." And his words had struck from half a world away and sent me out to weep beneath a streetlight for the elves which have departed, sailing to the West, returning not.

CONCLUSION

If this were a book on Tolkien, we could do whole chapters each on the biblical motifs of Creation, Fall, Redemption, Sacrifice, and Grace as they permeate the structure, the plot, the texture, the very flavor of Tolkien's tale. We could speak of the happy circumstance of having not one but three figures who recall for us different aspects of the life of Christ--Gandalf the prophet, Aragorn the king, Frodo the suffering servant--so that no one character has to shoulder the impossible burden of being the "Christ figure," and all three remain believable while yet together recapitulating the patterns laid down in the life of the Real Redeemer. (I think we must believe Tolkien when he tells us there was no such thing in his thoughts.[11] That is, he did not set out to create Christ figures; but when he set out to create his heroes they came out like *the* Hero in many respects because of the depth at which their maker had absorbed the ways of the Maker in the biblical text.)

But time is fleeting, so we will content ourselves with noticing how Tolkien's elves so wonderfully capture the biblical perspective on the way time is given value by its relation to eternity; with noticing, that is, how his fantasy precisely at its most fantastic is more like the real world than that world can sometimes seem itself. And in noticing that delicious irony, we see not only those tantalizing inklings of reality, not only the rich influence of biblical consciousness on a fertile mind, but also the ultimate vindication of Sir Philip Sidney's theology of literature.

Notes to Chapter 8

1. J. R. R. Tolkien, <u>The Hobbit</u>, <u>The Fellowship of the Ring</u>, <u>The Two Towers</u>, and <u>The Return of the King</u> (all N. Y.:: Ballantine, 1965).

2. William Shakespeare, "Sonnet 73," in G. B. Harrison, ed., <u>Shakespeare: The Complete Works</u> (N.Y.: Harcourt, Brace, & World, 1968), p. 1608.

3. C. S. Lewis developed this idea of unfulfilled desire as a key to the meaning of life in <u>Mere Christianity</u> (N. Y.: MacMillan, 1960), p. 120, and in his autobiography, <u>Surprised by Joy: The Shape of My Early Life</u> (N. Y.: Harcourt, Brace, & World, 1955). Cf. Peter J. Kreeft's fine study of the idea in "C. S. Lewis's Argument from Desire," in Michael H. McDonald & Andrew A. Tadie, eds., <u>G. K. Chesterton and C. S. Lewis: The Riddle of Joy</u> (Grand Rapids: Eerdmans, 1989), pp. 249-72.

4. Robert Frost, "Reluctance," in Edward Connery Lathem, ed., <u>The Poetry of Robert Frost</u> (N. Y.: Holt, Rhinehart, & Winston, 1969), pp. 29-30.

5. George Herbert, "The Pulley," in F. E. Hutchinson, ed., <u>The Works of George Herbert</u> (Oxford: Clarendon Pr., 1941), pp. 159-60.

6. Gerard Manley Hopkins, "The Leaden Echo and the Golden Echo," in W. H. Gardner & N. H. MacKenzie, eds., <u>The Poems of Gerard Manley Hopkins</u>, 4th ed. (London: Oxford Univ. Pr., 1967), pp. 91-93.

7. A. E. Housman, "Loveliest of Trees," in <u>The Collected Poems of A. E. Housman</u> (N. Y.: Holt, Rhinehart, & Winston, 1965), p. 11.

8. Cf. J. R. R. Tolkien, "On Fairy Stories," in The Tolkien Reader (N. Y.: Ballantine, 1966), pp. 71-73.

9. J. R. R. Tolkien, "Foreward" to The Fellowship of the Ring, op..cit., p. xi.

10. The best explications of this point are by C. S. Kilby, "Mythic and Christian Elements in Tolkien," in John W. Montgomery, ed., Myth, Allegory, and Gospel (Minneapolis: Bethany Fellowship, 1974), pp. 119-43, and especially in Kilby's Tolkien and the Silmarillion (Wheaton: Harold Shaw, 1976), pp. 55ff., where Tolkien himself confirms the basic approach we are taking.

11. Qtd. in Kilby, Tolkien and the Silmarillion, op. cit., p. 56.

Interlude

THE MINSTREL

The minstrel struck his golden harp;
The music sounded strong and clear,
Like edges keen and arrows sharp
    In hands of warriors bold.
Like rivers swift and mountains sheer,
Like the North Wind blowing cold,
It stirred the very blood to hear
    Him strike his harp of gold.

And then the bard began to sing:
If all alone his melody
Could build so bright and shimmering
    A vision in the heart,
What charms of might and mystery
The spoken spell, the subtle art,
The wisdom and the wizardry
    Of wordcraft could impart!

So deep was the enchantment laid,
So masterful the minstrelsy,
So strong the music that he made,
    The story that he told,
That all the gathered chivalry
Would hearken 'til the night was old,
Entranced and still, whenever he
    Took up his harp of gold.

                      -- D.T.W.

Conclusion

REGENERATION AND RIGHT THINKING:
The Fruit of Biblical Consciousness

"He who would not be frustrate of his hope to write well hereafter in laudable things ought himself to be a true poem."

--John Milton, <u>Apology for Smectymnus</u>

"The inquiry of truth, which is the love-making or wooing of it, the knowledge of truth, which is the presence of it, the belief of truth, which is the enjoying of it, is the sovereign good of human nature."

--Sir Francis Bacon, <u>Essays</u>.

We have argued in this book that we are not going to have revival without wholeness of vision, we are not going to have wholeness of vision without biblical consciousness, and we are not going to have biblical consciousness without becoming readers--of the Bible first, the classics of course, and the great heroes of the faith who have modeled biblical consciousness for us in the past as well. We have looked at a number of examples of writers whose work manifested that biblical consciousness richly.

These writers did not agree on everything; they did not have all the same emphases, and they did not all have the same style. They wrote in many different genres. But they all had minds nourished and structured by reading the world and literature through the lens of Scripture, which formed in them by its language the biblical paradigms of Creation, Fall, Incarnation, Sacrifice, Grace, and Redemption.   These ideas, more importantly, had a profound influence on the kinds of things they valued--truth over fame, people over things, tradition over novelty, God over all--and the fullness with which they lived life. And they all got that way because they were readers who wanted in their reading to find out what the author wanted to say to them and believed it was possible to do so.

But the right kind of reading by itself did not produce their biblical consciousness. It is a necessary but not a sufficient condition. And they testify to this truth frequently themselves. Calvin's humanism was a great boon to his ministry, but it did not bear the fruit of biblical consciousness until God by a sudden conversion subdued his mind and rescued him from so profound an abyss of mire.[1] Lewis described himself as having to be dragged kicking and screaming into the kingdom.[2] So this book about the value and crucial importance of reading and humane letters must conclude by stressing their impotence apart from something else.

My picture file includes a portrait of that great Puritan theologian and philosopher Jonathan Edwards, under which is the caption, "Where right thinking begins." This iconography is not intended to suggest that right thinking--or biblical consciousness, which is its prerequisite--had their origin with Jonathan Edwards. But he was a man who knew well where the possibility of right thinking does begin. It begins with regeneration, or the new birth.

Edwards discussed this point in his sermon "A Divine and Supernatural Light,"[3] which he preached at Northampton, Massachusetts, in August of 1733. The "light" about which he spoke is given directly to the soul by God at the moment of conversion, and from that point on makes the new Christian capable of understanding spiritual things. He will go on to do so--that is, to develop biblical consciousness--to the extent that this light is allowed to shine in a mind that is truly reading the world through Scripture without compartmentalizing. But without the light, nothing can happen. In Edwards' explanation, this light may be said to be the very cause of conversion, for before its arrival the sinner is the "natural man" of 1 Cor. 2:14, who does not receive the things of the Spirit.

This "light" is more than mere intellectual assent to the truth of the Gospel. That could be produced (at least in theory) by natural reason alone, and would be of no saving significance. It is rather an *application* of that truth by the Holy Spirit to the heart and will, issuing in an *acceptance* of the Gospel and *commitment* of the whole self to Christ as Lord. It is a sense of one's own sinfulness and helplessness before a righteous and holy God, coupled with an apprehension of and delight in the excellence of his majestic mercy and the salvation offered in Christ. It changes the heart which was once at enmity with God to one that now loves him, desires above all to do his will, and casts itself unreservedly upon his grace. This "divine and supernatural light" is in short Edwards' way of expressing the work of the Holy Spirit in converting and regenerating the sinful heart.

Edwards then proceeds to the relation of this "divine light" to right thinking: It is its essential prerequisite. The divine light is above natural reason, but is not contrary to it, and in fact frees it to be used as God intended. Since unregenerate man hates God, he therefore also hates the truth, and his pride and rebellious commitment to his own "autonomy" (to use a term popularized by Francis Schaeffer) tend to lead him to contradict true reason, which is on the side of the Gospel (and indeed of the whole teaching of Scripture).

But the divine light does not leave people in this state; it delivers them from it. In Edwards' own words:

> The prejudices that are in the heart, against the truth of divine things, are hereby removed; *so that the mind becomes susceptive to the due force of rational arguments* for their truth. . . . Hence was the different

effect that Christ's miracles had to convince the disciples from what they had to convince the Scribes and Pharisees. Not that they had a stronger reason, or had their reason more improved; but *their reason was sanctified* (emphasis added).[4]

"Their reason was sanctified." This is one of those rare phrases which seem to glow with an almost divine and supernatural light themselves, so succinctly and pertinently do they state the Truth that is too obvious to be seen. Note the judicious care with which Edwards constructed his sentences: Unbelievers are not totally irrational (we know that if we know unbelievers), but reason does not have its *due* force with them. Their sinful commitments tend to make them fight against the truth, especially at points where accepting reality would force them to bow before a sovereign God. Rationalizing, they cleverly make use of their reason to fight against what Reason really says.

Yet Reason still has some force with them. They cannot completely escape God's revelation in Nature even if they do discredit the Bible. They still have to live in the real world, which refuses to cooperate with their theories of humanity's essential goodness and perfectibility.

So non-Christians are not always wrong, nor are believers always right. Our reason is not always as "strong" or as "improved" as it ought to be, and we are still sometimes swayed by the "prejudices" which in principle we gave up at conversion. But the difference is that we have the *potential* to develop biblical consciousness; or, as Edwards put it, the difference is that our reason is sanctified. Believers alone have the full potential to think rightly and constructively about the world and the issues it raises. The question is, how far will we realize that potential? How open are we to wholeness of vision and biblical consciousness? Or, how sanctified, in other words, are we ready to allow our reasoning to become?

According to some polls, 40% of Americans claim to be born-again Christians, Evangelicals. But if this is true, then why do the inane arguments of secular humanism carry such weight in our society? Consider the argument that the foetus is "part of the mother's body" and that therefore abortion is a matter of her private choice with no moral overtones. Why doesn't the unanimous testimony of geneticists and embryologists that the facts are quite otherwise put an immediate stop to such nonsense? Or take the arguments of groups such as the A.C.L.U. that nativity scenes on public property or religious Christmas music in public school programs are violations of the separation of church and state. Any historian knows that the amendments in question were intended to prohibit the establishment of a national church, *not* to mandate an exclusion of religious influence from public life that amounts to a *de facto* censorship of Christian ideas. Why is this fact, even when it is admitted, somehow not allowed to count?

It is too simple just to say that the god of this world has blinded the eyes of the unbelieving. We must still explain why the influence of supposedly Bible-believing people is so small in proportion to their alleged numbers. For even if (as I suspect) the numbers of the supposedly saved are grossly inflated, it would only have taken a handful of righteous men to reverse the destiny of Sodom and Gomorrha. It doesn't take a ratio of four parts of salt to six of meat to flavor the dish, and even a small light shines brightly in pitch darkness. Thus part of the answer must be that hordes of professing believers have been satisfied to bottle up sanctification in their hearts and not allow it to reach their heads. Truth comes by hearing, and hearing by the Word of God. If we are spiritually impotent it is because we have allowed ourselves to become biblically illiterate or have compartmentalized our Bible knowledge in ways that hinder the development of real biblical consciousness and wholeness of vision--of really sanctified minds.

The very fact that you can still hear well-meaning but biblically illiterate preachers (why do we suffer such people in our pulpits?) drumming home the distinction between "head knowledge" and "heart knowledge" is symptomatic of the problem. Not only is such language unbiblical (for in Scripture the heart is the center of the whole person and encompasses emotions, will, *and* intellect, while these people seem to mean that we simply don't *feel* deeply enough about it as evidenced by a lack of tears at the altar), but it shows that Evangelicalism still disparages the mind. The result is good intentions but fuzzy-- that is, worldly--thinking on the issues.

When God gave you a new heart, did he give you a new mind as well? That is part of the package! "Be not conformed to this world [i.e., not only to its lifestyle but also its thought-patterns, the fallacious and sometimes wicked nonsense it blindly accepts as fact] but be transformed by the renewing of your *mind*." And how is this supposed to happen in people who are not readers? "Sanctify them in the *truth*," Jesus prayed; "Thy *Word* is truth." And, as we have seen, the Bible cannot have its full effect in people who read only the Bible. In our age of confusion and doubt, we have great need indeed for the vigorous exercise of "sanctified reason."

How, in practical terms, can we allow the divine and supernatural light which dawned in our hearts at conversion to have its full effect? The natural man will never attain biblical consciousness, but the redeemed man does not attain it automatically. How can we make sure that our reason becomes increasingly sanctified?

Perhaps the first step is simply to recognize the need for sanctified reason as well as the powerful and subtle forces that militate against it. We must realize in other words that, as Harry Blamires[5] and John Stott[6] have put it, we need not only to think about Christian things but also to think Christianly about things.

And because we live in a world permeated by secular thinking, this can only happen as a result of deliberate choice.

Second, we must certainly be diligent students of Scripture, but students of the right kind. We must read the Bible not primarily for a "blessing" but for *truth*, the message of its Author and its authors, expecting to find it and find it applicable to our own lives.. We must read *humbly*, with a willingness to bow in obedience when God requires us to change our way of thinking and living. We must read *intelligently*, making use of the helps that reverent scholarship can offer, but being slow to embrace the latest fads in interpretation. We must read with *faith* that, like Machiavelli reading Cicero, we can read *these* ancient authors and ask them the reasons for their actions and they will courteously answer us.

But if we want the Scriptures to transform our minds, if we want them to bear the fruit of biblical consciousness and wholeness of vision leading to effective service for God, we must also pursue the right kind of diet in our extrabiblical reading. We should allow the spiritual and intellectual junk food which gluts the shelves of most of our "Christian" book stores to stay there, and rather choose to nourish our minds on the rich vision of life in the great classics of human literature and on the wisdom of the great Christian thinkers of past generations. It is simply poor stewardship of your time to read the latest best seller if you have not read Augustine's Confessions or Calvin's Institutes or Bunyan's Pilgrim.

These giants of the past are indispensable not only because of their profound insights into the truth but because of the way familiarity with them protects us from what C. S. Lewis called "chronological snobbery,"[7] the assumption that the presuppositions of our own age are always right where they differ from those of the past. Former generations made their own errors, of course; but not the same ones we make. And it is easier to be aware of and critical of our own assumptions when we have something to measure them against. Reading the spiritual giants of the past gives us a critical distance which makes sanctified reasoning about the present much more possible. That way, when we do read modern books, view modern art, and hear modern music (as of course we will), we will be prepared to evaluate their message Christianly. We can not cut ourselves off from the great spiritual and intellectual heritage God has graciously given to his church and expect to have living biblical consciousness in the minds of our own generation.

Finally, we must beware of compartmentalization. We must deliberately, consciously, and continually be cross-referencing in our minds what the Bible is saying with everything else we read and hear, so that all our knowledge is constantly being evaluated by Scriptural perspectives and taking its place in the structure of the unified vision of the world that true biblical consciousness provides. Only thus does knowledge become understanding and wisdom; only thus does Bible reading make a difference in our lives.

C. S. Lewis has been one of the more prominent heroes in our story, for he was at the center of a group of friends called the Inklings who modeled the kind of Christian minds we are in need of. His friend and fellow Inkling Owen Barfield, in trying to describe what it was that made Lewis the great Christian thinker he was, said that the unity of Lewis's thought came from a quality Barfield called "presence of mind." By this he meant that "somehow what [Lewis] thought about everything was secretly present in what he said about anything."[8] When ideas are allowed to cross-pollenate each other like that, really penetrating insights can grow. And when the garden is full of the good seed which is the Word, they will be rooted in reality, will produce the peaceable fruit of righteousness, and will be found to come from the Tree of Life.

Notes to Conclusion

1. Cf. chp. 3, n.22.

2. C. S. Lewis, Surprised by Joy: The Shape of My Early Life (N. Y.: Harcourt, Brace, & World, 1955), pp. 228-29.

3. Jonathan Edwards, "A Divine and Supernatural Light, Immediately Imparted to the Soul by God, Shown to be both a Scriptural and a Rational Doctrine," in Sculley Bradley, Richmond Croom Beatty, & E. Hudson Long, eds., The American Tradition in Literature, 3rd ed. (N. Y.: Norton, 1967), 1:101-109.

4. Ibid., p. 106.

5. Harry Blamires, The Christian Mind (London: S.P.C.K., 1963).

6. John R. W. Stott, Your Mind Matters (Downers Grove, Il.: IVP, 1972).

7. Lewis, Surprised by Joy, op. cit., p. 213; cf. his essay "On the Reading of Old Books," in Walter Hooper, ed., God in the Dock: Essays in Theology and Ethics (Grand Rapids: Eerdmans, 1970), pp. 200-217.

8. Owen Barfield, "Preface" to Bruce Edwards, ed., The Taste of the Pineapple: Essays on C. S. Lewis as Reader, Critic, and Imaginative Writer (Bowling Green, Oh.: Bowling Green State Univ. Pr., 1988), p. 2.

Postlude

ON READING THE CLASSICS
Sonnets LXIX, LXX, LXXVI

I

(Commentary, Acts 17:23, Rom. 1:23, Col. 2:9)

The Ancients worshiped what they did not know:
    Corruptible men and beasts and creeping things
    Enthroned in splendor, deathless. From below,
    They scaled the sky with such imaginings,
But for that trip they needed stronger wings.
    The glimpses filled their hearts with holy dread;
    They could not see the way the King of kings
    Joined all the scattered hints into one Head:
Atropos, who snips thread after thread;
    Poseidon, master of the raging sea;
    Hera of the hearth and marriage bed;
    Life-giving power of Persephone;
Aphrodite's beauty, Ares' might;
    Zeus's thunder, and Apollo's light.

II
Faithful

The harsh will of the gods was the end of Troy;
    Most of the Greeks would never make it back.
    The ones who did met Clytemnestra, coy

With ten years' brooding vengeance to exact;
Or, like Odysseus, were blown off track
    To spend an extra decade wandering.
    But he kept his integrity intact:
    Calypso could not stay his voyaging;
Tied to the mast, he heard the Siren sing,
    But still sailed on toward Penelope.
    Lotus, Circe, Cyclops could not bring
    Despair, could not erase the memory
Which, after twenty years, still drove him on,
    Relentless as the rosy-fingered Dawn.

III
Atrophy

We seem incapable of concentration;
    More than a moment, we cannot be stirred.
    Not all our gigabytes of information
    Can keep the simplest thought from being blurred.
The ancient writers knew no punctuation;
    No space was used to set off word from word.
    Still, they preserved for future generations
    A chance to hear the cadence Homer heard.
But now, with electronic inundation,
    Is thought enhanced, or is it just deferred?
    We feed upon our own sophistication,
    And indigestion leaves us undeterred.
Have we the vision yet, the wide-eyed awe
    To see what Homer in his blindness saw?

                                        --D.T.W.

Appendix:
RELATED REVIEWS

Literature Through the Eyes of Faith. By Susan V. Gallagher and Roger Lundin. San Francisco: Harper & Row, 1989, xxvii + 193 pp., $9.95p.

Gallagher and Lundin set out to examine the implications of Christian faith for the study of literature. Their specific goals are threefold: "To help students of literature understand more clearly the nature of language and literature, to acquaint them with the tools of literary study, and to introduce them to the rich history of Christian reflection on literature, language, and the reading experience." It was perhaps inevitable that all three goals could not be achieved with equal success in such a small volume. As it is, the book has great strengths but also critical weaknesses as an introductory text in the area.

The authors' strongest performance is in the pursuit of their first aim, an understanding from a Christian perspective of the nature and purpose of literature. Taking their cue from Nicholas Wolterstorff's Art in Action: Toward a Christian Aesthetic (Grand Rapids: Eerdmans, 1980), they argue that the production and enjoyment of literature is not an artificial pursuit removed from the real world but a natural extension of normal activities common to (and distinctive of) all members of the human species. They show that all human beings tell stories and use metaphors to interpret their experiences (even when they use these very means to deny that they are doing so!), and that the Christian knows why. "In a universe created and ruled by a sovereign God all things are meaningful," so that "if we are convinced that our world has meaning, then . . . interpretation is not isolated from the rest of life but is at the very heart of our life" (pp. 3-5). The implications of these insights are worked out in generally helpful ways; there is wisdom here. Though a number of biblical motifs which could enrich a full-scale theology of literature are left relatively undeveloped (e.g., the incarnation, the *logos* doctrine, some aspects of the *imago dei*), the book is only an introduction after all, and what we do have here is essentially sound and healthy--a good place for students to start in their thinking.

The second task--acquainting students with the tools of literary study--is less well executed. Much good advice is given, though the authors at times bend over so far backward to avoid the idea that literary study can be "disinterested" that they veer too far toward a hermeneutic of subjectivity in which meaning is "created" rather than discovered by the reader. Giving equal time to someone such as E. D. Hirsch along with the more reader-centered approaches would have improved balance here. Also problematic is the superficiality of the authors' own reading at times. Those whose methods they reject, from the romantics to the structuralists, are presented in simplified caricatures as straw men easily demolished. Even those whose ideas are approved are not exempt from such treatment: C. S. Lewis's view of myth, for example, is oversimplified beyond recognition (pp. 155-58). And while some of their examples of literary analysis are helpful and insightful (e.g., of Benjamin Franklin's Autobiography), others (e.g., of Robert Frost a couple of times) are so incomplete as to be positively misleading. Here the introductory nature of the text cannot be pled as excuse, for it is precisely beginning students of literature who are most likely to come away with the false impressions which such lapses can generate.

It is as an introduction to the "rich history of Christian reflection" on language and literature that the book is at its weakest. The works *missing* from the rather extensive biography constitute precisely an honor roll of the best that has been written and thought by Christian literary scholars through the years. They include, incredibly, Sir Philip Sidney's <u>Defense of Poesy,</u> the indispensable starting point for any Christian theory of literature. Almost equally conspicuous by their absence are Milton's <u>Areopagetica</u> and "On Education," Dorothy L. Sayers' <u>The Mind of the Maker,</u> J. R. R. Tolkien's "Essay on Faerie Stories" with its seminal doctrine of sub-creation, and any of C. S. Lewis's writings on literary theory (his fiction appears, but <u>An Experiment in Criticism,</u> "Christianity and Literature," "Christianity and Culture," "Lilies that Fester," "On Stories," "*De Descriptione Temporum*," "*De Audiendis Poetis*," "On Reading Old Books," etc. are unaccountably absent). T. S. Eliot and Flannery O'Connor are mentioned in passing but get short shrift. That any book could be written on a Christian view of literature without extensive interaction with the thought of these giants is hard to imagine. That such a book should bill itself as an introduction to the heritage of Christian reflection on such things is almost beyond belief.

<u>Literature Through the Eyes of Faith</u> then offers a broad coverage of issues and contains much useful discussion, but is finally too thin to be reliable as a guide for beginning students. At too many points superficial treatment creates misleading impressions. In their discussion of literary curricula, for example, the authors stress the arbitrariness of the traditional literary canon and argue (quite rightly) for openness to the

importance of genres, media, and national or ethnic literatures which have generally not been included. But by totally failing to mention the role of *staying power* as the most important criterion of canonicity, they leave the impression that the traditional canon is much more arbitrary than it really is, and they also fail to give sufficient weight to the role of the canon as a preserver and transmitter of the central moral and cultural tradition of the West. With those who do not think such things are worth preserving and transmitting, we have no argument--for one cannot argue with barbarians. Gallagher and Lundin are not barbarians, but they have left gaps in their presentation through which the hordes will be glad to swarm. And "The Profession" (as English teachers like to call their collective ranks) is full of cultural relativists ready to do the swarming.

This then is a book with great virtues but also great failings. As a text for an introductory course in literary theory it would need to be used with great care.

The Bible Tells Them So: The Discourse of Protestant Fundamentalism. By Kathleen C. Boone. Albany: State Univ. of N. Y. Pr., 1989, 139 pp., $34.95/$12.95p.

Unresolved debates on translation, contextualization, and hermeneutics have made contemporary Evangelical scholars more sensitive than ever before to questions about how and to what extent the language we use constitutes as well as reflects the way we perceive the world. Not unrelated to these concerns is the rise of rhetorical criticism, which is in this book applied, not to the text of Scripture, but to the speech of the Evangelical movement itself.

Boone's book is an attempt to analyze and discover the grammar of the peculiar universe of discourse which Fundamentalists inhabit. By Fundamentalists she means anyone who believes in the inerrancy of Scripture. While admitting stylistic differences between Fundamentalists and Evangelicals, she (rightly, I think) perceives them as inhabiting the same universe of discourse, one which sets them apart from the modern world more effectively than either specific lifestyle or even doctrinal commitments. The necessity of justifying all one's truth claims by one inerrant and authoritative standard which is publicly accessible--or, what is possibly even more revealing, the necessity of rationalizing one's failure to do so in ways which disguise the fact if one is to continue with the discourse--sets us apart from the rest of society by virtue of its profound influence on the very structure of our language. That is Boone's thesis, buttressed with scores of quotations from practically the whole pantheon of Evangelical and Fundamentalist leaders from Warfield and Torrey down to John R. Rice, Carl F. H. Henry, and Francis Schaeffer.

Boone forthrightly dismisses inerrancy as impossible and cannot always hide her contempt for the doctrine, nor can she resist trotting out many of the tired old arguments against it we have heard before--but that is not her purpose. She manages in spite of that lack of sympathy to offer an amazingly objective study of why in the world such people would talk (and act) the way they do. In the course of it she comes to some fascinating conclusions. One which deserves some pondering is that participation in the kind of discourse generated by shared belief in an inerrant Scripture commits one of itself to a text-centered, determinative-meaning hermeneutic such as E. D. Hirsch's (he who has ears to hear, let him hear) as opposed to a reader-centered hermeneutic in which meaning is generated by the audience, as in Stanley Fish or Foucalt.

This conclusion, if true, has unending implications for many of the debates being carried on around us in the Evangelical movement right now. And Boone's primary reason for rejecting inerrancy--the fact that she has been convinced by Fish and Foucalt that determinative meaning is an illusion--has implications for the directions our apologetics may need to be taking. If meaning really is in the eye of the beholder, so is truth, and all absolutes--including the absolute authority of Scripture-- are inconceivable, no matter how many historical arguments or archaeological discoveries we can adduce. It may be that while we've been successfully defending the wall of Truth, the wall of Meaning had been breached, so that the Enemy has gotten in behind us and is thus beginning to be found *inside* the fort of Evangelicalism. One wonders: If Boone had studied the language of unknown Evangelical college and seminary professors as well as that of popularly recognized leaders, would she have noticed that even within the institutions supposedly existing to preserve the community, the universe of discourse is beginning to break up?

Be that as it may, Boone has given us a portrait of our movement which we ought to take a close look at. It often shows us as we are; it always shows us as we appear to those around us who ultimately speak a different language; and thus again it raises the unavoidable question: How do we communicate across that language gap without losing the distinctiveness of our message? This thought-provoking study shows that we do not have to be foreign missionaries to need the answer.

Spenser's Moral Allegory. By Sean Kane. Toronto: Univ. of Toronto Pr., 1989, xiii + 237 pp., $40.00.

Some of the greatest teachers of theology in the history of the Church have not (fortunately for the Church) been professional theologians. John Bunyan from a previous century and C. S. Lewis from our own come immediately to mind. Not as frequently invoked as those two but in some ways greater than either was "our sage and serious poet" Edmund Spenser, the Sixteenth-Century Protestant allegorist whom no less an authority than John Milton (perhaps the captain of the whole crew) dared to call "a better teacher than Scotus or Aquinas." Those who have read his Faerie Queene with understanding recognize a more sophisticated Bunyan, a man with a love for the glory of God and the doctrines of grace and a desire to see them manifested in practical ways in both the private and public lives of his readers.

Unfortunately, most contemporary literary scholarship has done little to elucidate this side of Spenser, preferring either to attempt awkward hermeneutical gymnastics in an effort to make him over into a modern secular humanist in Puritan's clothing or simply to use the vast landscape of his epic as a quarry from which to mine symbolic material for use in their own labyrinthine intellectual structures. In this context, Sean Kane's promise to "read Spenser as someone from the past, and primarily as inhabiting that past, while speaking to our own time" (p. ix) offers hope. It is a hope which, unfortunately, is only partially fulfilled.

Kane sees as the key to Spenser an uneasiness with the Renaissance philosophy of power which saw the world in Aristotelian terms as ruled by "polarities" or "oppositions": flesh vs. spirit, self vs. other, subject vs. object, etc. In this framework the self seeks to achieve mastery over the external world through the use of power and skill; the Renaissance drive for excellence, exploration, etc. is ultimately an expression of the will to power. The problem is that opposition, polarity, and antithesis can only lead to sterility and strife, the destruction of fragile things like harmony and beauty and tolerance--to the modern world, in other words. To this view of polarity Spenser, in Kane's analysis, opposed the older platonic doctrine of *hierarchy*: antitheses are contained and given meaning by higher levels of reality and are never to be seen as ultimate. Kane gives us a rather cryptic reading of the Faerie Queene as an attempt to wrestle with and mediate between these two world views.

Kane's thesis is not without some merit, especially in the insights it gives into one side of Renaissance thought and its relation to later developments which would have horrified the Renaissance humanists who opened the door to them. But as a study of Spenser's poem the execution is faulty. Kane presses his idea too hard, and it slips away from him. Preferring a view of hierarchy in which all polarity is transcended, all opposition is caught up in a higher harmony, he ironically makes the very opposition between hierarchy and polarity into an antithesis which has the ultimacy he denies to every other. He consequently ends up missing the point of what Spenser was doing.

Spenser would have been puzzled by the notion that hierarchy (which he believed in a strongly as anyone ever has) ruled out all polarities or somehow could resolve the antithesis between good and evil, darkness and light, etc. Thus in spite of his promise to present Spenser as a man of his time, Kane's Spenser comes out more Hegelian than any man of the Renaissance or the Reformation (and Spenser was solidly rooted in both) could ever have been. The end result is a reading in which Spenser "subtly disavows" (p. 40) the very meanings which the surface of his text projects. This is suspicious diction in any literary critic: It usually arises from a covert attempt to make an earlier author over into something he was not.

It is, moreover, difficult to understand how the text of an older writer is supposed to be elucidated by language which is more cryptic and obscure than that of the text it is supposed to be interpreting. Kane's book is full of utterances like the following: "Since this identity is superior to ourselves and our relationships, and superior in a way that takes us beyond the notion of superiority itself, the idea of hierarchy is difficult" (p. 9). I guess so. The question is not so much what this phraseology means as whether it means anything. The failure of this book, as of so much of modern literary criticism, is simply one of clarity of thought. Read Spenser instead.

Herbert's Prayerful Art. By Terry G. Sherwood. Toronto: Univ. of Toronto Pr., 1989, 190 pp., $45.00.

Widely recognized as the greatest Protestant devotional poet in the history of the English language, George Herbert has attracted a good deal of attention from literary historians attempting to relate him to the classical Protestant orthodoxy of the Seventeenth Century which nurtured his spirituality. Lewalski (Protestant Poetics and the Seventeenth-Century Religious Lyric, 1979), Strier (Love Known: Theology and Experience in George Herbert's Poetry, 1983), and Veith (Reformation Spirituality: The Religion of George Herbert, 1985) are among those who have admirably succeeded in showing how the richness of Herbert's art finds its roots in the fertile soil of that heritage. Sherwood tries to offer a corrective to their account by showing ways in which Herbert transcended the limitations of that heritage. But while he does offer some positive insights into Herbert's achievement, his efforts to nuance Herbert's relationship to orthodox theology stumble over forced readings of the texts in which that orthodoxy is expressed.

In the standard Pauline/Protestant paradigm, as Sherwood would have it, God reaches out to man in love, and man responds to God in faith. There is no room in this scheme for man to respond to God with love; his radically depraved and impotent soul is capable only of faith or trust in God's work (The Reformers would have been surprised, if ability is to be considered, to find they thought it capable even of that!). But Herbert emphasizes the human soul returning God's love, reaching out to communion with him in prayer, thus radically personalizing the more sterile and abstract model for the divine-human relationship set forth by Calvin. In Calvin, "Love is expressed to God only in an undeveloped way, since sola fide encouraged it to atrophy" (p. 34). Herbert, then, along with his contemporary Richard Sibbes, explores "developed notions of loving God" which are "absent in Calvin and Perkins" (p. 44). Herbert feels more clearly than Sibbes the tensions inherent in the idea of loving God in a Protestant framework and thus struggles to find the right way of expressing it, finally emphasizing friendship love rather than the embrace of heterosexual love as his model for man's response to God.

As a reading of Herbert, Sherwood's approach is not without some merit, highlighting certain aspects of his work that might otherwise be neglected. But his reading of the history of doctrine is highly questionable, and his errors there also cause problems in his interpretation of Herbert at points. The alleged Pauline paradigm becomes a Procrustean bed which the Reformers are forced to fit. When Calvin protests that we are united to Christ "by a faith which is not feigned, but which springs from sincere affection, which [Christ] describes by the name of *love*," and concludes that "no man believes purely in Christ who does not cordially embrace him," he is not allowed to speak for himself. Despite his clear statement that faith *entails* love and demands it rather than opposing it, Sherwood replies that "Calvin here reveals his true colors, . . . telling us that 'love' really means 'faith.'" Hence, as usual, "the importance of faith simply crowds out direct love of God" (p. 36). The hermeneutic by which we get from "springs from" to "crowds out" is a strange one, and it is hard to escape the feeling that Calvin would have had difficulty recognizing himself in the portrait Sherwood draws of him.

Sherwood's book illustrates how easy it is for a secular critic to become quite knowledgeable about theological texts while remaining incapable of appreciating the spirit in which they were written. While he usually confines his use of the hermeneutic of the preconceived notion to the theological treatises and commentaries he cites as background, his wooden caricatures of the Protestant paradigm can also cause him to miss the point of the Herbertian language with which he is more familiar. He refers with approval to readers who have "noted that Herbert does not regard man as depraved" (p. 149), totally ignoring the fact that Herbert is describing the *regenerate* rather than the natural man in the passage in question--which is rather like attributing to someone the opinion that corpses are not dead on the grounds that he thinks living men can walk.

What we have here, in short, is a phenomenon all too common in literary scholarship today: a critic who recognizes the importance of theological background for understanding older literature and who duly masters the data of it but lacks a framework of understanding which could tell him what it means or how to apply it. He then writes up an authoritative-sounding account buttressed by scores of footnotes which is nevertheless obtuse at points and which will mainly be read by scholars who are equally incapable of telling whether and when they have been led astray. That the rebuilding of that framework is a critical need to which Evangelical scholars must address themselves is one thing this book demonstrates beyond the shadow of a doubt.

Reading Between the Lines: A Christian Guide to Literature. By Gene Edward Veith, Jr. Turning Point Christian World view Series, no. 11. Wheaton: Crossway, 1990, 254pp., n.p.

It is highly ironic that conservative Protestants--who ought supremely to be a people of the Book--have always manifested ambivalent attitudes toward literature. Since Sir Philip Sidney's profoundly Christian Defense of Poesy defended imaginative literature from half-cocked Puritan moralizing in the Sixteenth Century, our movement has flirted with philistinism. Now, even the secular academic pursuit of letters is in a state of serious disarray, struggling to justify humane learning to a jaded culture. Increasingly the field is so dominated by Marxist and feminist hermeneutics, deconstruction, political correctness, and other forms of fad exegesis that the remnant who still believe that literature can be a powerful instrument for the preservation and transmission of the central Western Greco-Roman and Judaio-Christian traditions begin to feel like quaint and archaic anachronisms. Indeed, most of the current trends involve an implicit (and sometimes explicit) denial that those traditions are worth preserving and transmitting in the first place. In such times, the temptation to doubt that Athens has anything to do with Jerusalem grows even stronger than usual. The temptation to withdraw from culture rather than confront it may be one we yield to out of sheer frustration.

In short, the time is ripe for a reinfusion of sanity and common sense. And that is precisely what Gene Edward Veith, Jr., offers in Reading Between the Lines. The book is both an eloquent apology for quality reading and an introduction to how to do it. In a manageable paperback, he succeeds with amazing completeness and clarity in surveying the importance of reading, the forms of literature (nonfiction, fiction, poetry, drama, along with the purpose, value, and distinctiveness of each), the modes of literature (tragic vs. comic, realist vs. fantasy), and the major literary periods in the Western tradition, with a tourist's guide to the main attractions to be found in each.

The issues Veith addresses ought to be of concern to more than just teachers and students of literature. He argues persuasively that the whole nature of our civilization and Christianity's role in it may be at stake. "Words and images promote two different mind-sets." (Here he means words versus visual, i.e. electronic-media, images, not the images carried by words in literature.) "Christians must be people of the Word, although the temptation to succumb to 'graven images' is present in a new form in the television age. . . . As television turns our society into an increasingly image-dominated culture, Christians must continue to be people of the Word." Why? "When we read, we cultivate a sustained attention span, an active imagination, a capacity for logical analysis and critical thinking, and a rich inner life. Each of these qualities, which have proven themselves essential to a free people, is under assault in our TV-dominated culture" (xiv-xv). To the extent that we cease to be intelligent and discerning readers, we forfeit the unique contact we have with God himself through the Bible. "Whereas other religions may stress visions, experiences, or even the silence of meditation as the way to achieve contact with the divine, Christianity insists on the role of language" (17). Those who read *only* the Bible, though, cannot hope to read even the Bible very well, and they also lose the rich heritage of vicarious experience stored up in the literature which has survived the ravages of time.

The "how to" section contains an excellent introduction to the main types of literature and how they work and good, balanced treatments of may of the corollary issues such as censorship which are implicit in the topic. There are details one could quibble over: The definition of postmodernism is perhaps a bit too broad to be useful, Donne's Devotions Upon Emergent Occasions is cited as having been on "divergent" occasions, etc. But this is a book which deserves a wide readership among Evangelical scholars and lay persons alike. It is to be hoped they will carefully ponder the exhortation with which Veith leaves us, remembering that when "the Vandals trashed a civilization based on law and learning," it was the Church which cherished and preserved books--not only the Bible, but others as well. "The Vandal aesthetic may be coming back in the anti-intellectualism of the mass culture and in the Postmodern nihilism of the high culture. Christians may be the last readers. If so, they need to be in training" (224).

Realms of Gold: The Classics in Christian Perspective. By Leland Ryken. Wheaton: Harold Shaw, 1991, x + 230 pp., n.p.

In recent years there has been no more prolific apologist for the importance of literature to Evangelicals than Wheaton professor Leland Ryken. Realms of Gold covers much the same ground as his Triumphs of the Imagination (IVP, 1979). The newer book gives less attention to theory and more space to criticism and appreciation of classic literary texts from a Christian perspective. As such it complements Triumphs and provides a good introduction to Ryken's approach for those unfamiliar with his writings.

He discusses a potpourri of "classic" texts ranging from Homer's Odyssey to Camus' The Stranger, both analyzing and appreciating them for their own sake and dealing with the critical issues they raise. The pieces are chosen both for their inherent value and because of the issues they raise for Christian readers. Both an apology for the value of the classics and a how-to for rich and accurate reading emerge from the texts themselves.

Ryken's virtues are a good acquaintance with the thought of the great Christian critics from Sir Philip Sidney to C. S. Lewis, J. R. R. Tolkien, Dorothy L. Sayers, T. S. Eliot, and Flannery O'Connor; genuine enthusiasm; a modicum of common sense; and an avoidance of jargon. Letting critical issues emerge from the texts is a healthy and refreshing approach which keeps the reader's attention from flagging. The discussions are generally rewarding; those of Homer and Hawthorne are especially good.

The main weakness is thin treatments at isolated spots. That "readers collaborate with the author to produce" the work (p. 17) is an idea with pitfalls around which fences need to be placed. That Paul "alludes to Homer's Oddysey" (p. 43) by using the same word for men "feeling after God" (Acts 17:27) that Homer used to describe the blinded Cyclops groping for the door of his cave is an intriguing suggestion--but can we be sure it is true?

How rare was this word; might Paul have used it without reading Homer? We need more. The distinction between morality and taste (p. 60) needs more development. Etc.

All in all, the book is well worth reading, especially for students encountering these issues for the first time. I only wish the selection of texts made it easier to find a college course in which it could serve as a supplementary text. But then, that may be the fault of the courses.

Voicing Creation's Praise: Towards a Theology of the Arts. By Jeremy S. Begbie. Edinburgh: T. & T. Clark, 1991, xix + 286 pp., n.p.

Begbie begins by noting the modern fragmentation of the arts, the Church's ambivalence toward them, and the lack of much solid theological reflection on how to relate them to Christian faith. After studying two major exceptions to that dearth--Paul Tillich and the Dutch neo-Calvinists--and finding them helpful but incomplete, he tries to chart a course toward healing through a renewal of Christology and Trinitarian theology.

Tillich is revealed as a theologian who reflected much on the arts and saw them as central to a Christian view of the world: "As religion is the substance of culture, so culture is the form of religion" (qtd. on p. 7). He rightly saw that artists inevitably display to some degree their "ultimate concern" and that of their culture. But despite frequently penetrating insights, his views are rooted more in a complex, jargon-laden German idealist metaphysic than in Scripture, which is reduced to just one more artistic symbol of ultimate Being which, like all the others, must never be absolutized, for "the truth of a religious symbol has nothing to do with the validity of factual statements" (52).

Begbie's critique of Tillich is incisive: for him the biblical picture of Jesus as the Christ has "all the characteristics of an expressionist painting" (55). What is significant is not its factual truth but the fact that it mediates the power felt by the disciples. But, "if we can never demonstrate a correspondence between the historical information in the biblical picture and the actual life of the man it interprets as the Christ, how can we ever claim with any confidence that Jesus of Nazareth actually was the manifestation of the New Being?" (56). Thus Tillich's aesthetic is too abstract and insufficiently rooted in the objectivity of historical revelation (in other words, it does not take the *language* of Scripture seriously enough) to provide a framework for a Christian theology of the arts.

The Dutch neo-Calvinists (Abraham Kuyper, Herman Bavinck, Hans Rookmaaker, and Calvin Seerveld) labored, by contrast, to give art its due place in a comprehensive Christian philosophy rooted in the self-revealing God of the Bible. Begbie does a nice job of outlining how Dooyeweerd elaborated Kuyper's concept of sphere sovereignty and how it was differently applied by Rookmaaker and Seerveld. He appreciates the strengths of their approach, its comprehensiveness, its unity, its affirmation of the value of art and culture in terms of their place under the sovereignty of God over all of His creation. But he faults them for looking at God more as a Lawgiver than as "ecstatic, self-giving love" (159), and he thinks their distinctions between common and special grace or between the covenants of works and grace somehow "impair the constancy of God's character" (159). In this, it seems that Begbie has more of a problem with their theology than their view of art, and that he is unfairly trying to force them onto the horns of a false dilemma, as he never explains how an emphasis on God's love would allow us to operate without such distinctions in a fallen world. On the other hand, he rightly notes the inadequacy of their tendency to see beauty as the ultimate aim and criterion of artistic expression.

Begbie's own attempts to take us further show great promise which is only partially fulfilled. His Christocentric emphasis is positive, but his view of Christ is at least as imbalanced (in a different direction) as the one he accuses the neo-Calvinists of having. And one wonders why he gives great attention to Tillich and the Kuyperians but almost totally ignores the great tradition of Christian wrestling with these issues which includes people like Sidney and Milton and reaches its fullest expression in Lewis, Tolkien, and Sayers. Surely the Defense of Poesy, The Mind of the Maker, and the "Essay on Fairy Stories" could have prevented some needless spinning of wheels and lack of focus and clarity. Still, Begbies's study, while not as good as it could have been, is worthwhile reading on a topic too often ignored by Christian theology.

Recovering the Lost Tools of Learning: An Approach to Distinctively Christian Education. By Douglas Wilson. Wheaton: Crossway, 1991, 215 pp., n.p.

Public education is not only a dismal failure, but its very nature as a state-run bureaucracy insures that it must be; as long as it is public it is inherently unreformable. Christian private education is not simply an option for concerned parents but a biblical mandate. Such an education should be both Christian and classical, rooting the student in an integrated biblical World view and in the Greco-Roman tradition of the West. These conclusions sound radical, but Douglas Wilson makes a strong case for them, one that deserves a careful hearing.

Public education, he argues, cannot succeed in being true education on the whole or in the long run. In a pluralistic society it must of necessity be based on a lowest-common-denominator World view which has no place for ultimate truth commitments. And "In a world without truth, skill in thinking is a useless skill" (p. 61). Philosophically, then, public schools can train but not educate. Practically, they cannot even train very well. "All bureaucracies tend to replace their original task with the goal of self-perpetuation" (133). This truth applies to educational bureaucracies too. The only force strong enough to bring real change is the accountability of the free market--which is of course incompatible with the whole concept of state-run schools.

Private education, then, which is directly accountable to its consumers, is the only kind which can consistently produce quality. Private education is also free to teach all knowledge from a Christian perspective. Since Christian parents are responsible for the nurture of their children, they cannot turn them over to the state. Home schooling is an option of last resort, but the principle of the division of labor makes a good Christian school the best option.

Classical education--including language study--develops the mind and puts the student in touch with the wisdom of the past. He must know both the Bible and history to understand the present. Education is not just the accumulation of a mass of unrelated data but an integrated understanding of the world from a biblical perspective.

The case for these conclusions is well documented and carefully thought out. Wilson's experience as the founder of the

Logos School in Moscow, Idaho, keeps him from straying into merely theoretical discussion. His book is a practical blueprint for organizing a Christian school, complete with appendices containing sample philosophy statements and curriculum guides. It is also a ringing challenge to those who continue to support public education. He leaves some issues unaddressed, e.g., if public education were abolished, could private schools really reach everyone? What would be the consequences of Christians totally abandoning the public schools? Can we afford them? Not everyone will be convinced by all his arguments. He sometimes lapses into sarcasm and cuteness, which will put some readers off. But he is more willing than most to look straight at sacred cows and naked emperors and call a spade a spade. He includes Dorothy L. Sayers' classic essay "The Lost Tools of Learning" as an appendix, and he has learned its lessons well. He deserves to be heard.

A Final Word

LITERARY MOTIFS

Dusk to dusk and dawn to dawn,
Starlight, sunlight slip away.
Ubi sunt, where have they gone?
All the sages cannot say.

Many things will be restored:
Sanctity in flesh of men;
But hours squandered from the hoard
Never will return again.

Ubi Sunt, where have they gone?
All the sages cannot say.
Hence the message of the dawn:
Carpe diem! seize the day.

--D.T.W.

INDEX OF NAMES

Names of modern scholars used only as secondary sources, or who appear only in the notes, are not indexed.

Williams, Charles 60, 7

Williams, Donald T. .   '33,
    140, 200
Williams, Wi''iam Carl
Wither, Geo.   45, 1

h, William 57, 227

homas 148

32, 124, 128